I0131073

Foundations of Critical Theory

This second volume of Christian Fuchs' *Media, Communication and Society* book series outlines key concepts and contemporary debates in critical theory.

The book explores the foundations of a Marxist-Humanist critical theory of society, clarifying and updating key concepts in critical theory – such as the dialectic, critique, alienation, class, capitalism, ideology, and racial capitalism. In doing so, the book engages with and further develops elements from the works of Karl Marx, Friedrich Engels, Rosa Luxemburg, Max Horkheimer, Theodor W. Adorno, Herbert Marcuse, David Harvey, Michael Hardt, Antonio Negri, C.L.R. James, Adolph L. Reed Jr., and Cornel West.

Written for a broad audience of students and scholars, this book is an essential guide for readers who are interested in how to think critically from perspectives such as media and communication studies, sociology, philosophy, political economy, and political science.

Christian Fuchs is a critical theorist of communication and society. He is co-editor of the journal *tripleC: Communication, Capitalism & Critique*. He is author of many publications, including the books *Social Media: A Critical Introduction* (third edition 2021), *Communication and Capitalism: A Critical Theory* (2020), *Marxism: Karl Marx's Fifteen Key Concepts for Cultural and Communication Studies* (2020), *Nationalism on the Internet: Critical Theory and Ideology in the Age of Social Media and Fake News* (2020), *Rereading Marx in the Age of Digital Capitalism* (2019), *Digital Demagogue: Authoritarian Capitalism in the Age of Trump and Twitter* (2016), *Digital Labour and Karl Marx* (2014), and *Internet and Society* (2008).

Foundations of Critical Theory

Media, Communication and Society
Volume Two

Christian Fuchs

Routledge
Taylor & Francis Group

LONDON AND NEW YORK

First published 2022
by Routledge
2 Park Square, Milton Park, Abingdon, Oxon OX14 4RN

and by Routledge
605 Third Avenue, New York, NY 10158

Routledge is an imprint of the Taylor & Francis Group, an informa business

© 2022 Christian Fuchs

The right of Christian Fuchs to be identified as author of this work has
been asserted by him in accordance with sections 77 and 78 of the Copyright,
Designs and Patents Act 1988.

All rights reserved. No part of this book may be reprinted or reproduced
or utilised in any form or by any electronic, mechanical, or other means, now
known or hereafter invented, including photocopying and recording, or in
any information storage or retrieval system, without permission in writing from
the publishers.

Trademark notice: Product or corporate names may be trademarks or registered
trademarks, and are used only for identification and explanation without intent
to infringe.

British Library Cataloguing-in-Publication Data
A catalogue record for this book is available from the British Library.

Library of Congress Cataloging-in-Publication Data
Names: Fuchs, Christian, author.
Title: Foundations of critical theory: media, communication, and society: volume
two / Christian Fuchs.
Description: New York: Routledge, 2021. | Includes bibliographical references
and index.
Identifiers: LCCN 2021010354 (print) | LCCN 2021010355 (ebook) | ISBN
9781032057866 (hardback) | ISBN 9781032057897 (paperback) | ISBN
9781003199182 (ebook)
Subjects: LCSH: Critical theory. | Dialectic. | Ideology. | Social conflict.
Classification: LCC HM480.F83 2021 (print) | LCC HM480 (ebook) | DDC
142--dc23
LC record available at https://lccn.loc.gov/2021010354
LC ebook record available at https://lccn.loc.gov/2021010355

ISBN: 978-1-032-05786-6 (hbk)
ISBN: 978-1-032-05789-7 (pbk)
ISBN: 978-1-003-19918-2 (ebk)

DOI: 10.4324/9781003199182

Typeset in Univers
by MPS Limited, Dehradun

Contents

Figures

Tables

Acknowledgements

Chapter 2 is a combination and update of two previously published book chapters:

Fuchs, Christian. 2016. Critical Theory. In *International Encyclopedia of Communication Theory and Philosophy*, ed. Klaus Bruhn Jensen and Robert Craig. Hoboken, NJ: *Wiley-Blackwell*. DOI: https://doi.org/10.1002/9781118766804.wbiect002

Fuchs, Christian. 2016. Critical Theory. In *International Encyclopedia of Political Communication*, ed. Gianpietro Mazzoleni, Kevin Barnhurst, Ken'ichi Ikeda, Rouisley Mai and Hartmut Wessler. Hoboken, NJ: *Wiley-Blackwell.*

Reuse with permission of John Wiley and Son

Section 2.7.4. is a new addition not contained in any of the two previous articles the chapter builds on.

Chapter 3 is a combination of elements from two previously published articles:

Fuchs, Christian. 2021. Engels@200: Friedrich Engels and Digital Capitalism. How Relevant Are Engels's Works 200 Years After His Birth? *tripleC: Communication, Capitalism & Critique* 19 (1): 15–51. DOI: https://doi.org/10.31269/triplec.v19i1.1228

Fuchs, Christian. 2021. Engels@200: Friedrich Engels in the Age of Digital Capitalism. Introduction. *tripleC: Communication, Capitalism & Critique* 19 (1): 1–14. DOI: https://doi.org/10.31269/triplec.v19i1.1229

Reuse with permission of the journal *tripleC: Communication, Capitalism & Critique*

Chapter 4 is a reprint of a journal article:

Fuchs, Christian. 2018. Marx's Centenary (1918) in the Light of the Media and Socialist Thought. *tripleC: Communication, Capitalism & Critique* 16 (2): 406-414. *tripleC: Communication, Capitalism & Critique* 16 (2): 717–728. DOI: https://doi.org/10.31269/triplec.v16i2.1036

Reuse with permission of the journal *tripleC: Communication, Capitalism & Critique*

Chapter 5 is a reprint of a journal article:

Fuchs, Christian. 2018. Reflections on Sven-Eric Liedman's Marx-Biography "A World to Win: The Life and Works of Karl Marx". *tripleC: Communication, Capitalism & Critique* 16 (2): 406–414. *tripleC: Communication, Capitalism & Critique* 16 (2): 619–627. DOI: https://doi.org/10.31269/triplec.v16i2.1039

Reuse with permission of the journal *tripleC: Communication, Capitalism & Critique*

Chapter 6 is a reprint of a journal article:

Fuchs, Christian. 2018. Universal Alienation, Formal and Real Subsumption of Society Under Capital, Ongoing Primitive Accumulation by Dispossession: Reflections on the Marx@ 200-Contributions by David Harvey and Michael Hardt/Toni Negri. *tripleC: Communication, Capitalism & Critique* 16 (2): 454–467. DOI: https://doi.org/10.31269/triplec.v16i2.1028

Reuse with permission of the journal *tripleC: Communication, Capitalism & Critique*

Chapter 7 is a reprint of a journal article:

Fuchs, Christian. 2017. Critical Social Theory and Sustainable Development: The Role of Class, Capitalism and Domination in a Dialectical Analysis of Un/Sustainability. *Sustainable Development* 25 (5): 443–458. DOI: https://doi.org/10.1002/sd.1673

Copyright © 2017, 2017 John Wiley & Sons, Ltd and ERP Environment

Reuse based on the author agreement that allows re-use of the final, published article version of parts thereof in a book by the author

Chapter 8 has not been published previously.

Chapter 9 is a reprint of a journal article:

Fuchs, Christian. 2021. Cornel West and Marxist Humanism. *Critical Sociology*, DOI: http://doi.org/10.1177/0896920520988314

Published using a Creative Commons CC-BY licence that allows re-use without permission & reuse based on SAGE's Author Archiving and Reuse Guidelines that allow reuse of the final, published article version in a book by the author

Chapter 10 is a reprint of a journal article:

Luxemburg, Rosa. 2018/1903. Karl Marx. *tripleC: Communication, Capitalism & Critique* 16 (2): 729–741. With a postface by Christian Fuchs. DOI: https://doi.org/10.31269/triplec.v16i2.1018

Reuse with permission of the journal *tripleC: Communication, Capitalism & Critique*

Chapter One
Introduction

1.1 Critical Theory

This book deals with elements of the foundations of critical theory. It asks and investigates the following question: what are important elements of a Marxist-Humanist critical theory of society?

The book at hand is the second volume of a series of books titled "Communication & Society". The overall aim of *Communication & Society* is to outline foundations of a critical theory of communication and digital communication in society. It is a multi-volume theory social theory book series situated on the intersection of communication theory, sociology, and philosophy. The overall questions that "Communication & Society" deals with are: What is the role of communication in society? What is the role of communication in capitalism? What is the role of communication in digital capitalism?

Answers are given by engaging with some key thinkers and key topics of critical theory. The thinkers the present author engages with in this book include.

Karl Marx, Friedrich Engels, Rosa Luxemburg, Max Horkheimer, Theodor W. Adorno, Herbert Marcuse, David Harvey, Michael Hardt, Antonio Negri, C.L.R. James, Adolph L. Reed Jr., and Cornel West. The topics that are addressed include elements of critical theory (Chapters 2, 4, 5, 10), the dialectic (Chapters 3, 8), class struggles (Chapter 3), alienation (Chapter 6), formal and real subsumption (Chapter 6), primitive accumulation (Chapter 6), ideology (Chapter 9), racial capitalism (Chapters 8, 9), and culture (Chapter 9).

The engagement with the mentioned thinkers and topics has contributed to the present author's development of a Marxist-Humanist theory of communication and

DOI: 10.4324/9781003199182-1

society (Fuchs 2020a). This book together with the other volumes in the series of volumes together titled *Communication and Society* allows the reader to follow aspects of how the present author has arrived at his own critical theory of society as expressed in his major works such as *Communication and Capitalism. A Critical Theory* (Fuchs 2020a) and *Social Media: A Critical Introduction* (Fuchs 2021b, 2017, 2014) through engagement with key thinkers and key topics in critical theory and further development of critical theory by dialectical sublation (*Aufhebung*) of other critical theory approaches.

There are a number of key elements of a Marxist-Humanist version of critical theory (Fuchs 2021a):

- **The human being**

  Marxist Humanism is a humanism that stresses the importance of human interests, human needs, human practices, and social production in society. It builds on Marx's (1844) *Economic and Philosophic Manuscripts*.

- **The dialectic**

  Marxist Humanism builds on and uses dialectical philosophy as a means for critically understanding society. It is influenced by Hegel's dialectical philosophy, Marx's development of the dialectic into a critical theory of capitalism and society, and the tradition of Hegelian Marxism.

- **Praxis and class struggle**

  Marxist Humanism builds on Marx's insight that humans "make their own history, but they do not make it as they please; they do not make it under circumstances chosen by themselves, but under circumstances directly encountered, given and transmitted from the past" (Marx 1852, 103). In societies shaped by class and alienation, humans are exploited and oppressed by the ruling class. They can only achieve a better society through making their own history in the form of class struggles for a classless society. Praxis is class struggle for Democratic Socialism.

- **Alienation**

  Alienation is a key category in Marx's works and Marxist-Humanist thought. Alienation means conditions under which humans do not control, which means own, shape, govern and define, the systems that shape their everyday lives. The exploitation of humans in class relations is the key to understanding alienation and the economic form of alienation. But alienation also takes on the form of domination in the political system, where one group oppresses other groups, and the form of ideology in the cultural system (Fuchs 2020a). These forms of alienation interact. Capitalism, patriarchy, and racism are three types of power relations that each combine economic alienation, political alienation, and cultural alienation (Fuchs 2021a). In contemporary society, capitalism, patriarchy, and racism interact in capitalist society (Fuchs 2021a).

- **The critique of ideology**

   Marxist Humanism is also a critique of ideology. Ideology is the process of ideologue's construction and dissemination and reproduction of false knowledge that makes society appear different from what it is truly like in order to try to naturalise, justify, defend, and legitimate exploitation and alienation and to try to convince exploited and oppressed groups to accept and not question alienation and to accept the status quo. Ideology is the attempt to produce and reproduce alienated and reified consciousness (see Fuchs 2020b, Chapter 9; Fuchs 2020a, Chapters 9 and 10).

- **Democratic Socialism and Socialist Democracy**

   Marxist Humanism is a type of humanism. It understands humanism as the ethico-political stress on the importance of creating conditions in society that allow humans and society to realise their full potentials. For Marxist Humanism, humanism is socialism and socialism is a humanism. Socialism denotes a society of the commons where all humans benefit. Socialism is a realisation of the economic, political, and cultural commons: all humans live in wealth (economic commons), have democratic participation rights (political commons), and are respected (cultural commons). Democratic Socialism sees socialism as inherently humanist and democratic. It is anti-fascist, anti-Stalinist, and anti-capitalist. It is critical of the anti-democratic potentials and realities of these types of systems. Marxist Humanism doesn't limit the understanding of democracy to the political system, but argues for the extension of democracy to society at large, including the economy. Marxist/ Socialist Humanism stresses the democratic need for the collective self-management of the economy and society. It understands democracy as participatory democracy.

Each chapter in the book at hand contributes to the foundations of critical theory. Many of the essays compiled in this work have been previously published. It is therefore a collection of the present author's recent contributions to the development of a critical theory of society. It engages with a particular aspect of such a theory that allows us to gain new insights into elements of a Marxist-Humanist critical theory of society. Each chapter deals with one particular question:

- Chapter 2 asks: what is critical theory? It reconstructs the history and elements of critical theory;
- Chapter 3 asks: how relevant are Friedrich Engels's works today? It interprets Engels' works as contributions to Socialist Humanism;
- Chapter 4 asks: what can we learn from Marx's centenary in 1918? It reflects on the cultural forms through which Marx's centenary was reflected in 1918, including press articles, essays, speeches, rallies, demonstrations, music, and banners;
- Chapter 5 asks: how should one should best write biographies about Marx? It engages with Seven-Eric Liedman's Marx-biography *A World to Win: The Life and Works of Karl Marx* and compares it to the Marx-biographies written by Jonathan Sperber (*Karl Marx: A 19th-Century Life*) and Gareth Stedman-Jones (*Karl Marx: Greatness and Illusion);*
- Chapter 6 asks: how relevant are Marx's works for the critical analysis of society today? It gives an answer by engaging with a four-part debate between David Harvey and Michael Hardt/Antonio Negri on the relevance of Marx today on the occasion of Marx's 200th anniversary in 2018. This debate focused on Marx's categories of alienation, formal and real subsumption, and primitive accumulation. The chapter discusses the essence of these categories and their relations;
- Chapter 7 asks: what is the relationship of the notion of sustainability to critical theory? The chapter argues that although sustainability has a strongly ideological character, a critical theory of society should not simply discard this notion, but aim to sublate it. Some foundations of a way to integrate sustainability into a critical theory of society are presented;
- Chapter 8 asks: how relevant is C.L.R. James's dialectical philosophy today?
- It discusses key aspects of James's philosophy and relates them to moments of contemporary society such as Donald Trump, fascism and racism today, digital capitalism, digital ideology, and Black Lives Matter;
- Chapter 9 asks: how can Cornel West's works inform a contemporary Marxist-Humanist theory of society? Taking West's works as a starting point, what are key elements of a Marxist-Humanist theory of society?
- Chapter 10 asks: how did Rosa Luxemburg assess Karl Marx's works and how relevant is her interpretation of Marx today?

1.2 Critical Theorists

Readers in this book will have different pre-knowledge. Some will be familiar with single thinkers the work presents, others with several or almost all. I want to give a brief overview of who the main thinkers you encounter in this book are and why they matter.

Karl Marx (1818–1883) was a philosopher, economist, sociologist, journalist, and revolutionary socialist. In 1999, he won a BBC online poll that determined the millennium's "greatest thinker" (BBC 1999). His key works include *Economic and Philosophic Manuscripts*, *The Manifesto of the Communist Party* (together with Friedrich Engels), *Grundrisse*, and the three volumes of *Capital*.

Friedrich Engels (1820–1895) was Marx's closest comrade, collaborator, and friend. He co-wrote *The Manifesto of the Communist Party* together with Marx, funded and supported Marx's works, edited volumes two and three of Capital, and made original contributions to critical social theory with works such as *The Condition of the Working Class in England* and *The Origin of the Family, Private Property and the State*.

Rosa Luxemburg (1871–1919) was a Marxist theorist, revolutionary socialist, economist, philosopher, and anti-war activist. She was one the most important and influential thinkers and activists influenced by Marx and Engels in the 20th century. She saw the First World War as the result of and manifestation of imperialist capitalism and opposed the war as a project of competing nationalism where workers who should unite internationally to fight against capital kill each other. Luxemburg's most important works are *Social Reform or Revolution?*; *The Mass Strike, the Political Party and the Trade Unions*; *The Accumulation of Capital*, *The Junius Pamphlet: The Crisis of German Social Democracy*, *The Russian Revolution*, and *Introduction to Political Economy*.

Max Horkheimer (1895–1973) and Theodor W. Adorno (1903–1969) were philosophers and sociologists who are widely credited as the founders of what is often called Frankfurt School critical theory. Their Dialectic of Enlightenment is a classical work in critical theory that grounds foundations of the critique of ideology. Horkheimer and Adorno were dialectical philosophers who developed a particular version of the dialectic known as negative dialectic, which is also the name of one of Adorno's most widely read books. Horkheimer and Adorno contributed to the development of a critical theory of the authoritarian personality and explained how fascism and fascist consciousness work.

Critical Theorists

Herbert Marcuse (1898–1979) was the third major thinker in the first generation of the Frankfurt School. He was a philosopher and political theorist who contributed to the development of Marxist-Humanist philosophy and the critique of ideology. He was influenced by Hegel, Marx, and Freud. His major books are *Reason and Revolution: Hegel and the Rise of Social Theory, Eros and Civilization: A Philosophical Inquiry into Freud, One-Dimensional Man: Studies in the Ideology of Advanced Industrial Society, An Essay on Liberation*, and *Counterrevolution and Revolt*.

Jürgen Habermas (born in 1929) is a philosopher and sociologist who is by many seen as the major representative of the Frankfurt School's second generation. He has worked out a critical theory of the public sphere and a critical theory of communication. His major books are *The Structural Transformation of the Public Sphere: An Inquiry into a Category of Bourgeois Society, The Theory of Communicative Action, Between Facts and Norms: Contributions to a Discourse Theory of Law and Democracy*, and *This Too a History of Philosophy*.

David Harvey (born in 1935) is an economic geographer and economic and social theorist who has developed a particular version of Marxist-Humanist theory that focuses on issues such as space in capitalism, globalisation, imperialism, neoliberalism, and social struggles. Among Harvey's major books are *The Limits to Capital, The Condition of Postmodernity: An Enquiry into the Origins of Cultural Change, The New Imperialism, A Brief History of Neoliberalism, A Companion to Marx's Capital, The Enigma of Capital and the Crises of Capitalism, Seventeen Contradictions and the End of Capitalism*; and *Marx, Capital and the Madness of Economic Reason*.

Michael Hardt (born in 1960) is a political philosopher and literary theorist. Antonio Negri (born in 1933) is a political philosopher. Together, Hardt and Negri wrote Empire, which has by some been characterised as a communist manifesto for the 21st century and has influenced many left-wing activists and debates. Hardt and Negri followed up Empire with a sequence of related books, namely *Multitude: War and Democracy in the Age of Empire, Commonwealth, Declaration*, and *Assembly*.

Cyril Lionel Robert James (1901–1989) was a socialist theorist, activist, novelist, and journalist. He contributed to the development of Hegelian-Marxist Humanism. As socialist activist, James was engaged in anti-racist and anti-imperialist struggles. Among his best-known works are *The Black Jacobins: Toussaint L'Ouverture and the San Domingo Revolution, Beyond A Boundary, American Civilization*; *Mariners, Renegades and Castaways: The Story of Herman Melville and the World We Live In*;

Notes on Dialectics, A History of Pan-African Revolt, State Capitalism and World Revolution; and *World Revolution, 1917–1936: The Rise and Fall of the Communist International.*

Adolph L. Reed Jr. (born in 1947) is a political scientist and Marxist public intellectual. His work focuses on American and Afro-American politics, political thought, urban politics, and political development. He is known as a sharp commentator on political issues from a Marxist perspective, including US politics and left-wing politics. He stresses the importance of class politics and the need to situate racism and identity in the context of class and capitalism. Reed was a supporter of Bernie Sanders in the 2016 and 2020 US presidential primaries. He was involved in founding the United States Labor Party in 1996. His books include *W.E.B. Dubois and American Political Thought: Fabianism and the Color Line, Class Notes: Posing as Politics and Other Thoughts on the American Scene, Stirrings in the Jug: Black Politics in the Post-Segregation Era,* and *The Jesse Jackson Phenomenon: The Crisis of Purpose in Afro-American Politics.* He edited the collected volumes *Renewing Black Intellectual History: The Ideological and Material Foundations of African American Thought* (together with Kenneth W. Warren), *Without Justice for All: The New Liberalism and the Retreat from Racial Equality,* and *Race, Politics, and Culture: Critical Essays on the Radicalism of the 1960s.*

Cornel West (born in 1953) is a philosopher and one of the leading critical intellectuals today. He is an organic intellectual who has been highly visible in the public sphere through public interventions such as the support of the Bernie Sanders campaign, Black Lives Matter, and the Occupy movement. His work has been influenced by, has fused and has contributed to the development of anti-racist theory, Black Liberation Theology, Marxist theory, pragmatism, and existentialism. Among West's main works are *Prophesy Deliverance! An Afro-American Revolutionary Christianity, Prophetic Fragments, The American Evasion of Philosophy: A Genealogy of Pragmatism, The Ethical Dimensions of Marxist Thought, Keeping Faith: Philosophy and Race in America,* and Race Matters.

Critical Theory develops through the dialectics of theory that aim at critically understanding changes of society. Theoretical debates, controversies, and encounters are part of the dialectics of theory. In Chapter 1, we encountered several of these debates that have shaped critical theory in the 21st century. The present author does not necessarily agree with the different sides of these debates, but finds such encounters relevant as points that help clarifying what questions critical theory needs to ask today. In these debates, as presented in this book, we encounter Luc

Boltanski, Klaus Dörre, Nancy Fraser, Axel Honneth, Rahel Jaeggi, Stephan Lessenich, and Hartmut Rosa. The present author has benefited from reading these debates, but does not share particular positions or approaches advanced by the authors who contributed to them.

Luc Boltanski (born in 1940) is a sociologist who has developed an approach he terms the pragmatic sociology of critique that studies how humans experience and resist injustices. Among Boltanski's major works are the books *The New Spirit of Capitalism* (together with Ève Chiapello), *On Justification: The Economies of Worth* (together with Laurent Thévenot), *On Critique: A Sociology of Emancipation*, *Enrichment: A Critique of Commodities* (together with Arnaud Esquerre), *The Making of a Class. Cadres in French Society; Distant Suffering: Morality, Media and Politics; Love and Justice as Competences - Three Essays on the Sociology of Action; Mysteries and Conspiracies - Detective Stories, Spy Novels and the Making of Modern Societies.*

Klaus Dörre (born in 1957) is a sociologist and critical theorist who studies the contemporary economy and society. He has in this context coined the notion of *Landnahme* (capture/grabbing/seizure/appropriation/subsumption of territory). He is author of books such as *In der Warteschlange: Arbeiter*innen und die radikale Rechte* (*In the Queue: Workers and the Radical Right*), *Kampf um Beteiligung. Arbeit, Partizipation und industrielle Beziehungen im flexiblen Kapitalismus* (*Struggle for Participation. Labour, Participation and Industrial Relations in Flexible Capitalism*), *Sociology, Capitalism, Critique* (together with Stephan Lessenich and Hartmut Rosa), or *Was stimmt nicht mit der Demokratie? Eine Debatte* (*What's Wrong With Democracy? A Debate*; together with Nancy Fraser, Stephan Lessenich, and Hartmut Rosa).

Nancy Fraser (born in 1947) is a philosopher who has contributed to the development of critical theory by combining feminism and anti-capitalism. Among her major works are *Unruly Practices: Power, Discourse, and Gender in Contemporary Social Theory*, *Justice Interruptus: Critical Reflections on the "Postsocialist" Condition*, *Redistribution or Recognition: A Political-Philosophical Exchange* (together with Axel Honneth), *Scales of Justice: Reimagining Political Space in a Globalizing World*, *Fortunes of Feminism: From State-Managed Capitalism to Neoliberal Crisis*, *Feminism for the 99%: A Manifesto* (together with Cinzia Arruzz and Tithi Bhattacharya), and *Capitalism: A Conversation in Critical Theory* (together with Rahel Jaeggi).

Axel Honneth (born in 1949) is a philosopher who was the Frankfurt Institute for Social Research's director between 2001 and 2018. He is a major representative of the third generation of the Frankfurt School. Among his major works are *The Critique of Power: Reflective Stages in a Critical Social Theory, The Fragmented World of the Social, The Struggle for Recognition: The Moral Grammar of Social Conflicts, Redistribution or Recognition: A Political-Philosophical Exchange* (together with Nancy Fraser), *Reification: A Recognition-Theoretical View, Disrespect: The Normative Foundations of Critical Theory, Pathologies of Reason: On the Legacy of Critical Theory, The Pathologies of Individual Freedom: Hegel's Social Theory, The I in We: Studies in the Theory of Recognition, Freedom's Right,* and *The Idea of Socialism.*

Rahel Jaeggi (born in 1967) is a philosopher and critical theorist who has contributed to the analysis of alienation, capitalism, and forms of life. Among her works are the books Alienation, Critique of Forms of Life, *Capitalism: A Conversation in Critical Theory* (together with Nancy Fraser). She also edited collected volumes such as *Nach Marx: Philosophie, Kritik, Praxis (After Marx: Philosophy, Critique, Praxis;* together with Daniel Loick), *Karl Marx: Perspektiven der Gesellschaftskritik (Karl Marx: Perspectives for the Critique of Society;* together with Daniel Loick), *Sozialphilosophie und Kritik (Social Philosophy and Critique;* together with Rainer Forst, Martin Hartmann, Martin Saar), *Was ist Kritik? (What is Critique?,* together with Tilo Wesche).

Stephan Lessenich (born in 1965) is a sociologist who has contributed to critical theory based on the notion of activation. Among his works are the books *Living Well at Others' Expense: The Hidden Costs of Western Prosperity, Sociology, Capitalism, Critique* (together with Klaus Dörre and Hartmut Rosa), *Claus Offe and the Critical Theory of the State* (together with Jens Borchert), *Grenzen der Demokratie. Teilhabe als Verteilungsproblem* (Limits of Democracy), *Die Neuerfindung des Sozialen. Der Sozialstaat im flexiblen Kapitalismus (The Reinvention of the Social. The Welfare State in Flexible Capitalism), Dynamischer Immobilismus. Kontinuität und Wandel im deutschen Sozialmodell (Dynamic Immobilism. Continuity and Change of the German Social Model),* and *Was stimmt nicht mit der Demokratie? Eine Debatte (What's Wrong With Democracy? A Debate;* together with Klaus Dörre, Nancy Fraser, and Hartmut Rosa).

Hartmut Rosa (born in 1965) is a sociologist who has developed a theory of acceleration and resonance as contribution to critical theory. His major works

Critical Theorists

include *Resonance: A Sociology of Our Relationship to the World*, *Social Acceleration: A New Theory of Modernity*, *High-Speed Society: Social Acceleration, Power, and Modernity*; *Alienation & Acceleration: Towards a Critical Theory of Late-Modern Temporality*; *The Uncontrollability of the World*; *Sociology, Capitalism, Critique* (together with Klaus Dörre and Stephan Lessenich); *Was stimmt nicht mit der Demokratie? Eine Debatte* (*What's Wrong With Democracy? A Debate*; together with Klaus Dörre, Nancy Fraser, and Stephan Lessenich).

1.3 Overviews of the Chapters in this Book

Chapter 1: Introduction

This chapter introduces the book's goal and presents an overview of its structure and its single chapters. It points out key features of the Marxist-Humanist approach to critical theory, introduces critical theorists who the reader encounters in this book, and provides an overview of the chapters in this work.

Chapter 2: What is Critical Theory?

This chapter discusses critical theory and why it matters. Its substance is the analysis and questioning of power structures in order to overcome them and create a better society. It is inherently connected to Karl Marx's works, the works of the Frankfurt School and the Critical Political Economy of Media and Communication. Critical theory is dialectical, ethical, a philosophy of praxis, and a critique of domination, exploitation, domination, and capitalism.

The chapter also discusses how critical theory matters as foundation of a critical theory and critique of the political economy of communication, culture, information, and the media.

Chapter 3: Friedrich Engels Today

This chapter introduces Engels's life and works in the context of his 200th birthday in 2020. It shows that Engels class-struggle oriented theory can and should inform 21st-century social science. Based on a reading of Engels's works, the article discusses how to think of scientific socialism as critical social science today, updates Engels's *Condition of the Working Class in England,* and analyses the social murder of workers in the COVID-19 crisis. The chapter argues that Engels should be seen as a socialist humanist who stressed the important role of class struggles in society.

Chapter 4: Marx's Centenary (1918) in the Light of the Media and Socialist Thought

This chapter takes a historical view on Marx's 200th anniversary that we celebrated in 2018: it analyses how Marx's centenary (5 May 1918) was reflected in the media and socialist thought. 1918 not just marked Marx's 100th anniversary but was also the year in which the First World War ended. It was the year that saw the immediate aftermath of the Russian Revolution and the start of the Russian Civil War, the end of the Austro-Hungarian Empire; the formation of the Weimar Republic, Austria's First Republic, the Czech Republic, the Hungarian Republic, the Second Polish Republic; the founding of the Communist Party of Germany (KPD), and the independence of Iceland from Denmark. The cultural forms, in which Marx's centenary was reflected in 1918, included press articles, essays, speeches, rallies, demonstrations, music, and banners. The communists as well as left-wing socialists of the day saw themselves in the tradition of Marx, whereas revisionist social democrats based their politics on a criticism or revised reading of Marx. This difference resulted in different readings of Marx.

Chapter 5: Reflections on Sven-Eric Liedman's Marx-Biography *A World to Win: The Life and Works of Karl Marx*

This chapter discusses the English translation of Seven-Eric Liedman's Marx-biography *A World to Win: The Life and Works of Karl Marx* that was published in 2018. It presents reflections on Liedman's book and asks how one should best write biographically about Marx. The chapter compares Liedman's biography to the Marx-biographies written by Jonathan Sperber (*Karl Marx: A 19th-Century Life*) and Gareth Stedman-Jones (*Karl Marx: Greatness and Illusion*). A biography is a way of repeating a person's life, works, and age in a process of reconstruction and retelling. The question that arises is how to write a biography as a dialectical text.

Chapter 6: Universal Alienation, Formal and Real Subsumption of Society Under Capital, Ongoing Primitive Accumulation by Dispossession: Reflections on the Marx@200-Debate Between David Harvey and Michael Hardt/Toni Negri

This chapter presents reflections on a four-part debate between David Harvey and Michael Hardt/Toni Negri on the question of how relevant Marx is today. This debate was published in the journal *tripleC: Communication, Capitalism & Critique* on the occasion of Marx's 200th anniversary (Hardt and Negri 2018a; Harvey 2018a; Hardt and Negri 2018b; Harvey 2018b).

My reflection contextualises the debate by a) discussing the origin and genesis of Marx's concepts of alienation, formal/real subsumption, and primitive accumulation and b) situating the arguments in earlier works by Harvey, Hardt, and Negri. This chapter points out differences as well as the strong commonalities between the works of Michael Hardt/Toni Negri and David Harvey. It discusses how the categories of universal alienation, formal/real subsumption of society under capital, original/ongoing primitive accumulation of capital are related. Harvey and Hardt/Negri show that Marx's theory and politics are alive 200 years after his birth and will haunt capitalism as long as it exists. The chapter concludes by arguing that Harvey's concept of anti-value and the autonomous notion of self-valorisation point towards democratic, commons-based alternatives to capitalism.

Chapter 7: Critical Social Theory and Sustainable Development: The Role of Class, Capitalism and Domination in a Dialectical Analysis of Un/Sustainability

It is still a relatively open question if and how sustainability fits into a critical theory of society. This chapter's aim is to contribute to the critical social theory foundations of sustainability and to reflect on the links between capitalism, class, and sustainability. Sustainability has not been a very popular concept in sociological theory. One of the reasons may be that sociology has a strongly critical tradition focusing on the analysis and critique of power structures in modern society. It is therefore often sceptical of ideas coming from the policy world that are susceptible to have an administrative character. The chapter argues that although sustainability has a strongly ideological character, a critical theory of society should not simply discard this notion, but aim to sublate it. Some foundations of a way to integrate sustainability into a critical theory of society are presented.

Chapter 8: The Relevance of C.L.R. James's Dialectical, Marxist-Humanist Philosophy in the Age of Donald Trump, Black Lives Matter, and Digital Capitalism

This chapter asks: how relevant is C.L.R. James's dialectical philosophy today?

It discusses key aspects of James's philosophy and relates them to moments of contemporary society such as Donald Trump, fascism and racism today, digital capitalism, digital ideology, and Black Lives Matter.

Section 1.2 discusses James's concept of the dialectic and its focus on mediation and mediated communication. Section 1.3 analyses negative dialectics in the age of Donald Trump. Section 1.4 discusses ideology in the age of digital capitalism. Section 1.5's focus is on racism in the age of Black Lives Matter. Section 1.6 presents some conclusions.

Of particular relevance for critical analysis today are James's concepts of the dialectic as mediation, his negative dialectics of capitalism and barbarism, his focus on truth and the critique of ideology, and his analysis of the dialectic of capitalism and racism. In the age of racial, authoritarian, digital capitalism, C.L.R. James's dialectical, Marxist-Humanist philosophy remains an important inspiration for the critical analysis of capitalism and for struggles against barbarism and for socialism.

Chapter 9: Cornel West and Marxist Humanism

Humanity has experienced an explosion of anti-humanism in the form of authoritarian capitalism, postmodern filter bubbles, and global problems. Marxist/Socialist Humanism is the proper answer to the deep crisis of humanity. In this context, this chapter asks: how can Cornel West's works inform a contemporary Marxist-Humanist theory of society? Taking West's works as a starting point, what are key elements of a Marxist-Humanist theory of society?

Cornel West is one of the leading critical intellectuals today. He is an organic intellectual who has been highly visible in the public sphere through public interventions such as the support of the Bernie Sanders campaign, Black Lives Matter, and the Occupy movement. His work has been influenced by, has fused and has contributed to the development of anti-racist theory, Black Liberation Theology, Marxist theory, pragmatism, and existentialism.

This chapter especially focuses on West's understanding of humanism and culture. It shows how his works and praxis can inform the reinvigoration of Marxist Humanism in the age of authoritarian capitalism as a socialist response. West's thoughts can and should also inform the analysis of alienation, exploitation, domination, culture, the public sphere, the critique of ideology, and popular culture.

Chapter 10: Rosa Luxemburg and Karl Marx

Marx died on 14 March 1883. Exactly 20 years later, on 14 March 1903, Rosa Luxemburg's reflections on Karl Marx were published in German in *Vorwärts*, the newspaper of the Social Democratic Party of Germany. This chapter publishes an English translation of Luxemburg's essay on the occasion of Marx's bicentenary. Christian Fuchs reflects on the relationship of Karl Marx and Rosa Luxemburg by asking how we can make sense of Rosa Luxemburg's reading of Marx in 2018.

Chapter 11: Conclusion

This chapter draws some conclusions from the single chapters presented in the books. It points out important elements of a critical theory of society.

References

BBC. 1999. Marx the Millennium's "Greatest Thinker". *BBC*, 1 October 1999. http://news.bbc.co.uk/2/hi/461545.stm

Fuchs, Christian. 2021a. *Marxist Humanism and Communication Theory. Communication and Society Volume One*. New York: Routledge.

Fuchs, Christian. 2021b. *Social Media: A Critical Introduction*. London: Sage. Third edition.

Fuchs, Christian. 2020a. *Communication and Capitalism. A Critical Theory*. London: University of Westminster Press. https://doi.org/10.16997/book45

Fuchs, Christian. 2020b. *Marxism: Karl Marx's Fifteen Key Concepts for Cultural & Communication Studies*. New York: Routledge.

Fuchs, Christian. 2017. *Social Media: A Critical Introduction*. London: Sage. Second edition.

Fuchs, Christian. 2014. *Social Media: A Critical Introduction*. London: Sage. First edition.

Harvey, David. 2018a. Universal Alienation. *tripleC: Communication, Capitalism & Critique* 18 (2): 424–439. https://doi.org/10.31269/triplec.v16i2.1026

Harvey, David. 2018b. Universal Alienation and the Real Subsumption of Daily Life under Capital: A Response to Hardt and Negri. *tripleC: Communication, Capitalism & Critique* 18 (2): 449–453. https://doi.org/10.31269/triplec.v16i2.1027

Hardt, Michael and Antonio Negri. 2018a. The Powers of the Exploited and the Social Ontology of Praxis. *tripleC: Communication, Capitalism & Critique* 18 (2): 415–423. https://doi.org/1 0.31269/triplec.v16i2.1024

Hardt, Michael and Antonio Negri. 2018b. The Multiplicities Within Capitalist Rule and the Articulation of Struggles. *tripleC: Communication, Capitalism & Critique* 18 (2): 440–448. https://doi.org/10.31269/triplec.v16i2.1025

Marx, Karl. 1852. The Eighteenth Brumaire of Louis Bonaparte. In *Marx & Engels Collected Works* (MECW), 99–197. London: Lawrence & Wishart.

Marx, Karl. 1844. Economic and Philosophic Manuscripts of 1844. In *Marx & Engels Collected Works (MECW) Volume 3*, 229–346. London: Lawrence & Wishart.

Chapter Two
What is Critical Theory?

2.1 Introduction

One could say that all contemporary academic thought is critical because it questions opinions of other scholars. This understanding of critique stands in the tradition of Kantian enlightenment. Kant argued that modern society is an age of criticism. In contrast to Kant's general understanding of critique, Karl Marx formulated a categorical imperative of critical theory – the "categoric imperative to overthrow all conditions in which man is a degraded, enslaved, neglected, contemptible being" (Marx 1997, 257–258). For Marx, the "task of philosophy [...] is to unmask human self-alienation" (Marx 1997, 251). Marx points out a more specific understanding of being critical, namely the questioning of power, domination and exploitation, and the political demand and struggle for a just society. Critical theory is for him a critique of society. Scholars who refer to critical theory often mean this second understanding of the notion of critique. They employ the term "critical" in order to stress that not all science is critical, but that a lot of it has a more administrative character that takes power structures for granted, does not question them, or helps legitimatise them.

Critical theory is an approach that studies society in a dialectical way by analysing political economy, domination, exploitation, and ideologies. It is a normative approach that is based on the judgment that domination is a problem, that a society free from

DOI: 10.4324/9781003199182-2

domination is needed. It wants to inform political struggles that want to establish such a society.

All contemporary political communication is in a specific way critical because it consists of speech acts that normally question political opinions and practices of certain actors. Modern politics is a highly competitive system, in which elections and warfare are ways of distributing and redistributing power. This understanding of critique stands in the tradition of Kantian enlightenment that considered the enlightenment as an age of criticism. In contrast to Kant's general understanding of critique, Karl Marx and the Marxian tradition understands the categoric imperative as the need to overcome all forms of slavery and degradation and to unmask alienation. This school of thought points out a more specific understanding of being critical, namely the questioning of power, domination, and exploitation, the political demand and struggle for a just society. Critical theory is understood as a critique of society. Scholars in the Marxian-inspired tradition employ the term "critical" to stress that not all science is critical, but that a lot of it has a more administrative character that takes power structures for granted, does not question them or helps legitimatising them.

2.2 What is Critical Theory?

Some define critical theory as the Frankfurt School's works, a tradition of critical thinking that originated with the works of scholars like Herbert Marcuse, Max Horkheimer, and Theodor W. Adorno. Herbert Marcuse was a philosopher who lived in Germany from 1898 and fled Nazi Germany to the USA in 1934, where he spent the rest of his life. Max Horkheimer was director of the University of Frankfurt's Institute for Social Research in the years 1930–1959. This institute was the institutional home of what came to be known as the Frankfurt School. Theodor W. Adorno was one of the Institute's Directors from 1953 until his death in 1969. Also Horkheimer and Adorno emigrated together with the Institute to the USA, but other than Marcuse returned to Germany after the end of the Second World Ware. Critical theory's starting point is the work of Karl Marx. Critical theory was used as a camouflage term when the Frankfurt theorists were in exile from the Nazis in the USA, where they were concerned about being exposed as communist and Marxian thinkers and therefore took care in the categories they employed. Some definitions of critical theory couple the usage of this term exclusively to the Frankfurt School or Habermasian Frankfurt School.

Some introductory books to critical theory provide lists of different approaches such as the following: Marxist criticism, the Frankfurt School, psychoanalytic criticism, feminist criticism, new criticism, reader-response criticism, structuralist criticism, deconstructive criticism, new historical and cultural criticism, lesbian, gay, and queer criticism, African American criticism, postcolonial criticism, cultural studies, etc., structuralism/poststructuralism, feminism, post-foundational ethics/politics.

Critical theory is, by other scholars, understood as the works of the Frankfurt School, a tradition of critical thinking that originated with the works of scholars like Herbert Marcuse, Max Horkheimer, and Theodor W. Adorno. Its starting point is the work of Karl Marx. For Horkheimer and his colleagues, critical theory "was a camouflage label for 'Marxist theory'" (Wiggershaus 1995, 5) when they were in exile from the Nazis in the United States, where they were concerned about being exposed as communist thinkers and therefore took care in the categories they employed. There are definitions of critical theory that couple the usage of this term exclusively to the Frankfurt School or Habermasian Frankfurt School.

The entry for "Kritische Theorie" (critical theory) in the *Europäische Enzyklopädie zu Philosophie und Wissenschaften* (European Encyclopaedia of Philosophy and Science), a four-volume Marxist encyclopaedia of philosophy edited by Hans Jörg Sandkühler (1990), only provides a cross-reference to the entry Frankfurter Schule (Frankfurt School), which means that here one assumes an association of the terms "critical theory" and the "Frankfurt School". A second Marxist encyclopedia has taken a different approach. Gerhard Schweppenhäuser and Frigga Haug wrote the entry "Kritische Theorie" in the *Historisch-Kritisches Wörterbuch des Marxismus* (Historical-Critical Dictionary of Marxism), the largest encyclopaedic project of Marxism (see http://www. inkrit.de/hkwm/hkwm-index.htm), and defined critical theory as

> emancipatory social philosophy. It tries to unite in *one* movement of thought the analysis and critique of forms of practice as well as types of reason and rationality of bourgeois-capitalist societies since the middle of the 19th century until today. Its starting point is Marx's theory of the law of value as the foundation of commodity-producing societies that is derived from the analysis of the value-form. This theory is at the same time critique of the political economy, i.e. demonstration of the capability and limit of this science for the explanation of the value-form with its social and ideological consequences.
>
> (Schweppenhäuser and Haug 2012, 197)

The two authors stress the status of critical theory as critical philosophy and critical economics. They understand it as a broad approach that is grounded in Karl Marx's thought and works. However, they also acknowledge that the Frankfurt School introduced the term and therefore draw a distinction between critical theory as the more general approach and critical theory as the Frankfurt School approach.

An approach taken that neither lists approaches nor identifies critical theory only with persons associated with the Frankfurt School is to identify dimensions of critical theory at the content level. We can identify six dimensions of a critical theory:

- Critical ethics;
- Critique of domination and exploitation;
- Dialectical reason;
- Ideology critique;
- Critique of the political economy;
- Struggles and political practice.

These six dimensions can be grouped into three overarching dimensions of critical theory. The first concerns its epistemology, the next three its ontology and the latter two its praxeology. Epistemology is a theory of knowledge, it deals with how the very concepts that constitute a theory are constituted and organised. Ontology is a theory of being, it deals with the question how reality is organised and develops. Praxeology is the study of human action, especially political action and ethics.

EPISTEMOLOGY:

A) Dialectical reason;

ONTOLOGY:

B) Critique of the political economy;
C) Critique of domination and exploitation;
D) Ideology critique;

PRAXEOLOGY:

E) Critical ethics;
F) Struggles and political practice.

For grounding an understanding of critical theory that specifies dimensions of the critique of society, some foundational texts of the Frankfurt School are helpful: Marcuse's essay *Philosophy and Critical Theory* (1988, 134–158), Horkheimer's essay *Traditional and Critical Theory* (2002, 188–252), Marcuse's article *The Concept of Essence* (1988, 43–87), and the section *The Foundations of the Dialectical Theory of Society* in Marcuse's book *Reason and Revolution* (1941, 258–322).

Critical theory has a "concern with human happiness" (Marcuse 1988, 135) and uses the Hegelian method of comparing essence and existence because in capitalism "what exists is not immediately and already rational" (136). This essence can be found in man's positive capacities (such as striving for freedom, sociality, co-operation) and it has the ethical implication that universal conditions should be created that allow all humans to realise these capacities:

That man is a rational being, that this being requires freedom, and that happiness is his highest good are universal propositions whose progressive impetus derives precisely from their universality. Universality gives them an almost revolutionary character, for they claim that all, and not merely this or that particular person, should be rational, free, and happy (Marcuse 1988, 152).

2.2.1 Dialectical Reason

In Marx's works, concepts that describe the existence of capitalism (profit, surplus value, worker, capital, commodity, etc.) are dialectical because they "transcend the given social reality in the direction of another historical structure which is present as a tendency in the given reality" and represent the essence of man (Marcuse 1988, 86):

If, for instance, it is said that concepts such as wages, the value of labor, and entrepreneurial profit are only categories of manifestations behind which are hidden the "essential relations" of the second set of concepts, it is also true that these essential relations represent the truth of the manifestations only insofar as the concepts which comprehend them already contain their own negation and transcendence – the image of a social organization without surplus value. All materialist concepts contain an accusation and an imperative.

(Marcuse 1988, 86)

Marx's categories "are negative and at the same time positive" (Marcuse 1941, 295).

The concepts of contradiction (negation) and negation of the negation are crucial for critical theory: in capitalism, every fact is "a negation and restriction of real possibilities" (282). "Private property is a fact, but at the same time it is a negation of man's collective appropriation of nature" (Marcuse 1941, 282).

> The historical character of the Marxian dialectic embraces the prevailing negativity as well as its negation. [...] the negation of the negation [...] does not steadily and automatically grow out of the earlier state; it can be set free only by an autonomous act on the part of men.
>
> (Marcuse 1941, 315)

The dialectic of capitalism has a structural-objective part: capital accumulation's contradictions result in crisis. These contradictions can only be overcome by the subjective force of dialectic: political struggle (Marcuse 1941, 316–319).

2.2.2 Critique of the Political Economy

Kant's fundamental philosophical questions about man and his knowledge, activities, and hopes (What can I know? What ought I to do? What may I hope? What is the human being?) were treated by Marx in the form of a philosophy and theory that "demonstrate the concrete forces and tendencies that prevented and those that promoted" the goal of a society that benefits all (Marcuse 1941, 321). So Marx's reformulation of Kant's question was his categorical imperative – the critique of domination and exploitation.

2.2.3 Critique of Domination and Exploitation

Critical theory holds that "man can be more than a manipulable subject in the production process of class society" (Marcuse 1988, 153). The goal of critical theory is the transformation of society as a whole (Horkheimer 2002, 219) so that a "society without injustice" (221) emerges that is shaped by "reasonableness, and striving for peace, freedom, and happiness" (222), "in which man's actions no longer flow from a mechanism but from his own decision" (229), and that is "a state of affairs in which there will be no exploitation or oppression" (241).

2.2.4 Ideology Critique

"Basic to the present form of social organization, the antagonisms of the capitalist production process, is the fact that the central phenomena connected with this process do not immediately appear to men as what they are 'in reality', but in masked, 'perverted' form" (Marcuse 1988, 70). There are different definitions of ideology. Whereas ideology theories define ideology in a relatively general sense as worldviews or contested worldviews, ideology critique sees it as practice and strategy of those in power for trying to guard their interests by presenting reality in a manipulated or distorted manner. For the Frankfurt School, a critical concept of ideology requires a normative distinction between true and false beliefs and practices. It understands ideology as thoughts, practices, ideas, words, concepts, phrases, sentences, texts, belief systems, meanings, representations, artifacts, institutions, systems, or combinations thereof that represent and justify one group's or individual's power, domination, or exploitation of other groups or individuals by mis-representing, one-dimensionally presenting or distorting reality in symbolic representa-tions. Domination means in this context that there is a system that enables one human side to gain advantages at the expense of others and to sustain this condition. It is a routinised and institutionalised form of asymmetric power, in which one side has the opportunity to shape and control societal structures (such as the production and control of wealth, political decision-making, public discussions, ideas, norms, rules, values), whereas others do not have these opportunities and are facing disadvantages or exclusion from the opportunities of others. Exploitation is a specific form of domination, in which an exploiting class derives wealth advantages at the expense of an exploited class by controlling economic resources and means of coercion in such a way that the exploited class is forced to produce new use-values that the exploiting class controls. Ideology presupposes and comes along with the existence of class societies. Put in Hegelian terms, one can say that ideologies claim the class reality of society is its natural essence.

2.2.5 Struggles and Political Practice

"The materialist protest and materialist critique originated in the struggle of oppressed groups for better living conditions and remain permanently associated with the actual process of this struggle" (Marcuse 1988, 141). "The philosophical ideal of a better world and of true Being are incorporated into the practical aim of struggling mankind, where they take on a human form" (Marcuse 1988, 142).

2.2.6 Jürgen Habermas's Critical Theory

Jürgen Habermas (1984, 1987) built his approach on the classical Frankfurt School and at the same time worked out the concept of communicative rationality, by which he went beyond the classical tradition. Habermas distinguishes between instrumental (nonsocial, success-oriented), strategic (social, success-oriented), and communicative action (social, oriented on understanding). Habermas (1987, 333) argues that Horkheimer and Adorno did not take the discussion of communication into account, "failed to recognize the communicative rationality of the lifeworld". For Habermas (1987, 375), critical theory questions that steering media (money, power) attack "the communicative infrastructure of largely rationalized lifeworlds". He conceives instrumental action and communicative action as the two fundamental aspects of social praxis. What Habermas wants to express is that the human being is both a labouring and a communicating being and says that the reproduction of life depends on work and interaction/communication. Dallas Smythe expressed the same idea as foundation of a Marxist theory of media and communication.

In a way, Habermas retains the classical Marxist distinction between base and superstructure, but inverts it by putting the stress on communication. Doubts arise if labour can be so strictly separated from communication in a dualistic way. The 20th and 21st century have seen a rising importance of communicative and cultural work in the economy. But is such activity takes on value-generating form, then culture and communication must be part of the economy themselves, base and superstructure become integrated and labour and communication cannot be separated.

For Habermas, emancipatory interest is reflective and enables liberation from dogmatic dependence. In those passages where Habermas tries to define what critical theory is all about, his formulations remain often rather abstract and vague; he mainly points out the emancipatory role of communication and that the goal is undistorted communication. He thereby falls behind the concreteness of Horkheimer's, Adorno's, and Marcuse's notion of critical theory. These thinkers left no doubt that such a theory is all about questioning all structures of domination.

Communication is one of the crucial foundations of the economy: the latter is not just a system of the production of use-values and in class societies of exchange values. It is also a social system because production in any society takes on complex forms beyond individual self-sustenance. The only way for organising the relational dimension of the economy is via communication, in the form of symbolic interaction and/or anonymous forms of indirect communication (as for example via money, markets, the price system, etc.). Human thought is a precondition for human communication and existence. When humans produce in the economy, they do so with a purpose in mind, which means that they anticipate the form of the object and how it will be put to use. The economic existence of man requires anticipative thinking just like it requires communication. It is in these two specific senses – the importance of communication and thought – that the economy is always and fundamentally cultural. Capitalism has had a history of the commodification of culture and communication, especially since the 20th century. This is not to say that culture and communication necessarily take on the form of a commodity, but that in capitalism they frequently do so in the form of content commodities, audience commodities, and cultural labour power as commodity. In this sense culture has been economised, or, to be more precise commoditised, i.e. put under the influence of the commodity logic.

Communication is certainly an important aspect of a society that is free from domination. However, communication is, in capitalism, also a form of interaction in which ideology, with the help of the mass media, is made available to the dominated groups. Communication is not automatically progressive. For Habermas, the differentiation is between instrumental/strategic reason and communicative reason, whereas for Horkheimer the distinction is between instrumental reason and critical reason and, based on that, between traditional and critical theory. For Habermas communication is an emancipatory concept confined to the lifeworld that is not distorted and not shaped by the steering media money and power. Thus, Habermas splits off communication from instrumentality and thereby neglects the fact that in capitalism communication, just like technology, the media, ideology, or labour, is an instrument that is used by the dominant system to defend its rule. Communication is not pure and untouched by structures of domination; it is antagonistically entangled with them. For Horkheimer (based on Marx), critical theory's goal is man's "emancipation from slavery" (Horkheimer 2002, 249) and "the happiness of all individuals" (248). Horkheimer has in mind the emancipation of communication just like the emancipation of work, decision-making, and everyday life. His notion of critical rationality is larger than Habermas's notion of communicative rationality that risks becoming soaked up by noncritical approaches that use Habermas's stress on communication for instrumental purposes. The concept of communication can be critical, but is not necessarily critical, whereas the concept of a critique of domination is necessarily critical.

Whereas communication is not necessarily critical and a critical concept, there is a tradition of critical theory within media and communication studies: Robert T. Craig (1999) points out seven approaches in communication theory. Critical theory is one of them, the others are rhetorical, semiotic, phenomenological, cybernetic, sociopsychological, and sociocultural approaches. He stresses that critique here means the criticism of domination and ideology as well as attempts to change the world for the better by political praxis.

Marxist theory and politics was in the 1920s dominated by structuralist approaches that underestimated the importance of class struggle. Young radicals were looking for philosophical inspiration in order to renew Marxist theory and politics. Some of them, including Herbert Marcuse and Günther Anders, felt that Martin Heidegger's philosophy could help make Marxist theory a concrete philosophy. They therefore became his students in Freiburg. Heidegger's book *Sein und Zeit* [*Being and Time*] in particular influenced these scholars' thinking and works. Heidegger became a member of the Nazi Party (NSDAP) in May 1933 and stayed a member until the NSDAP was dissolved in 1945. For critical theorists like Marcuse and Anders, who were communist and came from Jewish families, Heidegger's entry into the Nazi Party was a big disappointment. Intellectually, they completely turned away from Heidegger and argued that his philosophy was only pseudo-concrete and that the revolution it promised was a Nazi society built on nationalism, racism, Führer-ideology, anti-Semitism, and a militant anti-Marxism suppressing the labour movement. In the introduction to his 1932 thesis, *Hegels Ontologie und die Grundlegung einer Theorie der Geschichtlichkeit* [*Hegel's Ontology and the Theory of Historicity*] that he was unable, due to the rise of National Socialism, to defend, Marcuse thanked Heidegger. After Marcuse had fled from Germany to the United States, he worked on another book about Hegel that was published in 1941: *Reason and Revolution: Hegel and the Rise of Social Theory*. In this book, Marcuse mentioned Heidegger only once in a list of National Socialist philosophers. This shift in perspective is an indication of how Marcuse's assessment of Heidegger as philosopher and political person had changed. When Marx's (1844) *Economic-Philosophical Manuscripts of 1844* were published in 1932, they deeply impressed Marcuse. He discovered that a truly revolutionary concrete Marxist philosophy could be grounded in the philosophical works of the young Marx and did not need Heidegger at all. The question how deeply influenced Heidegger's thought was by National Socialism remained a disputed question. On the one hand, there were apologists such as Hannah Arendt, Jean-Paul Sartre, Jacques Derrida, or Richard Rorty who felt inspired by Heidegger and defended and took up the content of his philosophical works. On the other hand, critical theorists, especially Theodor W. Adorno and Jürgen Habermas, argued that Heidegger was a fascist and that National Socialism also shaped his philosophy. This controversy remains topical even today. New insights were gained by the 2014 publication of Heidegger's *Black Notebooks*. In these notebooks, Heidegger wrote that Jews were calculating profiteers, and would have lived based on the principle of race but resisted the Nazis applying this principle to them. He wrote that the Nazis would only practice manner what the Jews would have practiced long before them. World Judaism would be uprooted and abstract and would not want to sacrifice the blood of Jews in wars, whereas the Germans would only have the choice to sacrifice what Heidegger describes as the best blood of all – German blood – in warfare.

Many commentators have argued that these notebooks show once and for all that Heidegger was a convinced Nazi, an anti-Semite, and a Nazi apologist. They criticise Heidegger for arguing that the Jews were themselves to blame for the Shoah. Critical theory can today only be critical without Heidegger. Critical theory is only possible against and in opposition to Heidegger and Heideggerians. Those who continue to refer positively to Heidegger or argue that these were just unpublished minor remarks become apologists for a fascist and anti-Semitic thinker themselves. Questions concerning racism, fascism, and anti-Semitism are not minor matters, but are for critical theory questions about the totality. Heidegger's works on technology and philosophy continue to influence scholars studying media, communication, information, and technology today. A critical theory of these phenomena is today also only possible without Heidegger.

2.3 Critical Theory and Karl Marx

The six dimensions of a critical theory of society can also be found in Karl Marx's works, which shows the importance of his thought for any critical theory.

2.3.1 Critical Theory Uses Dialectical Reasoning as Method of Analysis

The dialectical method identifies contradictions. Contradictions are "the source of all dialectics" (Marx, 1867, 744). Dialectics tries to show how contemporary society and its moments are shaped by contradictions. Contradictions result in the circumstance that society is dynamic and that capitalism ensures the continuity of domination and exploitation by changing the way these phenomena are organised. Dialectics "regards every historically developed form as being in a fluid state, in motion, and therefore grasps its transient aspects as well" (Marx, 1867, 103). The "movement of capitalist society is full of contradictions" (ibid.). In a contradiction, one pole of the dialectic can only exist by way of the opposed pole; they require and exclude each other at the same time. In a dominative society (such as capitalism), contradictions cause problems and are to a certain extent also the seeds for overcoming these problems. They have positive potentials and negative realities at the same time.

Critical Theory and Karl Marx

Marx analysed capitalism's contradictions, for example, the contradictions between non-owners/owners, the poor/the rich, misery/wealth, workers/capitalists, use-value/exchange-value, concrete labour/abstract labour, the simple form of value/the relative and expanded form of value, social relations of humans/relations of things, the fetish of commodities and money/fetishistic thinking, the circulation of commodities/the circulation of money, commodities/money, labour power/wages, subject/object, labour process/valorisation process, subject of labour (labour power, worker)/the means of production (object), variable capital/constant capital, surplus labour/surplus product, necessary labour time/surplus labour time, single worker/cooperation, single company/industry sector, single capital/competing capitals, production/consumption, productive forces/relations of production.

The tension between opposing poles can be resolved in a process that Hegel and Marx called "*Aufhebung*" (sublation) and "negation of the negation": a new/third quality or a new system emerges from the contradiction between two poles. Sublation can take place at different levels of society, either relatively frequently in order to enable a dynamic of domination or infrequently in situations of revolution when domination is questioned. So, in capitalism, there is for example a contradiction between use-value and exchange-value. The use-value of a commodity is a quality that satisfies human needs; for example, movies' use-value is that they satisfy our need to be informed, entertained, and educated. But in capitalism many use-values can only be obtained if we pay money for access to them. We can only get access to them via the commodities' exchange-value: we have to enter an exchange of use-values for money so that a certain quantity of a commodity equals a specific sum of money: x commodity A = y amount of money M. Exchange-value in capitalist society dominates use-value. So the dialectic of use-value and exchange-value in capitalism is that many use-values cannot be accessed without exchange-value and the exchange-values mediate use-values; for example, Hollywood wants to sell movies in the form of cinema displays and DVDs in order to accumulate capital. There are, however, strategies that people use to try to resist commodification: for example, a commodity like education can be turned into a public service that is funded by taxes and is made available to all without payment. Movies in digital format are often "pirated" and spread online, so they become pure use-values: hackers sublate the contradiction between use-value and exchange-value. At the same time, those working for a wage in the production of films, music, and other cultural goods means that cultural work is a commodity and depends on revenues. Therefore cultural workers do not always see downloading favorably and may fear that it deprives them of income. So a new contradiction is created between cultural wage work, downloading, and the industry's monetary profits and exploitation of cultural workers. Different forms of sublation have been suggested for this contradiction such as the introduction of a cultural flat rate for the use of the Internet and culture, royalty systems, or the introduction of a basic income for cultural workers. The problem is that capitalism is contradictory as such. Therefore Marx sees communism as a society without exchange-value that is based on high productivity, automation, free distribution of all use-values, and voluntary engagement in the creation of use-values. It is a society of use-values that have sublated exchange-values. Everyone gets what s/he needs and works according to his/her abilities.

There are also contradictions in capitalism that are persistent and not frequently sublated. They are at the heart of human misery in capitalism. Their sublation can only be achieved by political struggle that would mean the end of capitalism. These are the antagonisms between productive forces/relations of production, owners/non-owners, the poor/the rich, misery/wealth, workers/capitalists. The contradiction between productive forces and relations of production is partly sublated in crisis situations, but reconstitutes itself in the crisis. Its true sublation can only be achieved by the overthrow of capitalism. If in capitalism an important contradiction is the one between the owning class that exploits the non-owning class, then the goal of critical theory is the representation of the interest of oppressed and exploited groups and the overcoming of class society. "It can only represent a class whose historical task is the overthrow of the capitalist mode of production and the final abolition of all classes – the proletariat" (Marx, 1867, 98).

In formulating a critique of domination and exploitation, critical theory develops "new principles for the world out of the principles of the world" (Marx 1997, 214). Dialectical thinking argues that the foundations of a classless society are already developing within capitalism; that capitalism produces new forms of cooperation that are within class relations forms of domination. The forces of production in capitalism are at the same time destructive forces.

2.3.2 Critique of the Political Economy: Critical Theory is a Critique of the Political Economy

Critical theory analyses how capital accumulation, surplus value exploitation, and the transformation of aspects of society into commodities (commodification) work and what the contradictions of the capitalist mode of production are. "In the critique of political economy, therefore, we shall examine the basic categories, uncover the contradiction introduced by the free-trade system, and bring out the consequences of both sides of the contradiction" (Engels, 1843/1844, 175).

Karl Marx (1867) titled his opus magnum not *Capital. A Political Economy*, but rather *Capital. A Critique of Political Economy*. Political Economy is a broad field, incorporating also traditions of thinking grounded in classical liberal economic thought and thinkers like Malthus, Mill, Petty, Ricardo, Say, Smith, Ure, etc. that Marx studied, sublated and was highly critical of in his works. His main point of criticism of Political Economy is that it fetishises capitalism, its thinkers "confine themselves to systematising in a pedantic way, and proclaiming for everlasting truths, the banal and complacent notions held by the bourgeois agents of production about their own world, which is to them the best possible one" (Marx 1867, 175). They postulate that categories like commodities, money, exchange value, capital, markets, or competition are anthropological features of all society, thereby ignoring the categories' historical character and enmeshment into class struggles. Marx showed the contradictions of political economy thought and took classical political economy as starting point for a critique of capitalism that considers "every historically developed form as being in a fluid state, in motion" and analyses how "the movement of capitalist society is full of contradictions" (Marx 1867, 103), which calls for the "development of the contradictions of a given historical form" by political practice (619) and means that Marx's approach is "in its very essence critical and revolutionary" (Marx 1867, 103).

Marx developed a Critique of the Political Economy of Capitalism, which means that his approach is: a) an analysis and critique of capitalism, b) a critique of liberal ideology, thought and academia, and c) transformative practice.

2.3.3 Critical Theory is a Critique of Domination and Exploitation

Critical theory questions all thought and practices that justify or uphold domination and exploitation. Marx formulated the categorical imperative of critical theory as the need to overthrow conditions that enslave and alienate human beings (Marx 1997, 257–258). Critical theory wants to show that a good life for all is possible and that domination and exploitation alienate humans from achieving such a society. Therefore, for Marx, the "task of philosophy [...] is to unmask human self-alienation" (Marx 1997, 251). In deconstructing alienation, domination, and exploitation, critical theory also makes demands for a self-determined, participatory, and just democracy. Such a society is not only a grassroots political democracy but also an economic democracy, in which producers control the production process, and the means and outcomes of production. Critical theory wants to make the world conscious of its own possibilities. The "world has long dreamed of something of which it only has to become conscious in order to possess it in actuality" (Marx 1997, 214).

2.3.4 Ideology Critique: Critical Theory is a Critique of Ideology

Ideologies are practices and modes of thought that present aspects of human existence that are historical and changeable as eternal and unchangeable. Ideology critique wants to remind us that everything that exists in society is created by humans in social relationships and that social relationships can be changed. It wants to bring "problems into the self-conscious human form" (Marx 1997, 214), which means that it wants to make humans conscious of the problems they are facing in society and the causes of these problems. Arguments like "there is no alternative to capitalism, neoliberalism, competition, egoism, racism, etc. because man is egoistic, competitive, etc." forget about the social character of society and make it appear as though the results of social activity are unchangeable things. Critical theory provides an "analysis of the mystical consciousness that is unclear about itself" (Marx 1997, 214).

2.3.5 Critical Ethics: Critical Theory Has a Normative Dimension

Criticism "measures individual existence against essence" (Marx 1997, 61–62). This means that critical theory is normative and realistic; it argues that it is possible to logically provide reasonably grounded arguments about what a good society is, that the good society relates to conditions that all humans require to survive (the essence of humans and society), and that we can judge existing societies according to what extent they provide humane conditions or not.

2.3.6 Critical Theory is Connected to Struggles for a Just and Fair Society; it is an Intellectual Dimension of Struggles

Critical theory provides a "self-understanding [...] of the age concerning its struggle and wishes" (Marx 1997, 315); it can "show the world why it actually struggles" and is "taking sides [...] with actual struggles" (Marx 1997, 214). This means that critical theory can help to explain the causes, conditions, potentials, and limits of struggles. Critical theory rejects the argument that academia and science should and can be value-free. It rather argues that all thought and theories are shaped by political worldviews. The reasons why a person is interested in a certain topic, aligns himself/ herself with a certain school of thought, develops a particular theory and not another, refers to certain authors and not others, are deeply political because modern society is shaped by conflicts of interests and therefore, in order to survive and assert themselves, scholars have to make choices, enter strategic alliances, and defend their positions against others. Critical theory holds not only that theory is always political but also that critical theory should develop analyses of society that struggle against interests and ideas that justify domination and exploitation.

2.4 Critical Political Economy of Media and Communication

Critical political economy is an approach within media and communication studies that has given special attention to what it means to study society, the media, and communication critically, that is, in the context of capitalism, class, power and domination, and social struggles. Dwayne Winseck (2011) provides, in the introduction to the collected volume *The Political Economies of Media*, a mapping of the landscape of political economy research in media and communication studies by identifying four approaches and speaking of "political economies of media":

- Neoclassical political economy of the media;
- Radical political economy of the media;
- Schumpeterian institutional political economy of the media;
- The cultural industries school.

Within Winseck's second approach, there is no consensus on how to name this field. In his seminal introduction to the field, *Political Economy of Communication*, Vincent Mosco defines it as the "study of the social relations, particularly the power relations, that mutually constitute the production, distribution, and consumption of resources, including communication resources" (Mosco 2009, 2). Murdock and Golding (2005) argue that the critical political economy of communications analyses "the interplay between the symbolic and the economic dimensions of public communications" (2005, 60) and "how the making and taking of meaning is shaped at every level by the structured asymmetries in social relations" (62). Terms that have been used for naming this field have been "political economy of communication", "political economy of communications", "political economy of culture", "political economy of information", "political economy of mass communication", and "political economy of the media".

The political economy of communication studies media communication in the context of power relations and the totality of social relations and is committed to moral philosophy and social praxis (Mosco 2009, 2–5). It is holistic, historical, cares about the public good, and engages with moral questions of justice and equity (Murdock and Golding 2005, 61).

Important topics of the critical political economy of communication include, for example, media activism, media and social movements; the commodification of media content, audiences and communication labour; capital accumulation models of the media, media and the public sphere, communication and space-time, the concentration of corporate power in the communication industry, the media and globalisation, media policies and state regulation of the media; communication and social class, gender, race; hegemony; the history of communication industries, media commercialisation, media homogenisation/diversification/multiplication/integration, media and advertising, media power.

Given Marx's stress on the *critique* of the political economy of, it is best to speak of the critical/critique of the political economy of communication, culture, information, and the media if a critical approach is meant (as opposed to one grounded in liberalism, neoclassical economics, institutionalism, etc.).

Horkheimer's notion of instrumental reason and Marcuse's notion of technological rationality open up connections between the two approaches of the Frankfurt School and the critical political economy of the media. Horkheimer and Marcuse stressed that in capitalism there is a tendency for freedom of action to be replaced by instrumental decision-making on the part of capital and the state so that the individual is expected only to react and not to act. The two concepts are grounded in Georg Lukács's notion of reification, which is a reformulation of Marx's (1867) concept of fetishism. Reification means that social relations take on the character and are reduced to the status of things so that the fundamental social nature of society gets concealed behind things (such as commodities or money).

The media in capitalism are modes of reification in a double sense. First, they reduce humans to the status of consumers of advertisements. Second, culture is, in capitalism,

Critical Political Economy of Media and Communication

to a large degree connected to the commodity form, in the form of cultural commodities that are bought by consumers and in the form of audience and user commodities that media consumers/Internet prosumers become themselves. And third, in order to reproduce its existence, capitalism has to present itself as the best possible (or only possible) system and makes use of the media in order to try to keep this message (in all its differentiated forms) hegemonic. The first and the second dimensions constitute the economic dimension of instrumental reason, the third dimension the ideological form of instrumental reason. Capitalist media are necessarily means of advertising and commodification and spaces of ideology. Advertisement and cultural commodification make humans an instrument for economic profit accumulation. Ideology aims at instilling belief in the system of capital and commodities into humans' subjectivity. The goal is that human thoughts and actions do not go beyond capitalism, do not question and revolt against this system and thereby play the role of instruments for the perpetuation of capitalism. It is, of course, an important question to what extent ideology is always successful and to what degree it is questioned and resisted, but the crucial aspect about ideology is that it encompasses strategies and attempts to make human subjects instrumental in the reproduction of domination and exploitation.

2.5 Cultural Studies, Political Economy, and Critique

Some cultural studies scholars (like Lawrence Grossberg) argued that both the Frankfurt School and political economy have a simple model of culture in which people – audiences and consumers – are seen as passive, stupid, manipulated cultural dupes. Scholars who say that the Frankfurt School and the critical political economy of media and communication are pessimistic and elitist and neglect audiences have a simplified understanding of these two approaches. Dallas Smythe, for example, had a very balanced view of the audience: capital would attempt to control audiences, but they would have the potential to resist the powerful and the system of capitalism.

Some forms of cultural studies have, by rejecting Marxism, faced new problems. There is the danger that consumer choice, liberal pluralism, consumption as resistance, and commercial culture are affirmed and celebrated. If resistance lies in consumption and entertainment and is a cultural automatism, then why should people engage in collective political action in social movements or political parties? The danger of culturalism is that it rejects the importance of the analysis and critique of capitalism and class and the interactions of class and domination. The active audience hypothesis resulted in the assumption that the media in capitalism create a pluralistic society. The limit of this assumption is that there are dominant discourses and unequal access to discourses and skills needed for producing information and making it visible in the public. The aftermath of the 1968 social rebellions resulted not just in the emergence of a new left but also in a new radicalism in the social sciences and humanities. The rise of neoliberalism weakened the political left and critical social sciences and humanities. It was accompanied by a culturalistic turn and the rise of postmodern thought, which were intellectual reflections of a new flexible regime of accumulation coupled with neoliberal ideology. Both cultural studies and critical political economy were influenced by the radicalism of 1968. With the rise of the commodification of everything, rebellious ideas too became commodities, fashion, and entertainment. The radical character of cultural studies was weakened, which is one of the reasons why the late Stuart Hall called for a more radical cultural studies that engages with capitalism and Marx.

The logic of determinism that some cultural studies proclaims as being characteristic of critical theory and political economy is in fact at the heart of the approaches of some of its main representatives. There is no automatism that makes humans resist, there is no automatism that culture is interpreted in a politically progressive way, there is no automatism that people struggle. There is, however, the continuity of capitalism's attempts to commodify culture and of attempts to impose dominant worldviews on people. Both critical theory and critical political economy show these tendencies that are largely left out of the analysis by many cultural studies scholars. At the same time, critical theory and critical political economy see the potential of alternative media production and the role of media in struggles and point out the problems and limits that alternative media use and that interpretation is facing in capitalism.

2.6 Frankfurt School Critical Theory and Critique of the Political Economy of Communication, Culture, Information, and the Media

Frankfurt School critical theory and the critical political economy of media/communication have both developed critiques of the role of media communication in exploitation, as means of ideology and potential means of liberation and struggle. The largest difference is that the Frankfurt School is profoundly grounded in philosophy, especially Hegelian philosophy and social theory, whereas the Anglo-American tradition of the critical political economy approach has less affinity with philosophy and more grounding in economic studies and sociology. Both traditions are valuable and important, and are complementary approaches for studying social media critically.

The globalisation of capitalism, its new global crisis, the new imperialism, and the role of knowledge and communication in capitalism (anticipated by Marx's notions of the means of communication and the general intellect) have resulted in a renewed interest in Marx that should also be practiced in media and communication studies (Fuchs 2016; Fuchs 2011; Fuchs and Mosco 2012).

The task for a critical theory and critique of the political economy of communication, culture, information, and the media is to focus on the critique and analysis of the role of communication, culture, information, and the media in capitalism in the context of: (a) processes of capital accumulation (including the analysis of capital, markets, commodity logic, competition, exchange value, the antagonisms of the mode of production, productive forces, crises, advertising, etc.); (b) class relations (with a focus on work, labour, the mode of the exploitation of surplus value, etc.); (c) domination in general; (d) ideology (both in academia and everyday life) as well as the analysis of and engagement in (e) struggles against the dominant order, which includes the analysis and advancement of (f) social movement struggles and (g) social movement media that (h) aim at the establishment of a democratic socialist society that is based on communication commons as part of structures of commonly owned means of production (Fuchs 2011). The approach thereby realises that in capitalism all forms of domination are connected to forms of exploitation (Fuchs 2011).

The tradition of the Frankfurt School stresses the notions of technological rationality and instrumental reasons. These concepts open up connections between the two approaches of the Frankfurt School and the Critical Political Economy of the Media: in capitalism there is a tendency that freedom of action is replaced by instrumental decision-making on the part of capital and the state so that the individual is expected to only react and not to act. The two concepts are grounded in the notion of reification, which is a reformulation of Marx's (1867) concept of fetishism. The media in capitalism are modes of reification in a manifold way: first, they reduce humans to the status of consumers of advertisements. Second, culture is in capitalism to a large degree connected to the commodity form, in the form of cultural commodities that are bought by consumers and in the form of audience and user commodities that media consumers/Internet prosumers become themselves. Third, in order to reproduce its existence, capitalism has to present itself as the best possible (or only possible) system and makes use of the media in order to try to keep this message (in all its differentiated forms) hegemonic. The first and the second dimension constitute the economic dimension of instrumental reason, the third dimension the ideological form of instrumental reason. Capitalist media are necessarily means of advertising and commodification and spaces of ideology. Advertisement and cultural commodification make humans an instrument for economic profit accumulation. Ideology aims at instilling the belief in the system of capital and commodities into human's subjectivity. The goal is that human thoughts and actions do not go beyond capitalism, do not question and revolt against this system and thereby play the role of instruments for the perpetuation of capitalism. It is of course an important question to which extent ideology is always successful and to which degree it is questioned and resisted, but the crucial aspect about ideology is that it encompasses strategies and attempts to make human subjects instrumental in the reproduction of domination and exploitation.

2.7 Four Debates in and about Contemporary Critical Theory

There have been interesting debates in recent years about how to best conceptualise critical theory today that will now be introduced: one focuses on the relationship of redistribution and recognition (Nancy Fraser, Axel Honneth) an, one on the relationship of critical sociology and the sociology of critique (Luc Boltanski, Axel Honneth), one on the renewal of the critique of capitalism in critical theory (Klaus Dörre, Stephan Lessenich, Hartmut Rosa), and one on the question of what is capitalism (Nancy Fraser, Rahel Jaeggi).

2.7.1 Nancy Fraser and Axel Honneth: Recognition and Redistribution

Fraser and Honneth (2003) engaged in a debate about the role of recognition and redistribution in critical theory. The encounter between the two philosophers was published as a dialogic book. It focuses on the relationship between identity politics and class politics and how critical theory should position itself on this question. Nancy Fraser is professor of philosophy at the New School in New York City. She has been a leading intellectual who has had a major influence on the development of a feminist critical theory. Axel Honneth is professor of philosophy and director of the Frankfurt Institute of Social Research at the Goethe University in Frankfurt am Main. Some consider Honneth to be the successor of Habermas as the leading intellectual figure in German critical theory.

Both Fraser and Honneth question the uncoupling of political demands for the re-cognition of identities from demands for redistribution. For Fraser, gender-, race-, and class-domination are two-dimensional categories that have economic and cultural aspects. For her, all three categories are processes of malrecognition of status and maldistribution. Fraser treats economy and culture, maldistribution and malrecognition, as two equal levels of society and domination. She sees the two poles as impinging on one another (Fraser and Honneth 2003, 64). Honneth argues that with the exception of Habermas and Gramsci, critical theory has had a tendency to anti-normativism (Fraser and Honneth 2003, 128–129). Whereas Fraser wants to base critical theory on two equal dual categories, redistribution and recognition, Honneth looks for a normative monism that is based on one central category, the one of recognition. He bases his theory on the assumption that humans are psychological beings that strive for self-esteem, self-confidence, and self-respect, and suffer if they are disrespected. Honneth subdivides recognition into three forms: love, equality, achievement. Distribution struggles are for Honneth "a specific kind of struggle for recognition, in which the appropriate evaluation of the social contributions of individuals or groups is contested" (Fraser and Honneth 2003, 171).

Christian Fuchs (2011, chapter 2) argues for a third version of moral philosophy that differs from Fraser's dualism and Honneth's monism. Redistribution would be the process of establishing a more participatory society by redistributing economic re-sources, power, and definition-capacities from dominant groups to oppressed groups. Recognition would be a cultural redistribution process of definition-capacities and reputation. For understanding recognition, a cultural materialist approach would be needed that sees that there can be no recognition without economic redistribution and the other way around. Fuchs argues neither for a separation of the concepts of re-cognition and redistribution (Fraser) nor for the subordination of the redistribution concept under the recognition concept (Honneth), but for a moral philosophy that is based on the notion of redistribution and considers recognition as a cultural form of redistribution.

2.7.2 Luc Boltanski and Axel Honneth: Critical Sociology and Sociology of Critique

A second contemporary debate about how to conceptualise critical theory has involved Axel Honneth and Luc Boltanski. Boltanski is professor of sociology at the École des hautes études en sciences sociales (School for Advanced Studies in the Social

Sciences) in Paris. Boltanski was invited by Honneth to give the 2008 Adorno lectures in Frankfurt. In these lectures, Boltanski (2011) distinguished his approach of a pragmatic sociology of critique from critical sociology. In France, Pierre Bourdieu in particular would have taken the latter approach. But the Marxist tradition can in Boltanski's view in general be described as being close to critical sociology that tries to unmask domination, exploitation, and oppression as well as ideologies justifying these phenomena (Boltanski 2011, 6). Boltanski describes his approach of the pragmatic sociology of critique as "rigorous empirical sociology" (23) that does not assume an asymmetry between the sociologist and ordinary people and aims to describe the reality and experiences of the oppressed. It would make use "*of the point of view of the actors* [...], their ordinary sense of justice, to expose the discrepancy between the social world as it is and as it should be in order to satisfy people's moral expectations" (2011, 30, italics in original). Boltanski criticises the fact that critical sociology, in his view, has an "overarching character" and a "distance at which it holds itself from the critical capacities developed by actors in the situations of everyday life" (43). The pragmatic sociology of critique would fully acknowledge "actors'" critical capacities and the creativity with which

> they engage in interpretation and action *en situation*" (43) for "denunciations of injustice" (37).

In a conversation with Honneth (Boltanski and Honneth 2009), Boltanski points out that his approach is not to denounce Marxism, as Bruno Latour does, but to take it in a new direction. Just as Boltanski says that in his view Bourdieu's approach saw domination everywhere and failed to see the immanent contradictions of society, Honneth says that Habermas, whom he considers as his main influence, saw Horkheimer and Adorno's approach as a total critique where everything is domination. The conversation makes clear that Boltanski takes an explicitly empirically grounded approach, whereas Honneth has developed a moral philosophy. Honneth argues that the reality of actors using critical capacities would be unequally distributed so that critical sociology would have to analyse the limits that social conditions pose for humans (Boltanski and Honneth 2009, 105). Boltanski argues that his approach is not to use moral philosophy and normative critique, but to assume that there are immanent contradictions in reality, that there is always something in the world that "goes beyond reality" (107). Boltanski argues that ideologies would be something that only those in power needed, whereas everyday people would create many experiences that go beyond ideology (108).

Four Debates in and about Contemporary Critical Theory

Boltanski (2011) terms normative critical theory "meta-critical theory" (8) or metacritique (6) because it would need an exteriority in order to judge what is good and what is bad. He argues for a purely immanent critique that is grounded in the empirical observation of how humans experience suffering in society and thereby criticise society. Boltanski's pragmatic sociology of critique is purely immanent. Honneth, in contrast, is more skeptical and does not see critical capacities developing with necessity in society. He stresses the need for a normative critique and a critical theory grounded in immanent transcendence.

Honneth distinguishes between a constructive, transcendental critique, a reconstructive, immanent critique, and a Foucauldian genealogical critique. Critical theory would combine all three forms. In the debate with Fraser, he characterises this combination as immanent transcendence. Transcendence

> must be attached to a form of practice or experience which is on the one hand indispensable for social reproduction, and on the other hand – owing to its normative surplus – points beyond all given forms of social organization. [...] 'transcendence' should be a property of 'immanence' itself, so that the facticity of social relations always contains a dimension of transcending claims.
>
> (Fraser and Honneth 2003, 244)

Fraser sees the immanent element of contemporary society that can transcend it in social movements that engage in political struggles (Fraser and Honneth 2003, 205), whereas Honneth is very critical of new social movements (Fraser and Honneth 2003, 114–125), considers them as rather affirmative, and sees immanent transcendence in an objective morality that should be legally implemented in the form of laws.

2.7.3 Klaus Dörre, Stephan Lessenich, Hartmut Rosa: Sociology, Capitalism, and Critique

A new development in German critical theory is the emergence of a Jena School of critical theory at the University of Jena's Department of Sociology, where three professors (Klaus Dörre, Stephan Lessenich, and Hartmut Rosa) understand their work to stand in the tradition of the Frankfurt School and Marx's critique of capitalism. They want to renew this tradition by giving specific focuses to the critical analysis of society.

In a trialogue that was published as the book *Soziologie – Kapitalismus – Kritik* [*Sociology – Capitalism – Critique*], Dörre, Lessenich, and Rosa (2009) point out the commonalities and differences of their approaches. They stress that commonalities of their approaches are that "overcoming the system is the centre of our critique" (14 [translated from German by CF]), that they argue for a critical sociology and want to go beyond Boltanski's sociology of critique (15), and that the sociological critique of capitalism would have to be renewed. Their central categories are land grabbing (*Landnahme*, Dörre), acceleration (Rosa), and activation (Lessenich).

Klaus Dörre argues that capitalism uses primitive accumulation for grabbing, appropriating, and subsuming internal and external territories in order to expand. His work is influenced by Rosa Luxemburg and David Harvey's versions of the Marxist theory of imperialism. Precarious labour and precarious life would be the consequences of a finance-dominated regime of accumulation, which would express itself clearly in the austerity measures taken after the tax-financed bailout of banks and corporations that happened in 2008 and the years following.

Hartmut Rosa says that sociology's real subject would be the question about what constitutes or harms a good life. Capitalism would be based on the logics of growth and acceleration. Modern society would be based on three logics of acceleration: technological acceleration, the acceleration of social change, and the acceleration of the speed of life. Social struggles would today be struggles about performance, that is, to achieve more in less time. Acceleration would undermine capitalism's promise to guarantee and increase autonomy. The logic of acceleration would result in ecological crisis, social exclusion, and disruption of systems that do not function based on the logic of acceleration (such as education, the legal system, and the welfare system).

Stephan Lessenich argues that the state mobilises and activates humans for the purposes of capitalism. There would be a late-modern dialectic of mobility and control. He argues for a combination of Marx and Foucault in order to understand this phenomenon. He sees it as a crucial task of critical theory today to bring the analysis of the state back to social theory. The state would, in Fordist capitalism (a form of capitalism based on mass production and mass consumption of standardised commodities that was the dominant form of capitalism in the 20th century up until the 1970s), have provided absorption mechanisms in the form of the welfare state that curbed the negative effects of capitalism. Neoliberalism would have reduced these mechanisms and resulted in an activating state that defines responsibility in individualistic terms as self-care and thereby privatises the management of social risks.

Four Debates in and about Contemporary Critical Theory

The three authors mutually criticise each other by focusing on a discussion of the approaches' implications for society and politics. Lessenich argues that Dörre formulates a classical social critique by focusing on the critique of exploitation, whereas Rosa would formulate an artistic critique by focusing on the critique of alienation from others, society, work, nature, things, and one's own body, and that both need to be united.

Lessenich hereby makes use of Boltanski and Chiapello's (2005) distinction between artistic critique – the critique of alienation that calls for authenticity, creativity, freedom, and autonomy – and social critique – the critique of class that calls for equality and overcoming capitalism. Boltanski and Chiapello argue that the new spirit of capitalism characteristic of the neoliberal turn of capitalism has incorporated the anti-authoritarian claims of the 1968 movement into capitalism so that the outcome was network capitalism.

Dörre, Lessenich, and Rosa have different sociological perspectives, from which they draw differing political conclusions. Yet they stress that what unites them is the commitment to critical theory, and that *Landnahme* is the spatial, acceleration the temporal, and activation the social dimension of "a single economic, cultural and political process, whose foundation is constituted by the logic of capital movement" (Dörre, Lessenich, and Rosa 2009, 297 [translated from German by CF]). They conclude that "capitalism does not *have* a pathology, it is one" (300 [translated from German by CF]).

2.7.4 Nancy Fraser and Rahel Jaeggi: What is Capitalism?

In a book organised as a conversation, Nancy Fraser and Rahel Jaeggi (2018) discuss the question of what is capitalism. Their starting point is the fact that since the world economic crisis that started in 2008, there has been a rising interest in the analysis of capitalism. In contrast, during the time from the 1980s until the start of the crisis, capitalism and class were often ignored and their importance were downplayed.

As a consequence, there was little focus on "grasping society as a totality" (5) and more interest in micro-sociological analyses. At the same time, there was the rise of postmodern thought that just like liberalism ignored "the problematic of political economy" (6). Fraser and Jaeggi agree that the turn against economic reductionism enabled a focus on "gender, race, sexuality, and identity" (7) but say that this focus went too far by ignoring class. Fraser says that a "both/and" (7) approach is needed. She writes that in the 1980s, capitalism shifted from state-managed capitalism to financialised capitalism.

Fraser conceives of capitalism as an institutionalised social order, Jaeggi as a form of life. They agree that core features of capitalism are a) the private property of the means of production and the class relation between producers and owners, b) the labour market, c) capital accumulation, d) markets and the commodity form (15, 19, 28). The engine that drives capitalism is "the exploitation of labor" that "generates surplus value" (19). Fraser argues based on Karl Polanyi that capitalism contains both commodified and non-commodified spheres. Jaeggi adds that the totalisation of commodification creates contradictions and "real social conflicts" (23). For Fraser, class struggles emerge from the economy and boundary struggles from the points where production meets reproduction, economy meets polity, and humans meet nature (167). Such struggles against expropriation include struggles in the context of racism, imperialism, sexism, nationalism, and citizenship (165–166). Fraser's expanded notion of capitalism also implies an expended notion of class struggle that includes struggles by unpaid workers beyond wage-labour, including reproductive labour, labour that cultivates resources, and labour that sustains habits and nature (166).

Jaeggi and Fraser agree that capitalism extends beyond its economic core. For Fraser, capitalism is "an *institutionalized social order*" (52). The "economic foreground" has a "non-economic background" (29). Among those conditions of possibility of capitalism is social reproduction or what is also called reproductive labour. Fraser: "Wage labor could neither exist nor be exploited, after all, in the absence of housework, child-raising, schooling, affective care, and a host of other activities that produce new generations of workers, replenish existing generations, and maintain social bonds and shared understandings" (31). Besides social reproduction, the appropriation of nature as tap and sink, state power that operates as legal framework of private property and markets, imperialism, and racial oppression are background conditions of capitalism. For Fraser, expropriation means the confiscation of nature, sexual and reproductive capacity, human beings, and territory. She says that expropriation enables exploitation. Expropriation is for Fraser ongoing primitive accumulation, which is a parallel to Rosa Luxemburg and David Harvey (43). Capital benefits from expropriation by appropriating gratis resources, which allow increasing profit rates. Fraser argues that the background arenas of capitalist society are based on logics different from the commodity logic (49). Fraser talks about the background arenas' "divergence from the values associated with capitalism's foreground, such as growth, efficiency, equal exchange, individual choice,

Four Debates in and about Contemporary Critical Theory

negative liberty, and meritocratic advancement" (50). For Fraser, capitalism is based on four dualisms: production/reproduction, economy/polity, nature/human, exploitation/ expropriation (52–53). She argues that there are class struggles in the economy and boundary struggles in the non-economic spheres (69). She thinks of society and ca- pitalist society as consisting of "a plurality of" spheres, "each of which has its own 'inner logic' of development" (68).

Jaeggi argues for a "monistic social theory" (51) based on the concept of practices. Social practices congeal into institutions. For Jaeggi, there are economic and non- economic practices and institutions. She rejects the separation between action/lifeworld and system. Jaeggi conceives of capitalism as a form of life. Forms of life are "forms of human coexistence shaped by culture", "orders of human coexistence" that include an "ensemble of practices and orientations" and "their institutional manifestations and materialization" (Jaeggi 2018, 3), "ensembles of practices *marked by a certain form of inertia*" (Jaeggi 2018, 55), "*clusters of practices* that are *interconnected* and interrelated" (Jaeggi 2018, 41), "*collective* formations" that involve "socially shared practices" (Jaeggi 2018, 42), passive and active which means they are "pregiven and laid out in advance" and simultaneously created by human practices (Jaeggi 2018, 42).

Just like when Fraser speaks of capitalism as an institutionalised social order, speaking of capitalism as a form of life implies for Jaeggi that capitalism goes beyond the economy and "leaves its imprint not only on economic structures but also on how we conceive the world, on our relation to space and time, and on our relationship to nature in ways that affect our lives as a whole, without individuals even being aware of this as a specific imprint" (Jaeggi 2018, 4).

Forms of life are "social formations constituted through what I call 'ensembles' of practices, and these include economic practices as well as social and cultural ones. The whole point of a 'form of life' approach in this context is to understand economic practices as social practices – in a continuum with the other practices together and in connection to each other" (Fraser and Jaeggi 2018, 137). For Jaeggi, capitalism combines social, economic, and cultural practices (137).

Jaeggi is interested in an immanent crisis critique of capitalism that integrates ethical, functionalist and moral critiques of capitalism and analyses why "life under capitalism is 'bad' or an alienated life", "impoverished and meaningless" (Fraser and Jaeggi 2018, 127). For Jaeggi, alienation means "powerlessness" and "relations of relationlessness", an inability of humans to establish relations to other humans, things, and social institutions (134). Fraser argues that capitalism restricts human participation, democracy, and autonomy (131, which is a critique of capitalism centred on political in/justice (132).

The debate between Fraser and Jaeggi is important in several respects:

- Capitalism: The two social theorists ascertain the actuality of capitalism and argue that the debate on capitalism needs to be renewed. From the 1980s until the time of the start of the new world economic crisis in 2008, neoliberalism and postmodernism continuously undermined and destroyed the focus on class and capitalism, arguing that such analyses are outdated, economic reductionist, deterministic, totalitarian, etc. At the political level, these forces gave rise to neoliberal and postmodern identity politics. They discredited socialism as viable alternative to capitalism and Marx's theory. The rediscovery of class and capitalism underpins attempts to renew left-wing (anti-)class politics and the idea of socialism.
- Capitalist society: Both Fraser and Jaeggi argue that we live in a capitalist society. Such a stress is a countertendency to claims that we live in a radically new society and that everything has fundamentally changed. In this context, notions such as network society, information society, modern society, second modernity, reflexive modernisation, global society, etc. underestimate and downplay the importance of capitalism. Such terms sound very positive and affirm domination, whereas capitalism and capitalist society are inherently critical concepts of society.
- Alienation: Both theorists give attention to some version of Marx's concept of alienation. The focus on alienation allows to ground critical theories of society that stress capitalism and class, non-economic domination, and the dialectical mediation of both.

There are also limits and problems of the approaches that Fraser and Jaeggi advance. *First*, both approaches end up with multifactor analyses of society that cannot answer the question of what unites the different realms of capitalist society. Nancy Fraser advances a "perspectival dualism" (57) where multiple logics operate in parallel. What is missing is an answer to the question of what unites the different arenas of capitalist society. The result is a multi-factor analysis that is based on diversity of logics without unity. Fraser cannot explain what it is that makes non-economic spheres part of a *capitalist* society, which implies that capitalism is the key feature of society and is therefore not simply limited to the economy but shapes in a variety of ways also the non-economic spheres.

Four Debates in and about Contemporary Critical Theory

With an abstract notion of practices as "habitual, rule-governed, socially significant complexes of interlinked actions that have an enabling character and through which purposes are pursued" (Jaeggi 2018, 29), Jaeggi stresses the importance of both the economic and the non-economic in society. Both Fraser and Jaeggi have too much adopted the theoretical language of postmodernism that focuses on plurality and are too much giving in to this approach, which weakens their approach. They cannot explain what unites the diversity of realms in society and end up with ascertaining that there is a plurality of practices (Jaeggi) and arenas (Fraser) in society.

Second, both Fraser and Jaeggi cannot explain what is capitalist about the non-economic realms in capitalist society. They postulate multiple logics of alienation and domination operating in parallel that interact. It remains unclear what is the common denominator of these logics.

Third, both the approaches of Fraser and Jaeggi do not adequately incorporate the Marxian notion of society as capitalist totality. Fraser speaks of capitalism as an institutionalised social order and Jaeggi of capitalism as form of life. The concepts of "institutional social order" and "form of life" sound too much situated at the micro- and meso-levels of society. Critical theory needs to operate at the macro-level of society and dialectically mediate that level with the level of institutions, organisations, groups, and individuals. In order to make clear that capitalism is a totality, or what Marx calls *Gesellschaftsformation* (societal formation/formation of society), it is best to simply speak of capitalist society and not to coin notions such as institutional social order and form of life that relativise the focus on society as totality.

The present author has in contrast to dualist approaches advanced dialectical models of society and capitalism where social production is the practice that unites all spheres of society so that all of them are at the same time economic and have specific relative autonomous logics (Fuchs 2020). Marxist-Humanist approaches stress the importance of asking not just what society and capitalism are, but what the human being is and what its role is in society and in capitalist society. They are based on Marx's insights that humans are both social beings and producing beings. Social production is the materiality of humans and society. Social production is grounded in the economy, namely in the logic of human work processes, but goes beyond the economy in that it shapes all spheres of society and everyday life. Social production is the process of teleological positing by which humans produce and reproduce society through conscious, goal-oriented work processes by which humans transcend their individuality by producing together with and for others. In non-economic spheres, human production results in the creation and sustenance of structures that have their own logics and are dialectically mediated with the economy. Non-economic realms and practices are at the same time economic and non-economic. There is a dialectic of the economic and the non-economic in society.

Fraser and Jaeggi leave open the answer to the question of what exactly it is that unites and brings together the different realms of capitalist society. The present author has argued that the logic of accumulation unites the spheres of capitalist society (Fuchs 2020). It originates in the capitalist economy and shapes the spheres of capitalist society where accumulation takes on relatively autonomous logics that are based on and mediated with the logic of capital accumulation. The non-economic spheres of capitalist society are at the same time economic and non-economic, realms of production and accumulation and realms that have emergent qualities that go beyond capital accumulation and are dialectically mediated with capital accumulation.

Capitalist society is a society that is shaped by the logic of accumulation and instrumental reason. In the economy, accumulation means the accumulation of capital. In the political system, accumulation means the accumulation of decision-power. In the cultural system, accumulation means the accumulation of reputation and attention. Accumulation results in alienation that creates structures that cause injustices. Injustice means that humans are denied a good life, the realisation of their potentials, and control of the conditions that shape their lives. Accumulation and alienation are forms of inhumanity. Table 2.1 provides a brief overview of some aspects of the present author's model of society.

2.8 Conclusion

Habermas once wrote that "philosophy is preserved in science as critique" (Habermas 1971, 63). If we want to conduct a critical analysis of the media and communication then we require a critical philosophy as foundation. The most important critical philosophy tradition is the one that goes back to Hegel and Marx. This entry has shown that there are multiple ways of establishing a critical theory of society and applying such an approach to the study of media and communication. No matter which approach one takes, Marx's insights that class and domination interact and are foundational phenomena of modern society should lie at the heart of any attempt that sees itself as a critical approach for studying contemporary society and communication in contemporary society.

TABLE 2.1 Some foundations of a Marxist-Humanist, dialectical model of society

Sphere	General features	Structure	Process	Antagonism	Injustice
Economy	production of use-values	class relation between capital and labour	capital accumulation	capital vs. labour	Capitalist exploitation: capital's private ownership of the means of production, capital, and created products implies the working class' non-ownership and exploitation
Politics	production of collective decisions	nation-state	accumulation of decision-power and influence	bureaucracy vs. citizens	Domination: citizens' lack of influence on political decisions as consequence of the asymmetric distribution of decision-power
Culture	production of meanings	Ideologies	accumulation of reputation, attention and respect	ideologues and celebrities vs. everyday people	Invisibility, disrespect: lack of recognition as consequence of an asymmetric attention economy and ideological scapegoating

The three contemporary debates in critical theory that were introduced focused on the roles of recognition and redistribution, the sociology of critique and critical sociology, and the critique of capitalism today. All three debates matter for studying media and communication critically.

Fraser and Honneth's discussion is one about the relationship between identity politics and class in cultural studies, although in quite different ways that embrace either evolutionary economics, heterodox economics without Marx, or Marx (Fuchs 2014, chapter 3). The crisis has shown that inequality is shaping the world politics today. This question has shaped the conflict between cultural studies and critical political economy in media and communication studies. In light of the first world economic crisis in the 21st century, it became difficult to ignore the importance of capitalism and class. This has led to a return of the economy today and denies people material, political, and cultural recognition that they can only obtain via a redistribution of wealth, decision-power, and status. The question of how power, power inequalities, and power struggles shape and are shaped by the media is one about distribution and redistribution that entails the demands for equality, participation, and recognition.

The debate between Honneth and Boltanski, critical sociology and the sociology of critique, is one between a more normative and a more empirical sociological approach.

In media and communication studies (as in other parts of the social sciences), we find a kind of polarisation between theoretical approaches that focus on theorising communication and the media, and empirical approaches that engage in the observation and interpretation of the world through data collection and analysis. On the one hand, this situation reflects different traditions, but on the other, it is an expression of the fragmentation, individualisation, and neoliberalisation of the university. The university has increasingly been *seized* by the logic of capital, *accelerated* by the logic of performance measurement, with scholars *activated* to act as individuals and not so much as groups or collectives of scholars. As a consequence, there are few space, time, and social possibilities for critique and interdisciplinarity that, as suggested and practiced by the Frankfurt School, combines philosophy and empirical research in critical studies. Critical media and communication studies could under ideal circumstances operate as a *critical sociology of critique*. Such an approach combines critical sociology and the sociology of critique. It could be applied for studying media and communication in society with the help of a philosophically grounded normative critical theory. It could also be used for grounding empirical social research into human experiences in the context of mediated and communicative inequalities and struggles for equality. Such empirical studies could in turn inspire new theoretical knowledge.

Dörre, Lessenich, and Rosa, show the fruitfulness of debate between colleagues as well as the relevance of critically questioning capitalism. If we think of the media and communication, then capitalism is an all-present reality in the form of transnational media, communication and cultural corporations, media concentration, advertising and consumer culture, the information economy, and ideologies. Yet capitalism is only one existing political economy of the media. There is also a strong tradition of public service media in parts of the world and alternative media connected to social movements and activists who want to create a world of communicative, digital, and cultural commons. The question of capitalism is a core task for critical media and communication studies today. Studies of media and communication inspired by critical theory focus on the analysis of information phenomena in the context of Marxian topics such as dialectics; capitalism; commodity/commodification; surplus value, exploitation, alienation, class; globalisation; ideology/ideology critique; class struggle; commons; public sphere; communism; aesthetics (Fuchs 2011, 2012, 2014).

Conclusion

Fraser and Jaeggi point out the relevance of asking and discussing the question of what capitalism is. While talking about capitalism and class was ignored for a long time, the Fraser/Jaeggi-debate is symptomatic of a new interest in Marx and the analysis of capitalism and class. Fraser and Jaeggi stress that the society we live in is a capitalist and class society, which helps countering affirmative claims that we live in a postmodern society, knowledge society, network society, information society, modern society, society of reflexive modernisation, second modernity, risk society, global society, etc. Both Fraser and Jaeggi point out specific versions of the concept of alienation, which confirms the relevance of this Marxian notion.

Critical theory was a dominant approach in the social sciences in the years after the 1968 student protests. The rise of neoliberalism and postmodernism in the 1980s transformed universities in such a way that critical theory became less prevalent. This development was intensified after 1989 because many scholars saw the fall of the Soviet system as the historical victory of capitalism and were disillusioned about the feasibility of socialist alternatives. At the same time, the neoliberal mode of capitalism resulted in worldwide dramatic rises of inequality and precarious life and labour, which culminated in a new global economic crisis that started in 2008. Coming to grips with class, inequality, capitalism again became a crucial dimension of the social sciences. This development has resulted in a rising importance of critical theory-approaches both in the social sciences. Critical theory is an approach that is of crucial importance for understanding contemporary society.

References

Boltanski, Luc. 2011. *On Critique. A Sociology of Emancipation*. Cambridge: Polity Press.
Boltanski, Luc and Ève Chiapello. 2005. *The New Spirit of Capitalism*. London: Verso.
Boltanski, Luc and Axel Honneth. 2009. Soziologie der Kritik oder Kritische Theorie? In *Was ist Kritik?*, ed. Rahel Jaeggi and Tilo Wesche, 81–114. Frankfurt am Main: Suhrkamp.
Craig, Robert T. 1999. Communication Theory as a Field. *Communication Theory* 9 (2): 119–161.
Dörre, Klaus, Stephan Lessenich, and Hartmut Rosa. 2009. *Soziologie – Kapitalismus – Kritik. Eine Debatte*. Frankfurt am Main: Suhrkamp.
Engels, Friedrich. 1843/1844. Outlines of a Critique of Political Economy. In *Economic and Philosophic Manuscripts of 1844 and the Communist Manifesto.*, 171–202. Amherst, MA: Prometheus.
Fraser, Nancy and Axel Honneth. 2003. *Redistribution or Recognition? A Political-Philosophical Exchange*. London: Verso.
Fraser, Nancy and Rahel Jaeggi. 2018. *Capitalism. A Conversation in Critical Theory*. Cambridge: Polity.
Fuchs, Christian. 2020. *Communication and Capitalism. A Critical Theory*. London: University of Westminster Press. https://doi.org/10.16997/book45

Fuchs, Christian. 2016. *Reading Marx in the Information Age: A media and Communication Studies Perspective on "Capital, Volume 1"*. New York: Routledge.

Fuchs, Christian. 2014. *Digital Labour and Karl Marx*. New York: Routledge.

Fuchs, Christian. 2012. Towards Marxian Internet Studies. *triplec: Communication, Capitalism & Critique* 10 (2): 392–412.

Fuchs, Christian. 2011. *Foundations of Critical Media and Information Studies*. New York: Routledge.

Fuchs, Christian and Vincent Mosco, eds. 2012. Marx is Back. The Importance of Marxist Theory and Research for Critical Communication Studies Today. *triplec – Journal for a Global Sustainable Information Society* 10 (2): 127–632.

Habermas, Jürgen. 1987. *Theory of Communicative Action Volume 2*. Boston, MA: Beacon Press.

Habermas, Jürgen. 1984. *Theory of Communicative Action Volume 1*. Boston: Beacon Press.

Habermas, Jürgen. 1971. *Knowledge and Human Interest*. Boston, MA: Beacon Press.

Horkheimer, Max. 2002. *Critical Theory*. New York, NY: Continuum.

Jaeggi, Rahel. 2018. *Critique of Forms of Life*. Cambridge, MA: The Belknap Press.

Marcuse Herbert. 1988. *Negations: Essays in Critical Theory*. London: Free Association Books.

Marcuse, Herbert. 1941. *Reason and Revolution: Hegel and the Rise of Social Theory*. London: Routledge. Second edition.

Marx, Karl. 1997. *Writings of the Young Marx on Philosophy and Society*. Indianapolis, IN: Hackett.

Marx, Karl. 1867. *Capital. Volume I*. London, UK: Penguin.

Marx, Karl. 1844. *Economic and Philosophic Manuscripts of 1844*. Mineola, NY: Dover.

Mosco, Vincent. 2009. *Political Economy of Communication*. London: Sage. Second edition.

Murdock, Graham and Peter Golding. 2005. Culture, Communications and Political Economy. In *Mass Media and Society*, ed. James Curran and Michael Gurevitch, 60–83. London, UK: Hodder & Stoughton.

Sandkühler, Hans Jörg, ed. 1990. *Europäische Enzyklopädie zu Philosophie und Wissenschaften*. Hamburg. Felix Meiner Verlag.

Schweppenhäuser, Gerhard and Frigga Haug. 2012. Kritische Theorie. In *Historisch-Kritisches Wörterbuch des Marxismus*, ed. Wolfgang Fritz Haug and Peter Jehle, *Volume 8/1*, 197–223. Hamburg: Argument.

Wiggershaus, Rolf. 1995. *The Frankfurt School: Its History, Theories and Political Significance*. Cambridge, MA: MIT Press.

Winseck, Dwayne. 2011. The Political Economies of Media and the Transformation of the Global Media Industries. An Introductory Essay. In *The Political Economies of Media*, ed. Dwayne Winseck and Dal Yong Jin, 3–48. London: Bloomsbury Academic.

References

Chapter Three
Friedrich Engels Today

3.1 Introduction

Friedrich Engels was Karl Marx's closest comrade, intellectual collaborator, and friend. Just like critical theory is unthinkable without Marx, it would also not exist without Engels. Engels made original contributions to a critical theory of society, worked together with Marx, supported and funded Marx's works, edited the second and third volumes of Marx's *Capital*, and was a key figure in socialist politics.

This chapter asks: how relevant are Engels's works today? The introduction (Section 3.1) gives an overview of Engels's life. Section 3.2 provides an overview of Engels's works. Section 3.3 focuses on Engels's concept of history and the role of class struggles in history. Section 3.4 shows the relevance of Engels's book *The Condition of the Working Class in England* in the 21st century. Section 3.5 draws some conclusions.

Friedrich Engels was born on 28 November 1820 in Barmen, a city in North Rhine-Westphalia, Germany, that has since 1929 formed a district of the city Wuppertal. In the early 19th century, Barmen was one of the most important manufacturing centres in the German-speaking world. He was the child of Elisabeth Franziska Mauritia Engels (1797–1873) and Friedrich Engels senior (1796–1860). The Engels family was part of the capitalist class and operated a business in the cotton manufacturing industry, which was one of the most important industries. In 1837, Engels senior created a business partnership with Peter Ermen called Ermen & Engels. The company operated cotton mills in Manchester (Great Britain) and Engelskirchen (Germany).

DOI: 10.4324/9781003199182-3

Other than Marx, Engels did not attend university because his father wanted him to join the family business so that Engels junior already at the age of 16 started an apprenticeship in commerce.

Starting in September 1841, Friedrich Engels for one year served as a one-year volunteer soldier in the Prussian Army in Berlin. During this time, he attended lectures by Schelling, who held Hegel's philosophy chair. Like Marx, Engels became a "Young Hegelian", which was the name used for the followers of Hegel's philosophy who provided a left-wing interpretation of this approach.

From late 1842 until summer 1844 he stayed in Manchester in order to work in his father's business. During this stay, Engels conducted research for his book *The Condition of the Working Class in England* (Engels 1845b), built contacts to the League of the Just and the Chartist Movement, and met the Irish worker Mary Burns. Mary Burns (1821–1863) was Engels's partner until her death in 1863. After Mary's death, Friedrich Engels lived together in a partnership with her younger sister Lydia ("Lizzy", 1827–1878), whom he married one day before her death.

Marx and Engels first met in 1842. They became life-long friends, comrades, and collaborators when they again met for a ten-day period in Paris in August 1844. In 1847, Marx and Engels joined the League of the Just that was renamed to Communist League that commissioned the two thinkers to write the *Manifesto of the Communist Party*.

During the revolutionary times of 1848/1849, Engels contributed as journalist to the *Neue Rheinische Zeitung*, a radical democratic newspaper opposed to the monarchy and feudalism that was edited by Marx in Cologne. Engels actively participated in the revolutionary uprising against the Prussian regime in Elberfeld and Baden. After the defeat of the democratic revolution, Marx and Engels fled to England, where Engels started working for his father's company in 1850. He took over his father's management role in 1864. Engels junior hated work for the company because he did not share the capitalist worldview of the bourgeoisie. He saw the role as a strategic opportunity that allowed him to earn enough money for being able to fund Marx's research time and the socialist movement. In 1869, Engels left the company and the payout he received from selling his company share allowed him to fund his and Marx's work and the socialist movement until his death. He from then on dedicated his time to the socialist cause and socialist research.

In 1870, Engels moved to London so that he lived closer to Marx. Also in 1870, he became a member of the council of the First International (International Workingmen's

Association). After Marx's death in 1883, Engels became the intellectual leader of the international communist movement. Given that Engels and Marx's daughters Eleanor and Laura were after Marx' deaths the only people alive who were able to read Marx's terrible handwriting, Engels devoted the majority of his time to editing volumes 2 and 3 of *Capital*. Volume 2 was first published in 1885 and in a second edition in 1893. Volume 3 was first published in 1894. *Capital's* first volume had been published in 1867 and its second edition in 1872/1873. The French translation that contained many important editorial changes made by Marx had been published in 1875. Engels edited and published *Volume 1*'s third (1883) and fourth (1890) German editions as well as the first English translation that was published in 1886/1887. Marxist and non-Marxist critics of Engels often point out that Engels' editorial work vulgarised and distorted the meaning of Marx's *Capital*. But there is little evidence that Engels' additions and changes resulted in substantial changes of the meaning of what Marx wrote down in the manuscripts of *Capital* (see Fülberth 2020; Hecker 2018, 52–66, especially 64–66; Kopf 2017, 106–107). Without Engels's editorial work, there would be no second and third volume of *Capital*. Engels improved the readability of *Capital Volume 2 and 3* but did not change the theoretical meanings at the semantic level.

> If Engels [...] had committed forgeries, for example in the third volume of 'Capital', then the first publication in 1992 of Marx's main manuscript from the third rough draft of the 'Critique of Political Economy' in MEGA^2 Volume II/4.2 should have triggered a great flood of new, better solutions or presentations. But they do not exist, although more than two decades have passed. [...] Without Engels' great theoretical and methodological abilities, Marx would be a forgotten among other writers of the 19th century. Thanks to Engels, Marx's 'Capital' lives on in human memory throughout the centuries!
>
> (Kopf 2017, 106–107, 109, translation from German).

Suffering from cancer of the throat, Friedrich Engels died aged at the age of 74 on 5 August 1895.

3.2 Friedrich Engels's Work and Works

Engels on the one hand was the organiser and "manager" of Marx's intellectual works. On the other hand, he himself made important intellectual contributions to socialist theory. Engels together with Marx wrote the *Manifesto of the Communist Party*, *The German Ideology*, and *The Holy Family*. Engels also helped out Marx with writing newspaper articles that appeared under Marx's name. And he made a genuine contribution to critical theory with works such as *Anti-Schelling (Schelling and Revelation), Outlines of a Critique of Political Economy, The Condition of the Working Class in England, The Housing Question, Anti-Dühring, Socialism: Utopian and Scientific, Dialectics of Nature, The Origin of the Family, Private Property and the State; Ludwig Feuerbach and the End of Classical German Philosophy.*

At the age of 19, Engels (1839) published *Letters from* Wuppertal that documented the conditions the working class in Germany. Attending Schelling's lectures in Berlin, Engels published a series of three philosophical works that criticised Schelling's approach and defended Hegel against Schelling: Schelling on Hegel (Engels 1841), Schelling and Revelation: Critique of the Latest Attempt of Reaction against the Free Philosophy (Engels 1842a), Schelling, Philosopher in Christ (Engels 1842b). In 1843, Engels (1843) published the essay *Outlines of a Critique of Political Economy*, a foundational text of Marx's and Engels's approach to and critique of political economy, in which he formulated a critique of classical political economy. Marx (1859, 264) characterised the *Outlines* as "brilliant essay on the critique of economic categories" and directly referred to it several times in *Capital Volume I* (Marx 1867, 168 [footnote 30], 253 [footnote 5], 266–267 [footnote 20], 788 [footnote 15]). Michael Roberts (2020, 29) characterises the *Outlines* as "the first pioneering work of what we now call Marxian economics", where for the first time foundations of a Maxist theory of value were formulated.

Marx and Engels first joint works were *The Holy Family, or Critique of Critical Criticism. Against Bruno Bauer and Company* (Marx and Engels 1845) and *The German Ideology. Critique of Modern German Philosophy According to Its Representatives Feuerbach, B. Bauer and Stirner, and of German Socialism According to Its Various Prophets* (Marx and Engels 1845/1846). They wrote these manuscripts as a clarification of their own position towards contemporary German philosophy. Marx wrote the vast part of The Holy Family, but the book just like The German Ideology emerged from the joint thinking and discussions of Marx and Engels. The overall goal of both works was a critique of the contemporary left-wing thought of the 1840s as too much focused on the critique of ideas and religion. Marx and Engels argued for developing leftist critique towards a critique of capitalism and in doing so created foundations of a critical theory of ideology, capitalism, and communism. They focused their critique on the approaches of Carl Reichardt, Jules Faucher, Ernst Jungnitz, Edgar Bauer, Franz Zychlin von Zychlinski ("Szeliga"), Bruno Bauer, Ludwig

Feuerbach, Max Stirner, Karl Grün, and Georg Kuhlmann. *Holy Family* was published as book in 1845. Marx and Engels did not find a publisher for *German Ideology*. The entire book was first published in 1932 as part of the first German *Marx-Engels-Gesamtausgabe* (MEGA[1]).

In February 1845, Engels (1845a) gave two speeches in Elberfeld as part of communist gatherings led by Moses Hess, who was Germany's leading communist in the 1830s and 1840s and had major influence on Marx and Engels. Engels spoke about how communism differs from capitalism.

Engels conducted the research for his book *The Condition of the Working Class in England* (*CWCE* = Engels 1845b) during his stay in Manchester from 1842 until 1844, where he was supposed to learn his father's trade. Engels directly experienced the working class' conditions in England and got in touch with workers, from whom he learned about their everyday life and the problems they faced. In *CWCE*, Engels analyses the rise, early development and consequences of capitalism in England. The decisive features he mentions are a) the working class, b) industrial technologies such as the steam-engine as moving technology and manufacturing machinery as working technology that replaced handicraft, c) the capitalist class, and d) the division of labour.

In *CWCE*, Engels analyses the terrible conditions that the working class had to endure in industrial England, including long working hours, low wages, poverty, overcrowded and dirty slums and dwellings, poisonous and uneatable food, overwork, starvation, death by hunger, lack of sleep, air pollution, untreated illnesses, egotism and moral indifference, crime, alcoholism, bad clothes, unemployment, rape, homelessness, lack of clean water, drainage and sanitation, illiteracy, child labour, military drill in factories, overseers' flogging and maltreatment of workers, deadly work accidents, fines, etc.

Using factory inspectors' reports, parliamentary reports, observation, and the analysis of news reports, *The Condition of the Working Class in England* shows that Engels already in the 1840s practiced and pioneered empirical social research (Kurz 2020, 67; Krätke 2020, 29–34; Zimmermann 2020). In *Capital Volume 1*, Marx (1867) uses the same empirical method as Engels in *CWCE*, which shows that Engels's work had large influence on Marx. Marx (1867, 349 (footnote 15), 573, 755) explicitly refers positively to Engels's book several times. Working on *Capital*, Marx re-read Engels's *Condition* and wrote to him about the book: "With what zest and passion, what boldness of vision and absence of all learned or scientific reservations, the subject is still attacked in these pages!" (Marx 1863, 469).

Marx and Engels' (1848) *Manifesto of the Communist Party* has been their most influential work. Published on the eve of the 1848 revolutions, the Manifesto outlines the critique of class society and capitalism, introduces different forms of socialism and introduces foundations of communism. Draft of a Communist Confession of Faith (Engels 1847a) and Principles of Communism (Engels 1847b) were pre-works and drafts written by Engels that Marx used as foundations for writing the text of the *Manifesto* (Marx and Engels 1848). Eric Hobsbawm (2011) writes that the *Manifesto* "was almost certainly by far the most influential single piece of political writing since the French Revolutionary *Declaration of the Rights of Man and Citizen*" (102) and that it "still has plenty to say to the world in the 21st century" (107).

Engels specialised on and over the course of his life again and again wrote about wars and military strategy. Examples are his works *The Peasant War in Germany* (Engels 1850), *Po and Rhine* (Engels 1859), *Notes on the War* (Engels 1870/1871), or *Can Europe Disarm?* (Engels 1893). At the end of his life, Engels anticipated the First World War and stressed the need for general disarmament as potential way out. "For the past twenty-five years all Europe has been arming on a hitherto unprecedented scale. Every major power is seeking to surpass another in military might and readiness for war. [...] Is there no way out of this blind alley except through a war of destruction such as the world has never seen? I maintain: disarmament and thus a guarantee of peace is possible" (Engels 1893, 372).

In *The Housing Question*, Engels (1872) criticised Pierre-Joseph Proudhon's approach to social policy and pointed out that the housing problem that the working-class faces is inherent to capitalism. Almost 150 years later, housing remains a key problem of capitalism as the financialisation of housing and its role in the 2008 capitalist crisis showed.

In 1878, Engels (1878) published *Anti-Dühring. Herr Eugen Dühring's Revolution in Science*. Eugen Dühring (1833–1921) was a German theorist who was influential in the Social Democratic Workers' Party of Germany, critical of Marx, and embraced positivism, anti-Semitism, and racism. In *Anti-Dühring*, Engels outlines foundations of dialectical-materialist philosophy, the critique of political economy, and socialism. Marx wrote the tenth chapter of the books' part on political economy. Parts of *Anti-Dühring* that focused on utopian socialism, dialectics, and historical materialism were first published (in French) in 1880 under the title *Socialism: Utopian and Scientific* (Engels 1880). In the 1870s and 1880s, Engels worked on materials about the dialectics of nature. The work remained unfinished and was first published in 1925 under the title

Dialectics of Nature (Engels 1925). In 1886, Engels (1888) published *Ludwig Feuerbach and the End of Classical German Philosophy* in the socialist journal *Die Neue Zeit*. In 1888, the work was published as a separate book.

Lenin (1913, 24) characterised Engels's *Ludwig Feuerbach* and *Anti-Dühring* as "handbooks for every class-conscious worker". In the Soviet Union and in orthodox communist parties and movements, reading these works by Engels often was a substitute for engaging with Marx's writings and the entire oeuvre of Marx and Engels. Stalinism eulogised elements from some of Engels's works. In his essay "Dialectical and Historical Materialism" published in the *History of the Communist Party of the Soviet Union Bolsheviks: Short Course* – the ideological bible of Stalinism – Stalin (1945) references and quotes from Engels's *Anti-Dühring*, *Dialectics of Nature*, and *Feuerbach and the End of Classical German Philosophy*.

For Stalin, socialism as science does not mean a science of society that is different from the natural sciences, but deterministic and mechanical social laws of nature operating in society. The implication is for Stalin that history develops in a linear manner, it is for him a "process of development from the lower to the higher" (Stalin 1945, 109). Stalin argues that the Soviet Union followed capitalism and therefore was a socialist system: "[T]he U.S.S.R. has already done away with capitalism and has set up a Socialist system" (Stalin 1945, 119). His implication was that anyone critical of him was bourgeois and anti-socialist. The mechanical interpretation of the dialectic legitimated Stalin's terror against his opponents.

The concepts of *Aufhebung* (sublation) and the negation of the negation are missing in Stalinist dialectics. They are however key features of Engels's dialectics. Stalin referred to Engels, but Engels's interpretation of dialectics was other than Stalin's not based on mechanical and deterministic concepts. Engels is not be blamed for Stalinism (see Liedman 2018, 467–525). For Engels, dialectics operates in nature, consciousness, and society. These dialectics are connected but not the same. In society, there are conscious human actors who act and struggle based on intentions and interests that cannot always be realised as planned because society is complex and dynamic. For Engels just like for Marx, history is the history of class struggles. "In modern history at least it is, therefore, proved that all political struggles are class struggles, and all class struggles for emancipation, despite their necessarily political form – for every class struggle is a political struggle – turn ultimately on the question of *economic* emancipation" (Engels 1888, 387–388, 391). Scientific socialism does not mean for Engels that society develops based on natural laws and mechanical determinism. Rather, society has its own dialectical logic. It is one of the laws of society that change happens through human practices and that in class society, class struggle is the decisive practice of transformation.

The operation of dialectics in nature means that nature has the capacity to produce itself – nature is a complex, dynamic, self-producing system (Fuchs 2003). In society, the dynamic character of production is based on conscious, social actions of human beings who are producing, social, conscious, thinking, creative, moral, anticipatory-imaginative (i.e. capable of imagining the future and acting based on such anticipations) beings. Society is based on a dialectic of human practices and structures, in which human processes of social production play a key role. The dialectic of production and communication is another dialectic through which humans shape society (Fuchs 2020a). Humans engage in a metabolism with nature, which means that there is a nature-society-dialectic (Fuchs 2006), where humans live based on nature and shape and transform nature. The specific dialectics that are at play in society include the dialectic of human practices and social structures, the dialectic of production and communication, the dialectic of nature and society, and the dialectic of human freedom and structural necessity/conditioning. Society and humanity are a particular form of the existence of matter that have their own, specific manifestation of dialectical principles with emergent qualities. Society and human beings cannot be reduced to nature. They are part of nature and have emergent qualities. Society is a sublation (*Aufhebung*) of nature (Fuchs 2006).

Elmar Altvater (2015; 2016, 150) argues that Engels' dialectical approach to nature and society anticipated red-green socialist thought. What Altvater and others term the Capitalocene, the subsumption of nature under capital, Engels (1925) reminds us, only appears as "human victories over nature" (460) in the first place, but in the "second and third places [...] has quite different, unforeseen effects which only too often cancel the first" (461). The climate crisis is such an unforeseen, negative effect of the Capitalocene that reminds us of the circumstance that humans "by no means rule over nature like a conqueror over a foreign people, like someone standing outside nature – but that we, with flesh, blood and brain, belong to nature, and exist in its midst " (Engels 1925, 461).

Engels also conducted multiple historical studies. We can just mention two of them. In *On the History of Early Christianity*, Engels (1894b) analysed early Christianity as a movement of the oppressed, including slaves and the poor, and draws parallels to the modern working-class movement. In his book *The Origin of the Family, Private Property and the State* that was first published in 1884, Engels (1891) analyses the history and historical origins of the family, class, and the state. He based his analysis on the studies of the American anthropologist Lewis H. Morgan. Engels (1891, 131) argues that according "to the materialist conception, the determining factor in history is, in the last resort, the production and reproduction of immediate life", that reproduction such as housework is an important aspect of the economy and material life, and that patriarchy was history's first class relation:

> In an old unpublished manuscript, the work of Marx and myself in 1846, I find the following: 'The first division of labour is that between man and woman for child breeding'. And today I can add: The first class antithesis which appears in history coincides with the development of the antagonism between man and woman in monogamian marriage, and the first class oppression with that of the female sex by the male.
>
> (Engels 1891, 173)

Engels's analysis of patriarchy has been influential on and led to discussions in Marxist and socialist feminism (e.g. Barrett 1980, 48–49, 131–132; Eisenstein 1979; Federici 2012, 1; Fraser and Jaeggi 2018, 32; Gimenez 1987; Haug 2015; Leacock 2008, 13–29; Notz 2020; Rowbotham 1973, 47; Sayers, Evans and Redclift 1987; Vogel 1996).

Without Engels' editorial work there would be no second and third volume of *Capital*. Engels was one of the few people who was able to read Marx's terrible handwriting. After Marx's death in 1883, Engels spent the last 12 years of his own life on editing Marx's manuscripts, which resulted in volumes 2 and 3 of Capital.

Some observers and analysts claim that Engels vulgarised Marx's works and distorted the content of Marx's original manuscripts. Two examples follow that refer to a passage in Chapter 15 of *Capital Volume 3*, where we find a discussion of the internal contradictions of the tendency of the rate of profit to fall. Table 3.1 shows the German and English versions of this passage and both what Marx's wrote in the original German manuscript and Engels's version of it. The passage focuses on the impacts of the tendency of the rate of profit to fall on capitalist production and the role of the countervailing tendencies that are discussed in *Capital Volume 3*'s Chapter 14.

Michael Heinrich's analysis of this passage is the first example. Carl-Erich Vollgraf's and Jürgen Jungnickel's analysis is the second example. Heinrich is a representative of the Neue Marx-Lektüre approach (New Marx Reading) that goes back to the works of Helmut Reichelt and Hans-Georg Backhaus, Vollgraf and Jungnickel are two of the editors of the second Marx/Engels Gesamtausgabe (*MEGA²*).

TABLE 3.1 A passage from *Capital Volume 3* about the tendential fall in the rate of profit

Language	Marx's original manuscript	Engels' 1894 edition
German original	"[...] Dieser Proceß würde bald die capitalistische Production zum Klappen bringen, wenn nicht widerstrebende Tendenzen beständig wieder decentralisirend neben der centripetalen Kraft wirkten.)" (Marx 1863-1865a, 315).	"Dieser Prozeß würde bald die kapitalistische Produktion zum Zusammenbruch bringen, wenn nicht widerstrebende Tendenzen beständig wieder dezentralisierend neben der zentripetalen Kraft wirkten" (Marx 1894a, 256)
English translation	"This process of divorce of the conditions of labour from the producers (which would soon shake capitalist production if counteracting tendencies were not constantly at work alongside this centripetal force, in the direction of decentralisation)" (Marx 1863-1865b, 350)	"This process would soon bring about the collapse of capitalist production if it were not for counteracting tendencies, which have a continuous decentralising effect alongside the centripetal one". (Marx 1894b, 245). "This process would entail the rapid breakdown of capitalist production, if counter acting tendencies were not constantly at work alongside this centripetal force, in the direction of decentralization" (Marx 1894c, 355)

Authors such as Backhaus (1997) argue that Engels in his preface to and materials accompanying the third volume of *Capital* argues incorrectly that Marx in Chapter 1.3's value form analysis describe a historical development from simple commodity production to capitalism (for this discussion, see also Hecker 2018, 189–206). In reality, Marx would have provided an analysis of the logic of capital. Engels' misunderstanding would have grounded an evolutionary and mechanistic interpretation of Marx typical for Soviet Marxism, in which the identity of the historical and the logical moment of capital(ism) implies that the crisis-ridden nature of capitalism that is part of its antagonistic logic results in its natural law-like historical breakdown and the rise of communism. Marx certainly provides an analysis of capital(ism)'s dialectical logic, but he sees capital as historical system whose development is shaped by praxis, many historical examples form part of the analysis (see also Haug 2003). Engels's interpretation in prefaces and accompanying materials do not imply that he is the inventor of Stalinist and revisionist evolutionism.

Heinrich (2006, 360, footnote 55), argues that Engels' substitution of the term "Klappen" (folding) by "Zusammenbruch" (breakdown, collapse) enabled Henryk Grossman and others to claim that Marx saw "immanent breakdown tendencies" (translation from German) of capitalism. Heinrich (2006, 359 [translation from German]) writes that Engels "exacerbated" ("verschärft") Marx's formulations. Vollgraf and Jungnickel (2002, 62), in a manner comparable to Heinrich, claim:

One word correction by Engels had a big effect on the reception. In discussing the tendency of the rate of profit to fall, Marx had stated in parentheses that centralization would cause capitalist production to 'shake,' if there were no countervailing effects. Engels, who as mentioned broke Marx's continuous exposition into subsections, removed these parentheses, made the idea the final sentence of the introductory subpoint he titled '1. General,' and replaced 'shake' with 'collapse,' with an eye to his own purposes. By just this one editorial intervention, Engels probably gave sustenance (e.g. with Bebel) to the breakdown expectations widespread in the Second International (as in Kautsky), and also gave a boost to the debate over whether Marx had a breakdown theory.

The English translations are somewhat imprecise. In fact, the only changes that Engels made are that he removed the parenthesis and substituted the German term "Klappen" by "Zusammenbruch". The English translation of "Klappen" as "shake" is imprecise. According to the Oxford English Dictionary German/English, the precise translation is "to fold".[1] Marx probably had the English term "folding" or "collapse" in mind when writing the sentence in question and translated it as "Klappen". But in German to speak of "Klappen" of a system is very uncommon, which is why Engels seems to have used the more common term "Zusammenbruch". "Engels thus replaced a rather colloquial expression from oral language ('Klappen') – which even today would seem strange e.g. in a scientific text – by a more term ('Zusammenbruch') that is more common in written form" (Fülberth 2018, 107, translation from German).

In the English language, according to the Oxford Dictionary one of the meanings of the verb "to fold" is that something economic is ceasing "trading or operating as a result of financial problems".[2] Engels's editorial change is feasible and does not change the meaning of the sentence. Neither Engels's edition of the passage nor Marx's original wording imply that capitalism automatically collapses because the key point is that Marx says that there are counteracting tendencies so that there is a dialectic of the tendency of breakdown and the tendency of stabilisation in the capitalist economy. This dialectic results in crises, from which capitalism can recover if the capitalist class manages to succeed in class struggles against the proletariat by various measures (that Marx calls "countervailing tendencies", "entgegenwirkende Ursachen") such as lowering wages, increasing the rate of exploitation, cheapening constant capital, etc.

Authors such as Heinrich, Vollgraf, and Jungnickel, who follow particular interpretations of Marx and Engels, blame Engels for having introduced a breakdown theory to Marx, while in reality Engels did not change the meaning of Marx's writing, but he simply used a German term that is more common and better understandable, but expresses the same meaning. "klappen" and "zusammenbrechen" have quite similar German meanings in respect to an economic system. Engels was a thorough, organised, and systematic intellectual worker, who made an important original contribution to socialist theory. Without his support of Marx and his editorial work, there would be no *Capital* at all.

Functionalist Marxists such as Henryk Grossmann, who assumed that capitalism would automatically break down, interpreted the passage in question from *Capital Volume 3* as breakdown law of capitalism (Grossmann 1929, 79). Even if Engels had left the term "klappen" instead of "Zusammenbruch", Grossmann and others would have made the same interpretation. The absolute breakdown is an (incorrect) interpretation of Marx and Engels that can neither be found in Marx's original manuscripts nor in Engels' edition.

Marx and Engels stress the importance of the structural conditions of class struggles in society, capitalism, and history. Capitalism's antagonisms again and again result in crises, but the results of these crises are relatively open because class struggle is an element of conditioned and relative chance whose results are not determined in advance. In editing *Capital Volumes 2 and 3*, Engels "did a solid job of interpreting Marx's drafts and there was no real distortion" (Roberts 2020, 110).

3.3 Engels on History and Class Struggles

Positions on the intellectual relationship of Marx and Engels are split. There are on the one hand those who argue that Engels misunderstood, manipulated and vulgarised Marx's theory and thereby not just turned Marx into Marxism but also laid the grounds for Stalinism (see e.g. Carver 1981, 1983, 1990; Levine 1975, 2006; Schmidt 1971). And there are those who say that Engels made his own contributions to socialist theory, but that there is no major theoretical difference between Marx and Engels (see e.g. Blackledge 2019; Fülberth 2018; Kopf 2017; Krätke 2020; Mayer 1935). The representatives of this position hold that Engels was a not just Marx's best friend but also his closest intellectual companion so that there would be not Marx without Engels.

Terrell Carver and Norman Levine are two of the theorists who hold the first position Carver (1981, 93) writes that Marx and Engels had "different approaches to social science and perhaps politics itself". "Engels's influence has chiefly been on the theoretical side of Marxism, and his 'dialectics' and 'materialism' are notably memorialized in official Soviet philosophy" (Carver 1990, 257). Levine (2018, 195–196) argues that Engels neglected: "Engelsian Leninism was founded upon the belief that the meteoric advancement of science made socialism attainable and therefore led to the prioritization of the forces of production. [...] Engelsian Leninism rested upon depoliticization" (Levine 2018, 195–196). Levine's arguments imply that there is a lack of focus on class struggle in Engels's works.

Stalinism eulogised elements from some of Engels's works. In his essay "Dialectical and Historical Materialism" published in the *History of the Communist Party of the Soviet Union Bolsheviks: Short Course* – the ideological bible of Stalinism – Stalin (1945) references and quotes from Engels's *Anti-Dühring*, *Dialectics of Nature*, and *Feuerbach and the End of Classical German Philosophy*.

Stalin (1945) directly applies some aspects of the dialectics of nature to society and claims that this means that revolutions and the transition to socialism are inevitable:

> "If the connection between the phenomena of nature and their interdependence are laws of the development of nature, it follows, too, that the connection and interdependence of the phenomena of social life are laws of the development of society, and not something accidental. Hence, social life, the history of society, ceases to be an agglomeration of 'accidents', for the history of society becomes a development of society according to regular laws, and the study of the history of society becomes a science" (114).

> "Further, if the passing of slow quantitative changes into rapid and abrupt qualitative changes is a law of development, then it is clear that revolutions made by oppressed classes are a quite natural and inevitable phenomenon" (111).

For Stalin, socialism as science does not mean a science of society that is different from the natural sciences, but deterministic and mechanical social laws of nature operating in society. The implication is for Stalin that history develops in a linear manner, it is for him a "process of development from the lower to the higher" (Stalin 1945, 109). Stalin argues that the Soviet Union followed capitalism and therefore was a socialist system: "[T]he U.S.S.R. has already done away with capitalism and has set up a Socialist system" (Stalin 1945, 119). His implication was that anyone critical of him was bourgeois and anti-socialist. The mechanical interpretation of the dialectic legitimated Stalin's terror against his opponents.

Engels on History and Class Struggles

The concepts of *Aufhebung* (sublation) and the negation of the negation are missing in Stalinist dialectics. They are however key features of Engels's dialectics. Stalin referred to Engels, but Engels's interpretation of dialectics was other than Stalin's not based on mechanical and deterministic concepts. Engels is not be blamed for Stalinism.

In Engels's canonical works, there are some problematic formulations. For example, he writes that "the capitalist mode of production has likewise itself created the material conditions from which it must perish" (Engels 1878, 122) or that there is the "inevitable downfall" of the capitalistic mode of production (Engels 1880, 305). Such formulations create the impression that society is governed by mechanistic and deterministic laws.

But Engels (1878) stresses in the same works where the mentioned problematic formulations can be found that there is a difference between the negation of the negation in nature and in society. The dialectic has in each realm of the world "specific peculiarities" (Engels 1878, 131). The "history of the development of society turns out to be essentially different from that of nature" because humans "are all endowed with consciousness, are men acting with deliberation or passion, working towards definite goals" (Engels 1888, 387). Humans would act with intentions towards specific goals, but the outcomes would often be quite different from the intentions, which is an element of chance in society that is, however, "governed by inner, hidden laws" (Engels 1888, 387). He describes the proletarian revolution as the solution of capitalism's contradictions (Engels 1880, 325): "To accomplish this act of universal emancipation is the historical mission of the modern proletariat". A mission does not necessarily succeed. In these passages, Engels stresses that society operates on dialectical laws that are different from the laws of nature. The question is, however, what a law is in society. The more problematic formulations that can be found in these works can imply that capitalism automatically breaks down. But more frequently Engels stresses in the same works that history is the history of class struggles, for example: "In modern history at least it is, therefore, proved that all political struggles are class struggles, and all class struggles for emancipation, despite their necessarily political form – for every class struggle is a political struggle – turn ultimately on the question of *economic* emancipation" (Engels 1888, 387–388, 391). It is one of the laws of society that change happens through human practices and that in class society, class struggle is the decisive practice of transformation.

This assumption is also in line with Marx's and Engels's view of history in their early works. In *The Holy Family*, the first work that Marx and Engels co-authored, Engels writes: "*History* does *nothing*, it 'possesses *no* immense wealth', it 'wages *no* battles'.

It is *man,* real, living man who does all that, who possesses and fights; 'history' is not, as it were, a person apart, using man as a means to achieve *its own* aims; history is *nothing but* the activity of man pursuing his aims" (Marx and Engels 1845, 93). In *The Manifesto of the Communist Party,* Marx and Engels (1848, 482) say: "The history of all hitherto existing society is the history of class struggles". Marx added to the law of class struggle the law of the dialectic of structures and agency, of societal conditions and practices. Humans "make their own history, but they do not make it just as they please; they do not make it under circumstances chosen by themselves, but under circumstances directly encountered, given and transmitted from the past" (Marx 1852, 103). Society's transformation is based on dialectics of chance/necessity, freedom/determination, discontinuity/continuity, practices/structural conditions. In capitalism, the class contradiction and the contradiction between productive forces and relations of production with necessity call forth crises. The outcome of such crises is not determined and depends on the results of class struggles. Society's dialectic is a dialectic of objective contradictions and the human subjects' practices.

If Marx and Engels had assumed that capitalism would automatically break down and socialism would emerge inevitably, why would they have engaged in practical revolutionary activity? Engels participated, for example, active in the 1849 revolutionary uprising for democracy in Elberfeld and Baden. Marx and Engels were leaders of the League of the Just, the Communist League, and the First International. Engels's single deterministic historical formulations seem to have served the rhetorical-political purpose of motivating revolutionary optimism among activists.

In a letter to Borgius, Engels (1894a) stresses that humans "make their history themselves, only in given surroundings which condition it and on the basis of actual relations already existing, among which the economic relations" form "the red thread which runs through them". The notion of the economic as read thread allows us to see the economic, i.e. social production, as the universal and common element of all social realms. Social production takes on different forms with emergent meanings but also is the red thread of society and its various spheres (see Fuchs 2020a).

Blackledge (2019, 240) stresses that by scientific socialism Engels did not understand "empiricism or positivism" and "a mechanical and fatalistic model of agency. "Engels was neither an empiricist nor a positivist. And as regards the charge of reductionism, he held to a stratified view of natural and social reality according to which emergent properties at each level could neither be reduced to laws governing the levels below them, nor could the laws through which they operated be understood in an empiricist or positivist fashion".

Engels stresses in *Socialism: Utopian and Scientific* in line with Marx's *Grundrisse* and *Capital* that science and technology are on the one hand "the most powerful weapon in the war of capital against the working-class" (Engels 1880, 314) and on the other hand important means of emancipation from capitalism and class society that support the establishment and reproduction of "the kingdom of freedom" beyond necessity (Engels 1880, 324).

Taken together, there is no doubt that there are some problematic formulations in Engels's canonical works. But a more pertinent reading is that he and Marx interpreted history as a dialectic of class struggles and structural conditions, which implies that there is no automatic breakdown of capitalism. The implication is also, as Tristam Hunt (2009, 361) stresses in his Engels-biography that Engels and Marx are not to blame for Stalin's terror:

> In no intelligible sense can Engels or Marx bear culpability for the crimes of historical actors carried out generations later, even if the policies were offered up in their honor. Just as Adam Smith is not to blame for the inequalities of the free market West, nor Martin Luther for the nature of modern Protestant evangelicalism, nor the Prophet Muhammad for the atrocities of Osama bin Laden, so the millions of souls dispatched by Stalinism (or by Mao's China, Pol Pot's Cambodia, and Mengistu's Ethiopia) did not go to their graves on account of two 19th-century London philosophers.

Although there are single problematic passages in Engels's works that imply that capitalism must automatically collapse, there are other passages that stress the difference of dialectical laws in nature and society and that a key social law found in class societies is that humans make their own history under given conditions and in class societies do so in the form of class and social struggles. Scientific socialism doesn't mean that society is governed by mechanical laws, but that socialist research studies society based on the combination of critical social theory and critical empirical social research.

3.4 The Condition of the Working Class Today

The Condition of the Working Class in England (*CWCE*) is for many Engels's most influential book. Eric J. Hobsbawm writes that "the *Condition* is probably the earliest large work whose analysis is systematically based on the concept of the Industrial Revolution" (Hobsbawm 1969, 17). It "remains an indispensable work and a landmark in the fight for the emancipation of humanity" (Hobsbawm 1969, 17). David McLellan (1993, xix) writes that the *Condition* is "the first book to have dealt comprehensively with the industrial working class as a whole rather than just with particular groups or industries". Engels's method was a "[r]ich and complex" form of interdisciplinarity that combined "economics, philosophy, and labour history" (McLellan 1993, xix). Engels integrated a "rich mass of material" into "an extraordinary unity [...] articulated [...] under [...] general principles" (Mayer 1935, 62).

Engels came from a bourgeois family. His father Friedrich Engels senior (1796–1860) owned the cotton factory Ermen & Engels that operated two cotton mills, one in Engelskirchen (Rhineland) and one in Manchester (United Kingdom).

Engels junior conducted the research for his book *The Condition of the Working Class in England* (*CWCE* = Engels 1845b) during his stay in Manchester from 1842 until 1844, where he was supposed to learn his father's trade. Engels directly experienced the working class' conditions in England and got in touch with workers, from whom he learned about their everyday life and the problems they faced. Family status does not determine one's political worldview. Born into a capitalist family, Engels became one of the international leaders of the communist movement. There is no 1:1 relationship and no mechanic determination of culture by the economy. Engels junior became his father's representative in the Manchester business. After the death of his father in 1860, Engels became the co-owner of the Manchester establishment. He managed the company, funded Marx's life in London, financially and intellectually supported the socialist movement, and was active as a writer. In 1869, Engels had accumulated enough wealth in order to be able to sustain himself and Marx and family, and support the socialist movement. He sold his share in Ermen & Engels, retired from the company, and entirely devoted himself to the socialist movement and theory.

In *CWCE*, Engels analyses the rise, early development and consequences of capitalism in England. The decisive features he mentions are a) the working class, b) industrial technologies such as the steam-engine as moving technology and manufacturing machinery as working technology that replaced handicraft, c) the capitalist class, and d) the division of labour.

In *CWCE*, Engels analyses the terrible conditions that the working class had to endure in industrial England, including long working hours, low wages, poverty, overcrowded and dirty slums and dwellings, poisonous and uneatable food, overwork, starvation, death by hunger, lack of sleep, air pollution, untreated illnesses, egotism and moral indifference, crime, alcoholism, bad clothes, unemployment, rape, homelessness, lack of clean water, drainage and sanitation, illiteracy, child labour, military drill in factories, overseers' flogging and maltreatment of workers, deadly work accidents, fines, etc.

Engels characterises the misery the working class faces as "a condition unworthy of human beings" (*CWCE*, 43), conditions where humans cannot "think, feel, and live as human beings" (*CWCE*, 220), degradation to "the lowest stage of humanity" (*CWCE*, 73), treatment of workers "as mere material, a mere chattel" (*CWCE*, 66). Engels characterisation of capitalism as dehumanising resembles Marx's introduction of the notion of alienation in the *Economic and Philosophic Manuscripts of 1844*, where Marx (1844, 517) speaks of one aspect of alienation as "*alienation of the human being* from being *human*".[3] Out of such words speaks the deep humanism of Engels and Marx. They both understand socialism is a humanist society that enables a good life for all humans.

Using factory inspectors' reports, parliamentary reports, observation, and the analysis of news reports, *The Condition of the Working Class in England* shows that Engels already in the 1840s practiced and pioneered empirical social research (Kurz 2020, 67; Krätke 2020, 29–34; Zimmermann 2020). In *Capital Volume 1*, Marx (1867) uses the same empirical method as Engels in CWCE, which shows that Engels's work had large influence on Marx. Marx (1867, 349 (footnote 15), 573, 755), explicitly refers positively to Engels's book several times. For example, Marx (1867, 349 [footnote 15]) writes:

> How well Engels understood the spirit of the capitalist mode of production is shown by the Factory Reports, Reports on Mines, etc. which have appeared since 1845, and how wonderfully he painted the circumstances in detail is seen on the most superficial comparison of his work with the official reports of the Children's Employment Commission, published eighteen to twenty years later (1863-7).

Working on *Capital*, Marx re-read Engels's *Condition* and wrote to him about the book: "With what zest and passion, what boldness of vision and absence of all learned or scientific reservations, the subject is still attacked in these pages!" (Marx 1863, 469).

The 2020 COVID-19 crisis has resulted in radical changes of society and the economy. In many countries, societies were "shut down" in order to lower the infection risk. Many people stayed at home and worked from home. The economy and society thereby underwent substantial changes (Fuchs 2020b). Working at a physical distance mediated by Internet-based communication and co-operation technologies became widespread. Many knowledge and service workers, who normally conduct their work face-to-face in offices, started working at a distance from home. Workers such as academics, teachers, general practitioners, engineers, lawyers, consultants, artists, etc. became digital workers, who conduct services at a distance from their homes. Their homes became a supra-locale where working life, private life, education, leisure, etc. converged (Fuchs 2020b).

In the coronavirus crisis, being a digital worker who can work from home is a privilege that reduces the risk of unemployment, illness, and death. Other workers, especially those in the tourism industry, personal services, the hospitality industry, and the culture and entertainment industry, who cannot conduct their services from a distance, lost their jobs. Key sector workers such as food workers, supermarket workers, or health care workers, who work in industries that are absolutely essential for society, couldn't work from a distance and a shutdown of these realms of work was impossible. Because of a lack of personal protective equipment, workers in key sectors faced a much higher risk to get infected by and die from COVID-19.

Amazon's online shopping business boomed during the coronavirus-crisis. In the first financial quarter of 2020, its revenues increased from US $59.7 billion from the same period in 2019 to $75.5 billion, which is an increase by 26.5%.[4] Amazon's stock price increased from US $1,900 at the start of 2020 to $3,200 in the middle of July 2020.[5] Amazon is the world's 22nd largest transnational corporation with annual profits of US $10.6 billion in 2019.[6] In 2020, Amazon founder and CEO Jeff Bezos was with a total wealth of US $113 the world's richest person.[7] Amazon workers are precarious service workers who according to reports faced the risk of getting infected by COVID-19:

> In order to meet the demands of a country in which homes must suddenly be retrofitted to accommodate classrooms, co-working spaces, gyms, hair salons and so on, Amazon announced last month that it would hire 100,000 additional workers in its fulfillment centers and delivery networks, jobs for which many people will be desperate, given the decimated state of the retail and service industries. [...] Though the company has increased pay by $2 an hour, employees around the country at Amazon warehouses and its subsidiary, Whole Foods, have been staging walkouts to demand better health protections during the pandemic. For years, Amazon has resisted the efforts of organized labor. [...] In a letter to Mr. Bezos, [...] labor leaders also addressed concerns that conditions at Amazon warehouses were unsafe: workers there were 'reporting crowded spaces, a required rate of work that does not allow for proper sanitizing of work spaces, and empty containers meant to hold sanitizing wipes'. [...[various colleagues coming to work [...] [were] unwell: fatigued, lightheaded, nauseous [...] Later in the month, one

The Condition of the Working Class Today

of his colleagues, Barbara Chandler, tested positive for the coronavirus. She was advised by those in human resources at the facility to keep the news on the 'down low',' she told me. Frustrated by what he perceived as the company's lack of transparency, Mr. Smalls made it his mission to disseminate information about cases of Covid-19 at the warehouse.

(Bellafante 2020)

Amazon workers in countries such as the USA, France, and Italy protested against these conditions. Amazon has not released data on the number of its workers that got infected and the number of those that died. In the Amazon warehouse in Shakopee, Minnesota, 88 out of 1,000 employees got infected within 70 days (García-Hodges, Kent and Kaplan 2020).

Tönnies Holding is a German meat processing corporation that has more than 16,500 employees and. Its headquarters are in Rheda-Wiedenbrück, a town in the German state of North Rhine-Westphalia, where the company also operates a large meat processing plant. In 2018, the company achieved annual revenues of 6.65 billion Euros.[8] In 2020, the wealth of Clemens Tönnies and Robert Tönnies, who are the two major owners the Tönnies Holding, was US\$ 1.8 billion each, which equally placed them as the world's 1196th richest persons in 2020.[9] In summer 2020, there were more than 1,500 COVID-19 cases among workers in the Tönnies factory in Rheda-Wiedenbrück, among them many low-paid migrant workers who are bogus self-employed and live in crowded accommodations.

The agglomeration of workers in crowded spaces played a role in the spread of COVID-19 among Tönnies-workers. A report in *Der Spiegel* describes the conditions that the predominantly Eastern European Tönnies-workers faced in Rheda-Wiedenbrück:

> They tend to be hired by subcontractors, they are poorly paid, quickly replaced and inadequately protected – even during the current coronavirus pandemic. [...] Now, Clemens Tönnies – sometimes referred to as the Pork Chop Prince or the Meat Baron – has a problem. For years, he has ruthlessly pursued efficiency, but now, the entire country wants to know what goes on behind his factory gates. He has perfected the art of extracting all he can out of both his employees and the animals they process, transforming living creatures into an industrial product. His strategy was volume, volume, volume and he cut his costs to the bone, becoming the favorite supplier to Germany's discount grocery chains. The company enjoys a 30% share of the pork market in Germany. [...] A Polish

worker in Rheda-Wiedenbrück has a bit more to say, though he is fearful of speaking openly. He says he earns 1,600 euros for 190 hours of work per month. His shifts begin at 3 a.m. and end at 1 p.m., with a 30-minute break every three hours. 'We stand at the conveyor belt about 20 to 30 centimeters apart, right next to each other. Often, the speed of the belt is ratcheted up and the supervisor watches us closely'. [...] Like the Romanians in the white-plastered house near Münster, many workers aren't actually Tönnies employees, instead working for subcontractors, and without them [...] According to Tönnies Holding, 50% of its workers are actually employees of such a company.

(Becker et al. 2020, 10–11 & 11 & 14)

Romanian Tönnies workers described the housing conditions they faced:

Romanian worker: "It was always very crowded; there were sometimes 10, 12, occasionally even 14 people in one apartment. The monthly rent was 200 euros each. The buildings belonged to the subcontractors. [...] But it just isn't fair to cram so many people into one apartment!"

(Welle 2020a)

Most workers interviewed, many of whom were very upset, have been either employed by the huge meat producer Tönnies or its subsidiaries. They have described extremely exhaustive work and aggressive language. The workers accused managers of not putting enough protective measures in place in the wake of the COVID-19 pandemic. Some have also said that the shared accommodation, in which they were forced to live, was cramped and inhumane.

(Welle 2020b)

In *CWCE*, Engels introduces the notion of social murder, by which he means poor working conditions that endanger the lives of workers. Social murder means that workers die "indirectly, far more than directly" (*CWCE*, 38) through social structures that cause the death of workers and that "society places hundreds of proletarians in such a position that they inevitably meet a too early and an unnatural death, one which is quite as much a death by violence as that by the sword or bullet; when it deprives thousands of the necessaries of life, places them under conditions in which they *cannot* live" (*CWCE*, 106). Capitalism places

the workers under conditions in which they can neither retain health nor live long; that it undermines the vital force of these workers gradually, little by little, and so hurries them to the grave before their time. I have further to prove that society knows how injurious such conditions are to the health and the life of the workers, and yet does nothing to improve these conditions. That it *knows* the consequences of its deeds; that its act is, therefore, not mere manslaughter, but murder.

(*CWCE*, 107)

CWCE's second chapter "The Great Towns" focuses on spatial conditions of working class life. It is an analysis of everyday urban life. Engels described how in English working class districts "many human beings here lived crowded into a small space" (*CWCE*, 39) where there is "little air – and *such* air!" to breathe (*CWCE*, 65). 175 years after Engels published CWCE in 1845, poor working conditions and the racist exploitation of migrant workers have in the COVID-19 crisis created new forms of social murder where workers cannot keep social distance and working conditions result in COVID-19 that makes it hard for infected poor workers to breathe and results in the death of a specific share of those who caught the virus.

The Tönnies-scandal shows that 170 years after Engels's report on the conditions of the working class, poor and highly exploited workers still face threats to their health and life due to the agglomeration of many workers in cramped spaces. In the COVID-19 crisis, the poorest cannot afford social distancing and are forced to risk their lives. Capital draws profits from these risks because space is considered as a production factor of capital so that crowding workers into small work and living spaces increases profitability. Tönnies makes profits by low wages for long hours. And subcontractors in addition rob parts of the workers' wages by charging high rents for overcrowded substandard accommodation. Renting out small places to extremely vulnerable workers allows rentiers to divide space into small compartments and to command a high rental price for these compartments. In addition, by keeping the compartments in a shabby condition, the rentier tries to keep his investment costs low in order to be able to maximise their gains.

Amazon and Tönnies are examples of companies that have been criticised by observers in the context of COVID-19. These observers have argued that workers were put at risk of catching the virus by a lack of protective measures. Work inequalities have been reinforced on the COVID-19 crisis. Migrant workers and unskilled workers are more likely to have jobs that cannot be conducted over a distance. Slaughtering animals and packing books into parcels have not-yet been fully automated and robotised. They cannot be conducted at a distance via the Internet. Low-paid, low-skill workers who cannot work from a distance have faced an increased risk of catching COVID-19 and dying from the virus. In the COVID-19 crisis, social murder has taken on new forms.

3.5 Conclusion

Friedrich Engels's works remain highly relevant today. Engels should not be seen as a vulgariser of Marx but rather as Marx's most important comrade, collaborator, and supporter. Without Engels there would be no Marx. Engels supported Marx financially and intellectually, struggled together with Marx, and edited volume 2 and 3 of *Capital*.

It is a mistake to assume that Engels is to blame for Stalinism and was the first vulgariser of Marx. But it is also an error to assume that his works are flawless. There are problematic, deterministic formulations in his works. But by and large he has stressed the importance of class struggles in and against capitalism and that the basic social law of society is that humans make their own history based on and shaped by given conditions. Engels did not formulate a theory of the automatic collapse of capitalism. Scientific socialism is not a natural science theory of society, but an anti-positivist dialectical social analysis the uses the dialectics of subject/object, agency/ structures, practices/conditions, experience/reason, empirical research/social theory, chance/necessity, discontinuity/continuity, disorder/order, diversity/unity, individual/ society, local/global, spontaneity/organisation, etc.

Scientific socialism doesn't mean that society is governed by mechanical laws, but that socialist research studies society based on the combination of critical social theory and critical empirical social research. For Engels just like for Marx, there is a difference between natural dialectics and societal dialectics. The basic law of society is that humans make their own history under given conditions. In class society, class and social struggles are the processes, by which humans make their own history. Engels should be seen as a socialist humanist who stresses the important role of class struggles in society.

Engels in *The Condition of the Working Class in England* outlines concepts and analyses that can inspire critical labour analysis in the 21st century. Engels's concept of social murder matters for understanding how in the COVID-19 crisis, the profit imperative combined with a lack of protective measures and social distancing in capitalist corporations put low-paid, low skilled workers at risk of infection and death.

Notes

1 https://www.linguee.com/english-german/search?source=auto&query=klappen+, accessed on 4 August 2020.

2 https://www.lexico.com/definition/fold, accessed on 4 August 2020.

3 Übersetzung aus dem Deutschen [CF]: "die *Entfremdung des Menschen* von dem *Menschen*", accessed on 11 July 2020.

4 Amazon Inc., SEC filings, form 10-Q for the quarterly period ending 31 March 2020, https://ir.aboutamazon.com/sec-filings, accessed on 11 July 2020.

5 Data source: Yahoo! Finance, https://finance.yahoo.com/quote/AMZN, accessed on 11 July 2020.

6 Data source: Forbes 2000 list for the year 2020, https://www.forbes.com/global2000, accessed on 11 July 2020.

7 Forbes World's Billionaires List for 2020, https://www.forbes.com/billionaires/, accessed on 11 July 2020.

8 Data source: https://toennies.de/en/home/, accessed on 11 July 2020.

9 Data source: Forbes World's Billionaires List for the year 2020, https://www.forbes.com/billionaires/, accessed on 11 July 2020.

References

Altvater, Elmar. 2016. The Capitalocene, or, Geoengineering against Capitalism's Planetary Boundaries. In *Anthropocene or Capitalocene? Nature, History, and the Crisis of Capitalism*, ed. Jason W. Moore, 138–152. Oakland, CA: PM Press.

Altvater, Elmar. 2015. *Engels neu entdecken. Da hellblaue Bändchen zur Einführung in die "Dialektik der Natur" und die Kritik von Akkumulation und Wachstum*. Hamburg: VSA.

Backhaus, Hans-Georg. 1997. *Dialektik der Wertform: Untersuchungen zur Marxschen Ökonomiekritik*. Freiburg: Caira.

Barrett, Michèle. 1980. *Women's Oppression Today. Problems in Marxist Feminist Analysis*. London: Verso.

Becker, Markus et al. 2020. Corona in the Slaughterhouse: The High Price of Cheap Meat. *Der Spiegel*, 26 June 2020. https://www.spiegel.de/international/business/corona-in-the-slaughterhouse-the-high-price-of-cheap-meat-a-ad16d0df-c1c8-4f82-93df-573fdc2c8bd6

Bellafante, Ginia. 2020. "We Didn't Sign Up For This": Amazon Workers on the Front Lines. *The New York Times*, 3 April 2020. https://www.nytimes.com/2020/04/03/nyregion/coronavirus-nyc-chris-smalls-amazon.html

Blackledge, Paul. 2019. *Friedrich Engels and Modern Social and Political Theory*. Albany, NY: State University of New York Press.

Carver, Terrell. 1990. *Friedrich Engels: His Life and Thought*. New York: St. Martin's Press.

Carver, Terrell. 1983. *Marx and Engels Their Intellectual Relationship*. Brighton: Wheatsheaf Books.

Carver, Terrell. 1981. *Engels. A Very Short Introduction*. Oxford: Oxford University Press.

Eisenstein, Zillah. 1979. Developing a Theory of Capitalist Patriarchy and Socialist Feminism. In *Capitalist Patriarchy and the Case for Socialist Feminism*, ed. Zillah Eisenstein, 5–40. New York: Monthly Review Press.

Engels, Friedrich. 1925. Dialectics of Nature. In *Marx & Engels Collected Works (MECW) Volume 25*, 311–588. London: Lawrence & Wishart.

Engels, Friedrich. 1894a. Letter to Borgius. 25 January 1894. https://www.marxists.org/archive/marx/works/1894/letters/94_01_25.htm

Engels, Friedrich. 1894b. On the History of Early Christianity. In *Marx & Engels Collected Works (MECW) Volume 27*, 445–469. London: Lawrence & Wishart.

Engels, Friedrich. 1893. Can Europe Disarm? In *Marx & Engels Collected Works (MECW) Volume 26*, 367–393. London: Lawrence & Wishart.

Engels, Friedrich. 1891. The Origin of the Family, Private Property and the State. In the Light of the Researches by Lewis H. Morgan. In *Marx & Engels Collected Works (MECW) Volume 26*, 129–276. London: Lawrence & Wishart.

Engels, Friedrich. 1888. Ludwig Feuerbach and the End of Classical German Philosophy. In *Marx & Engels Collected Works (MECW) Volume 26*, 353–398. London: Lawrence & Wishart.

Engels, Friedrich. 1880. Socialism: Utopian and Scientific. In *Marx & Engels Collected Works (MECW) Volume 24*, 281–325. London: Lawrence & Wishart.

Engels, Friedrich. 1878. Anti-Dühring. Herr Eugen Dühring's Revolution in Science. In *Marx & Engels Collected Works (MECW) Volume 25*, 5–309. London: Lawrence & Wishart.

Engels, Friedrich. 1872. The Housing Question. In *Marx & Engels Collected Works (MECW) Volume 23*, 317–391. London: Lawrence & Wishart.

Engels, Friedrich. 1847a. Draft of a Communist Confession of Faith. In *Marx & Engels Collected Works (MECW) Volume 6*, 96–103. London: Lawrence & Wishart.

Engels, Friedrich. 1847b. Principles of Communism. In *Marx & Engels Collected Works (MECW) Volume 6*, 341–357. London: Lawrence & Wishart.

Engels, Friedrich. 1845a. Speeches in Elberfeld. In *Marx & Engels Collected Works (MECW) Volume 4*, 243–264. London: Lawrence & Wishart.

Engels, Friedrich. 1845b. *The Condition of the Working Class in England*. Oxford: Oxford University Press.

Engels, Friedrich. 1843. Outlines of a Critique of Political Economy. In *Marx & Engels Collected Works (MECW) Volume 3*, 418–443. London: Lawrence & Wishart.

Engels, Friedrich. 1842a. Schelling and Revelation: Critique of the Latest Attempt of Reaction against the Free Philosophy. In *Marx & Engels Collected Works (MECW) Volume 2*, 189–244. London: Lawrence & Wishart.

Engels, Friedrich. 1842b. Schelling, Philosopher in Christ. In *Marx & Engels Collected Works (MECW) Volume 2*, 245–264. London: Lawrence & Wishart.

Engels, Friedrich. 1841. Schelling on Hegel. In *Marx & Engels Collected Works (MECW) Volume 2*, 181–187. London: Lawrence & Wishart.

Engels, Friedrich. 1839. Letters from Wuppertal. In *Marx & Engels Collected Works (MECW) Volume 2*, 7–25. London: Lawrence & Wishart.

Federici, Silvia. 2012. *Revolution at Point Zero: Housework, Reproduction, and Feminist Struggle*. Oakland, CA: PM Press.

References

Fraser, Nancy and Rahel Jaeggi. 2018. *Capitalism: A Conversation in Critical Theory.* Cambridge: Polity.

Fuchs, Christian. 2020a. *Communication and Capitalism. A Critical Theory.* London: University of Westminster Press. https://doi.org/10.16997/book45

Fuchs, Christian. 2020b. Everyday Life and Everyday Communication in Coronavirus Capitalism. *tripleC: Communication, Capitalism & Critique* 18 (1): 375–399. https://doi.org/10.31269/triplec.v18i1.1167

Fuchs, Christian. 2006. The Dialectic of the Nature-Society-System. *tripleC: Communication, Capitalism & Critique* 4 (1): 1–39. https://doi.org/10.31269/triplec.v4i1.24

Fuchs, Christian. 2003. The Self-Organization of Matter. *Nature, Society, and Thought* 16 (3): 281–313.

Fülberth, Georg. 2020. Wie zwei ein Compagniegeschäft betrieben. Friedrich Engels' Beitrag zum Werk von Karl Marx. In *"Die Natur ist die Probe auf die Dialektik": Friedrich Engels kennenlernen*, 54–68. Hamburg: VSA.

Fülberth, Georg. 2018. *Friedrich Engels.* Köln: PapyRossa.

García-Hodges, Ahiza, Jo Ling Kent, and Ezra Kaplan. 2020. Amazon Warehouse in Minnesota Had More Than 80 COVID-19 Cases. *NBC News,* 24 June 2020. https://www.nbcnews.com/tech/tech-news/amazon-warehouse-minnesota-had-more-80-covid-19-cases-n1231937

Gimenez, Martha. 1987. Marxist and Non-Marxist Elements in Engels's Views on the Oppression of Women. In *Engels Revisited. New Feminist Essays,* ed. Janet Sayers, Mary Evans and Nanneke Redclift, 37–56. London: Tavistock.

Grossmann, Henryk. 1929. *Das Akkumulations- und Zusammenbruchsgesetz des kapitalistischen Systems.* Leipzig: Verlag von C.L. Hirschfeld.

Haug, Frigga. 2015. Gender Relations & The Marx Within Feminism. In *Marxism and Feminism,* ed. Shahrzad Mojab, 33–101. London: Zed.

Haug, Wolfgang Fritz. 2003. Historisches/Logisches. *Das Argument* 251: 378–396.

Hecker, Rolf. 2018. *Springpunkte. Beiträge zur Marx-Forschung und "Kapital"-Diskussion.* Berlin: Dietz.

Heinrich, Michael. 2006. *Die Wissenschaft vom Wert.* Münster: Westfälisches Dampfboot. Fourth edition.

Hobsbawm, Eric J. 2011. *How to Change the World. Reflections on Marx and Marxism.* New Haven, CT: Yale University Press.

Hobsbawm, Eric J. 1969. Introduction. In *Friedrich Engels:The Condition of the Working Class in England: From Personal Observation to Authentic Sources,* 7–17. London: Panther.

Hunt, Tristam. 2009. *Marx's General. The Revolutionary Life of Friedrich Engels.* New York: Metropolitan Books.

Kopf, Eike. 2017. *Marxismus ohne Engels?* Köln: PapyRossa.

Krätke, Michael. 2020. *Friedrich Engels oder: Wie ein "Cotton-Lord" den Marxismus erfand.* Berlin: Dietz.

Kurz, Heinz D. 2020. Der junge Engels über die "Bereicherungswissenschaft", die "Unsittlichket" von Privateigentum und Konkurrenz und die "Heuchelei der Oekonomen". In *Arbeiten am Widerspruch – Friedrich Engels zum 200. Geburtstag*, ed. Rainer Lucas, Reinhard Pfrim and Hans-Dieter Westhoff, 65–120. Marburg: Metropolis.

Leacock, Eleanor Burke. 2008. *Myths of Male Dominance. Collected Articles on Women Cross-Culturally*. Chicago, IL: Haymarket Books.

Lenin, Vladimir I. 1913. The Three Sources and Three Component Parts of Marxism. In *Lenin Collected Works Volume 19*, 21–28. Moscow: Progress.

Levine, Norman. 2018. Engels' Co-option of Lenin. In *The Palgrave Handbook of Leninist Political Philosophy*, ed. Tom Rockmore and Norman Levine, 161–199. Basingstoke: Palgrave Macmillan.

Levine, Norman. 2006. *Divergent Paths. Hegel in Marxism and Engelism. Volume 1: The Hegelian Foundations of Marx's Method*. Oxford: Lexington Books.

Levine, Norman. 1975. *The Tragic Deception. Marx Contra Engels*. Oxford: Oxford University Press.

Liedman, Sven-Eric. 2018. *A World to Win: The Life and Works of Karl Marx*. London: Verso.

Marx, Karl. 1894a. *Das Kapital. Dritter Band. Marx Engels Werke (MEW) Band 25*. Berlin: Dietz.

Marx, Karl. 1894b. *Capital. Volume III. Marx & Engels Collected Works (MECW) Volume 37*. London: Lawrence & Wishart.

Marx, Karl. 1894c. *Capital Volume III*. London: Penguin.

Marx, Karl. 1867. *Capital. Volume I*. London: Penguin.

Marx, Karl. 1863-1865a. *Ökonomische Manuskripte 1863–1867. Teil 2. Manuskript 1863/65 zum 3. Buch des "Kapital". Marx/Engels Gesamtausgabe (MEGA) II.4/2*. Berlin: De Gruyter.

Marx, Karl. 1863-1865b. *Marx's Economic Manuscript of 1864-1865*. Leiden: Brill.

Marx, Karl. 1863. Marx to Engels, 9 April 1863. In *Marx & Engels Collected Works (MECW) Volume 41*, 466–469. London: Lawrence & Wishart.

Marx, Karl. 1859. A Contribution to the Critique of Political Economy. Preface. In *Marx & Engels Collected Works (MECW) Volume 29*, 261–265. London: Lawrence & Wishart.

Marx, Karl 1852. The Eighteenth Brumaire of Louis Bonaparte. In *Marx & Engels Collected Works (MECW) Volume 11*, 99–197. London: Lawrence & Wishart.

Marx, Karl and Friedrich Engels. 1848. The Manifesto of the Communist Party. In *Marx & Engels Collected Works (MECW) Volume 6*, 477–519. London: Lawrence & Wishart.

Marx, Karl and Friedrich Engels. 1845/1846. The German Ideology. Critique of Modern German Philosophy According to Its Representatives Feuerbach, B. Bauer and Stirner, and of German Socialism According to Its Various Prophets. In *Marx & Engels Collected Works (MECW) Volume 5*, 19–539. London: Lawrence & Wishart.

Marx, Karl and Friedrich Engels. 1845. The Holy Family, or Critique of Critical Criticism. Against Bruno Bauer and Company. In *Marx & Engels Collected Works (MECW) Volume 4*, 5–211. London: Lawrence & Wishart.

Mayer, Gustav. 1935. *Friedrich Engels. A Biography*. London: Chapman & Hall.

McLellan, David. 1993. Introduction. In *Friedrich Engels:The Condition of the Working Class in England*, ix–xx. Oxford: Oxford University Press.

Notz, Gisela. 2000. Auseinandersetzung mit Friedrich Engels' "Ursprung der Familie ..." ... und was er uns heute noch zu sagen hat. In *Arbeiten am Widerspruch – Friedrich Engels zum 200. Geburtstag*, ed. Rainer Lucas, Reinhard Pfrim and Hans-Dieter Westhoff, 397–416. Marburg: Metropolis.

Roberts, Michael. 2020. *Engels 200 – His Contribution to Political Economy*. London: Lulu.com.

Rowbotham, Sheila. 1973. *Woman's Consciousness, Man's World*. Harmondsworth: Penguin.

Sayers, Janet, Mary Evans, and Nanneke Redclift, eds. 1987. *Engels Revisited. New Feminist Essays*. London: Tavistock.

Schmidt, Alfred. 1971. *The Concept of Nature in Marx*. London: NLB.

Stalin, Joseph V. 1945. Dialectical and Historical Materialism. In *History of the Communist Party of the Soviet Union*, 105–131. Moscow: Foreign Languages Publishing House.

Vogel, Lise. 1996. Engels's *Origin*: Legacy, Burden and Vision. In *Engels Today. A Centenary Appreciation*, ed. Christopher J. Arthur, 129–151. Basingstoke: Macmillan.

Vollgraf, Carl-Erich and Jürgen Jungnickel 2002. Marx in Marx's Words: On Engels's Edition of the Main Manuscript of Book 3 of *Capital. International Journal of Political Economy* 32 (1): 35–78.

Welle, Deutsche. 2020a. Germany: Former Abattoir Worker 'Heard Colleagues Cry at Night'. *Deutsche Welle*, 25 June 2020. https://www.dw.com/en/germany-former-abattoir-worker-heard-colleagues-crying-at-night/a-53943595

Welle, Deutsche 2020b. Germany: Romanian Workers Reveal Dire Conditions at Slaughterhouses. *Deutsche Welle*, 3 July 2020. https://www.dw.com/en/germany-meat-industry-conditions/a-54033187

Zimmermann, Clemens. 2020. Die Lage der arbeitenden Klasse in England. In *Friedrich Engels: Ein Gespenst geht um in Euopa. Begleitband zur Engelsausstellung 2020*, ed. Lars Bluma, 70–83. Remscheid: Bergischer Verlag.

Chapter Four
Marx's Centenary (1918) in the Light of the Media and Socialist Thought

4.1 Introduction

This chapter takes a look at some aspects of Marx's centenary in 1918. 1918 marked not just Marx's 100th anniversary but also the year in which the First World War ended. It was the year that saw the immediate aftermath of the Russian Revolution and the start of the Russian Civil War, the end of the Austro-Hungarian Empire; the formation of the Weimar Republic, Austria's First Republic, the Czech Republic, the Hungarian Republic, the Second Polish Republic; the founding of the Communist Party of Germany (KPD), and the independence of Iceland from Denmark.

The communists as well as left-wing socialists of the day saw themselves in the tradition of Marx, whereas revisionist social democrats based their politics on a criticism or revised reading of Marx. This difference resulted, as we will see, in different readings of Marx.

4.2 Communists and Left Socialists on Marx's Centenary

After the Social Democratic Party of Germany (SPD) had in August 1914 voted for war credits that had enabled the mobilisation of the German army in the First World War, Rosa Luxemburg, Hermann Duncker, Hugo Eberlein, Julian Marchlewski, Franz Mehring, Ernst Meyer, Wilhelm Pieck and Karl Liebknecht founded the Gruppe Internationale (Group International) that in 1916 became the Spartacus League. Spartacus in 1917 became part of the Independent Social Democratic Party of Germany

DOI: 10.4324/9781003199182-4

(USPD), a split-off from the SPD, and turned at the end of 1918 into the Communist Party of Germany (KPD).

4.2.1 Rosa Luxemburg and Franz Mehring

Rosa Luxemburg was imprisoned from 18 February 1915 until 9 November 1916. She was jailed for two speeches in which she had called for conscientious objection. After she had served the sentence, she was not immediately released because she was considered a security threat. At the time when Marx's centenary was celebrated, Rosa Luxemburg was a political prisoner. Writing was, as one can imagine, difficult in prison, but Luxemburg managed to secretly write the *Junius Pamphlet: The Crisis in the German Social Democracy* (Luxemburg 1916) in 1915. The pamphlet was published anonymously in 1916 and distributed illegally in Germany.

Luxemburg had written the chapter on *Capital Volumes 2 and 3* for Franz Mehring's Marx biography that was published in May 1918 (Mehring 2003/1936). In a letter to Mehring, Luxemburg (2011, 458) wrote on 30 December 2017: "How fine that your *Marx* [...] will soon appear, which is truly a gleam of light in these sorry times. I hope the book will be a stimulus and an encouragement for a great many people and at the same time a nostalgic reminder of that lovely time when one did not yet have to be ashamed to call oneself a German Social Democrat". Convinced by the book's excellence, she nonetheless had doubts about its effectiveness, as she wrote in a letter to Clara Zetkin on 29 June 1918: "I find it magnificent and promise myself it will have a powerful impact on the masses. If only they will read it!" (Ibid., 463).

In her chapter in Mehring's book, Luxemburg points out that the achievement of *Capital* is that "Marx showed for the first time how profit originated and how it flowed into the pockets of the capitalists. He did so on the basis of two decisive economic facts: first, that the mass of the workers consists of proletarians who are compelled to sell their labour-power as a commodity in order to exist, and secondly that this commodity labour-power possesses such a high degree of productivity in our own day that it is able to produce in a certain time a much greater product than is necessary for its own maintenance in that time" (Rosa Luxemburg, quoted in Mehring 2003/1936, 372). The second volume of *Capital* investigates how a whole is developed from the innumerable deviating movements of individual capital" (Ibid., 375). "In the first volume he [Marx] deals with the production of capital and lays bare the secret of profit-making. In the second volume he describes the movement of capital between the factory and the market, between the production and consumption of society. And in the third volume he deals with the distribution of the profit amongst the capitalist class as a whole. [...] In the first volume we are in the factory, in the deep social pit of labour where we can trace the source of capitalist wealth. In the second and third volumes we are on the surface, on the official stage of society. Department stores, banks, the stock exchanges, finance and the troubles of the 'needy' agriculturalists take up the foreground" (Rosa Luxemburg, quoted in Mehring 2003/1936, 376, 377).

"The investigations which Marx pursues in the second and third volumes of *Capital* offer a thorough insight into the nature of crises" (Rosa Luxemburg, quoted in Mehring 2003/1936, 378). 100 years later after this analysis of Luxemburg was published in the year of Marx's centenary, capitalism has gone through several more crisis stages, of which the latest began in 2008 and created a great recession. New authoritarianisms and new nationalisms emerged in the context of this crisis. Marx and Luxemburg remind us that the capitalist system is inherently crisis-ridden and that crises can within that system at a maximum be suspended temporarily and sooner or later always come back in new forms.

Franz Mehring was author of one of the first biographies of Karl Marx (Mehring 2003/1936) and a comrade of Rosa Luxemburg, Karl Liebknecht, and Clara Zetkin. Mehring was one of the people who together with Luxemburg founded the Spartacus League that became the Communist Party of Germany (KPD). Mehring published on the occasion of Marx's centenary an article in *Leipziger Volkszeitung* on 4 May 1918. He wrote: "Karl Marx's centenary directs our view from a gruesome presence to a brighter future just like a bright sunbeam that breaks through dark and apparently impenetrable cloud layers [...] Tireless and restless critique [...] was his true weapon. [...] To continue working based on the indestructible foundations that he laid is the most worthy homage we can offer to him on his one hundredth birthday"[1] (Mehring 1918, 11, 15).

4.2.2 Max Adler

The Austro-Marxist philosopher and politician Max Adler was a left socialist who was part of the left wing of Austrian social democracy. In May 1918, he published the pamphlet *Die sozialistische Idee der Befreiung bei Karl Marx* (*Karl Marx's Socialist Idea of Liberation*). He wrote: "The poet's words 'For I have been a man, and that Means I have been a combatant'[2] has for the proletariat through Karl Marx gained the deeper historical meaning that *the proletariat only as struggling class reaches humanity*. The World War's inhumanity has given the proletariat a terrible object lesson of this circumstance. [...] It is only in this context that Marx will again become teacher and leader. The true celebration of his centenary consists not in mere commemoration of his works and teachings, but in keeping alive his revolutionary spirit"[3] (Adler 1918, 489).

4.2.3 Antonio Gramsci

Italy at the time of Marx's centenary fought as part of the Allied Powers in the First World War. Antonio Gramsci was at that time a member of the Italian Socialist Party (PSI), lived in Turin, where he was PSI secretary, and was the editor of the Socialist Party's weekly *Il Grido del Popolo* (*The People's Cry*). On 4 May 1918, Gramsci (1918) published the essay "Il nostro Marx" ("Our Marx") on the occasion of Marx's centenary.

In this article, Gramsci writes that Marx's "only categorical imperative" is, "'Workers of the world, unite!' The duty of organizing, the propagation of the duty to organize and associate, should therefore be what distinguishes Marxists from non-Marxists" (Gramsci 1918, 36). Organisation and political action as such are not necessarily progressive. Also fascists organise in political groups and movements that act politically in public. So what Gramsci leaves out is that for Marx not political practice, but praxis – socialist political practice – is decisive.

Gramsci stresses that for Marx, ideas are not immaterial or fictitious, but grounded in the economy: "With Marx, history continues to be the domain of ideas, of spirit, of the conscious activity of single or associated individuals. But ideas, spirit, take on substance, lose their arbitrariness, they are no longer fictitious religious or sociological abstractions. Their substance is in the economy, in practical activity, in the systems and relations of production and exchange" (Gramsci 1918, 37).

Knowledge labour has today become a key feature of capitalist society. The intersection of ideas and labour in the contemporary economy strengthens Gramsci's interpretation of Marx, in which there is no strict base/superstructure separation and ideas operate within the economy.

Marx "is a monolithic bloc of knowing and thinking humanity [...] who constructs iron syllogisms which encircle reality in its essence and dominate it, which penetrate people's minds, which bring the sedimentations of prejudice and fixed ideas crumbling down and strengthen the moral character" (Ibid., 39). Today, we see the rise of new nationalisms and authoritarianisms that use prejudices for trying to divide humanity and distract attention from class conflicts and class structures. Marx's humanism and method of ideology critique are today of key importance for challenging these developments.

4.2.4 Eugene V. Debs

Eugene V. Debs was one of the founders of the International Workers of the World (IWW) and of the Socialist Party of America and its predecessor parties. The Socialist Party opposed the USA's entry into the First World War, which resulted in the First Red Scare. Debs on 4 May 1918, (Debs 1918) published an article that commemorated Marx for struggling "to destroy despotism in all its form" and to emancipate humankind "from the slavery of the ages". In November 1918, Debs was sentenced to ten years in prison for sedition. He was released at the end of 1921. Debs and his socialist contemporaries struggled against the authoritarian tendencies of their time. He considered Marx's works and life as a guiding light for the struggle against authoritarianism. 100 years later, new authoritarian dangers have emerged. Also today, Marx reminds is of the need "to destroy despotism".

In Russia, the Soviet government signed the Peace Treaty of Brest-Litovsk with Germany, Austria-Hungary, Bulgaria and the Ottoman Empire on 3 May 1918. Seven members of the Central Committee of the Communist Party of the Soviet Union had voted in favour of such a treaty, four against, four members abstained. The Central Soviet Executive passed the resolution with 112 votes in favour, 84 oppositional votes, and 24 abstentions. Not everyone agreed with this decision. In April 1918, a group of Left Communists led by Nikolai Bukharin and Karl Radek published "Theses on the Current Situation" (Left Communists 1918), in which they argued that the Peace Treaty was a "capitulation to international imperialism" and had "negative effect on the spiritual and psychological development of the international revolution" (Ibid.).

4.2.5 Lenin

On the day of Marx's centenary, Lenin (1918) wrote a response to the Left Communists under the title *"Left-Wing" Childishness and the Petty-Bourgeois Mentality*. Lenin disagreed with the Left Communists' hasty call for world revolution: "For, until the world socialist revolution breaks out, until it embraces several countries and is strong enough to overcome *international imperialism*, it is the direct duty of the socialists who have conquered in one country (especially a backward one) *not* to accept battle against the giants of imperialism. Their duty is to try to avoid battle, to wait until the conflicts between the imperialists weaken them *even more*, and bring the revolution in other countries even nearer" (Ibid., 327).

Lenin refers to Marx in order to stress that "Marx was profoundly right when he taught the workers the importance of preserving the organisation of large-scale production, precisely for the purpose of facilitating the transition to socialism" (Ibid., 345). "Socialism is inconceivable without large-scale capitalist engineering based on the latest discoveries of modern science" (Ibid., 339).

Lenin is certainly right in stressing with Marx that post-capitalism needs to use modern technologies for establishing a post-scarcity society so that emancipation from toil and true freedom become possible. But the problem was that Lenin on the occasion of Marx's centenary did not read Marx thoroughly enough. He adopted an uncritical celebration and uptake of Taylorism, including its de-humanising aspects such as re-petitive, monotonous labour. Soviet labour was not less alienated than labour in Western capitalist societies.

The point is that socialist technology needs to be a sublation of capitalist technology, i.e. a simultaneous preservation of the best elements, elimination of negative design features, and the development of new qualities. Marx and Engels spoke in this context already in *The German Ideology* of the appropriation of technology. They make clear that appropriation means a transformation that is at the same time revolution/overthrow/ceasing-to-be and development/coming-to-be: "The appropriation of a to-tality of instruments of production is, for this very reason, the development of a totality of capacities in the individuals themselves. [...] This appropriation is further de-termined by the manner in which it must be effected. It can only be effected through a union, which by the character of the proletariat itself can again only be a universal one, and through a revolution, in which, on the one hand, the power of the earlier mode of production and intercourse and social organisation is overthrown, and, on the other hand, there develops the universal character and the energy of the proletariat, without which the revolution cannot be accomplished; and in which, further, the proletariat rids itself of everything that still clings to it from its previous position in society. Only at this stage does self-activity coincide with material life, which corresponds to the development of individuals into complete individuals and the casting-off of all natural

limitations. The transformation of labour into self-activity corresponds to the transformation of the earlier limited intercourse into the intercourse of individuals as such.
With the appropriation of the total productive forces through united individuals, private
property comes to an end" (Marx and Engels 1845/46, 87–88).

Marx further developed the idea of appropriation as dialectical becoming in the
Grundrisse. Only a dialectic of old and new elements of technology makes possible
that what Hardt and Negri (2017) based on Marx call the appropriation of fixed capital
results in "*disposable time*" ceasing to have "an *antithetical* existence" (Marx 1857/
58, 708), "the powers of social production" – including the "general intellect" – becoming "the real life process" (Ibid., 706), the "free development of individualities"
that "then corresponds to the artistic, scientific etc. development of the individuals in
the time set free" (Ibid.). Social production means for Marx that human subjects exist
"in mutual relationships, which they equally reproduce and produce anew" in a
"constant process of their own movement, in which they even renew themselves even
as they renew the world of wealth they create" (Ibid., 712). In a society of the
commons, humans produce truly in an open, dynamic process and so do not stop
developing technologies, but give new qualities to old technologies and create entirely
new technologies.

In the age of digital capitalism, we cannot simply in a Leninist manner appropriate
capitalist digital technologies by stopping at socialising the ownership of Facebook,
Google, Amazon, Apple, etc. One also needs qualitative changes of digital technologies. So for example turning Facebook into a co-operative ownership does not automatically change its individualistic structures that enable the accumulation of online
reputation. Socialisation and co-operation has to include a qualitative transformation
of Facebook's platform design structures and policies.

4.2.6 Socialist Party of Great Britain

Jack Fitzgerald was in 1904 one of the founders of the Socialist Party of Great Britain.
He was the editor of the Party's journal *Socialist Standard*, where he in May 1918
published an article on "The Centenary of Marx". In it, Fitzgerald (1918) wrote: "Of
Capital it is no exaggeration to say that no work ever written on economics has
attracted so much attention and attempted criticism. Every professor of political
economy and every petty journalist feels bound to criticise, without having troubled to
read, Marx's unanswerable exposure of the present system. The two great features of

Capital are the solving of the riddle of Value and the demonstration of the appropriation of Surplus-Value". 2017 was the 150th anniversary of the publication of *Capital Volume 1*'s first edition. Fitzgerald's judgment certainly also holds true 100 years later: Marx and *Capital* are heavily discussed, but too many people make claims about both without having thoroughly engaged with them.

4.3 Reformist and Revisionist Social Democracy on Marx's Centenary

Arbeiter-Zeitung, the daily newspaper of the Austrian social democrats, wrote on the day of Marx's centenary: "And yet, we do not celebrate a dead person today when we commemorate Marx. His name is today still a battle cry as good as it was then when the thirty-year old threw his Communist Manifesto into the world. He is still today awakening sleeping souls and is today still collecting, uniting and spearheading the proletarians of all countries"[4]

(*Arbeiter-Zeitung* 1918, 1).

Other than Luxemburg, Liebknecht and Zetkin, Karl Kautsky did not clearly oppose the German Social Democrats' support of war credits. From 1916 onwards, Kautsky opposed the First World War, which led in 1917 to the creation of the Independent Social Democratic Party of Germany (USPD). Kautsky's criticism of Marxists' nationalist support of the First World War on the occasion of Marx's centenary was at the same time also a piece of self-criticism: "The celebration of the 100th birthday of our master will be the first act since the outbreak of the World War for which the proletarians of all countries unite"; Marxism was "partly dispersed into national parties that abet national hatred and the national lust for conquest of their governments and dominant classes"[5] (Kautsky 1918, 1). Kautsky reminded the readers that Marx had opposed Realpolitik and had favoured revolutionary politics. For Marx, the proletariat was revolutionary and therefore "constantly driven by a wide goal that transcends existing society"[6] (Kautsky 1918, 3).

Joseph Schumpeter was in 1918 professor of political economy at the University of Graz and worked in a commission of the German government that prepared the nationalisation of some parts of German industry. He was not a follower of Marx's theory, but in a newspaper article published on the day of Marx's centenary he praised Marx as political economist and sociologist. "What is unique about him is that he was the inseparable penetration of researcher and fighter, that he only conducted research in order to give direction to struggles and only struggled in order put the results of his research into action"[7] (Schumpeter 1918, 3).

Since 1876, *Vorwärts* has been the newspaper of the Social Democratic Party of Germany. Wilhelm Liebknecht was one of the founding editors. *Die Neue Zeit* was the Party's theoretical journal and existed from 1883 until 1923. At the time of Marx's centenary, German social democracy was split into the Spartacus League that later in the same year became the Communist Party of Germany, the centrist Independent Social Democratic Party of Germany (USPD) and the rightist Social Democratic Party of Germany (SPD). Interestingly, *Die Neue Zeit* and *Vorwärts* formulated different positions on how to think about Marx's centenary.

Heinrich Cunow, who in the years from 1917 until 1932 edited *Die Neue Zeit* – the academic publication of German social democracy – wrote about Marx's 100th birthday: "Marx protrudes among the geniuses whose names are engraved into the plaques of honour and who lived during the 19th century's second half as conquering the realm of the intellectual history. [...] His work has not come to an end. The spirit of this man, whose mortal remains have now been covered by Highgate Cemetery's lawn since more than 35 years, still exerts vital power. [...] Marx's enormous influence on theoretical-political economy, the interpretation of history and proletarian struggles in almost all European states proves well enough his importance"[8] (*Die Neue Zeit* 1918, 97–98).

On the day of Marx's centenary, *Vorwärts* reported on its title page that Marxists were deeply split: in Russia, the Bolsheviks and Mensheviks would kill each other. In France, the celebrations planned by Marx's grandson Jean-Laurent-Frederick Longuet would have been circumvented by war-supporting socialists. In Germany, "the split of the Party is an accomplished fact"[9] (*Vorwärts* 1918, 1). "In Germany, the Marx celebrations must limit themselves to appraisals of the master in the press and festivities in closed circles"[10] (*Vorwärts* 1918, 1). The article on the one hand justifies rightist German Social Democrats' support of the First World War. On the other hand, it is a deeply pessimist piece that expresses sorrow over the bad status of Social Democracy and its 1917 split into two parties (the USDP and the SPD). Marx was in the article seen as someone who did not matter in 1918, but would matter again in the future: "So Karl Marx's intellectual work can be a measure for the greatness of the working class at a later time"[11] (*Vorwärts* 1918, 2). It becomes evident how class struggle and socialism formed a mere lip service for revisionist social democrats.

At the time of the split of the Party into a pro- and an anti-First World War faction in 1915, Rudolf Hilferding was the newspaper's chief-editor and *Vorwärts* supported the anti-war position. But Hilferding was replaced by Friedrich Stampfer as chief-editor in

1916 so that the newspaper at the time of Marx's centenary represented the Party's mainstream positions of Friederich Ebert and Philipp Scheidemann. Scheidemann was Chancellor of the Weimar Republic when right-wing paramilitaries under Waldemar Pabst murdered Rosa Luxemburg and Karl Liebknecht in 1919, which was tolerated by Scheidemann's Minister of Defence Gustav Noske.

4.4 How the News Media Reported on Marx's Centenary

In London, where Marx lived from 1849 until his death in 1883, socialists planned a celebration of his centenary in Finsbury Park. An advertisement printed in the *Daily Herald* on 4 May (see Figure 4.1) makes clear that eight trade councils and over one hundred trade union branches and co-operatives supported the event that was planned to take place in Finsbury Park on 5 May. It should have featured speakers on eight platforms. The Herald also printed the resolution that the organisers (The North London Labour Demonstration Committee) planned to read out on all eight platforms:

> This mass meeting of London workers, on the centenary of the birth of Karl Marx, recalls with gratitude his devoted labours on behalf of the cause of International Socialism. Having no quarrel with the workers of any country, it extends fraternal greetings to them all, paying particular tribute to those Russian comrades who have waged such a magnificent struggle for their Social and Political emancipation. It emphatically protests against the continuation of the present Capitalistic war, and urges the workers of all lands immediately to meet in conference and arrange a 'Peoples' Peace' on the basis of 'no annexations and no indemnities'. It further vigorously protests against the continued imprisonment of those holding a conscientious objection to military service, and demands their immediate and unconditional release. It demands full political and civil rights for all workers, including soldiers, sailors, and civil servants. Finally, it reaffirms its belief in the solidarity of the workers of all lands, in the cause of International Brotherhood and goodwill amongst all peoples. Workers of London rally behind your Banners! Demonstrate your belief in the Solidarity of the Working Class the World over – of Internationalism, Brotherhood and Goodwill amongst all Peoples. Rally! Rally!! Rally!!!
>
> (*Daily Herald*, 4 May 1918, 11)

MAY CELEBRATION

GREAT RANK & FILE LABOUR
DEMONSTRATION
IN
FINSBURY PARK,
SUNDAY NEXT, MAY 5th, 3.30 p.m.
Supported by 8 Trade Councils and over 100 Trade Union Branches,
Co-operative Societies, &c.

8 Platforms	50 SPEAKERS	7 Processions

WELL-KNOWN SPEAKERS IN THE TRADE UNION AND POLITICAL WORLD

GREAT PROCESSIONS
with Bands and Banners will start from the following points:

Edmonton Town Hall, 1.30 p.m.	Holloway Prison, 2.45 p.m.
Camden Town N. L. Rly. Stn., 2.15 p.m.	Tottenham, Northumberland Pk., 2 p.m.
Hackney Town Hall, 1.30 p.m.	Walthamstow, Standard Corner, Black-
Highgate Archway Tavern, 2.30 p.m.	horse Road, 1.30 p.m.

FIGURE 4.1 Advertisement for a rally celebrating Marx's centenary in London's Finsbury Park. (source: *Daily Herald*, 4 May 1918)

The Home Secretary prohibited the public event. In the US, the *New York Herald* reported that in London, the "celebration of the centenary of the birthday of Karl Marx, the German Socialist, arranged to be held in a London park tomorrow, has been prohibited by the Home Secretary on the ground that it would be likely to cause disorder and make undue demands on the police. The principal organiser of the meeting was a pacifist weekly paper and several trade unions cooperated. There were to have been bands and banners and speeches, with resolutions against a 'capitalistic war'" (Marx Celebration Halted, *New York Herald*, 5 May 1918, 2).

How the News Media Reported on Marx's Centenary

In the US, the *New York Times* on the same day ran an overall appreciative piece titled *Today is 100th Anniversary of Marx's Birth*: "Few men have more profoundly influenced the life and thought of their own and succeeding generations than the great author of 'Das Kapital', upon whom the world has, with questionable accuracy, conferred the title 'Father of Modern Socialism'. [...] The great war seems destined to mark the close of the era of Marxism in Socialist history. [...] The centennial of Marx's birth may be regarded, at the same time, as the end of Marxian socialism" (Spargo 1918, 11–12).

The Globe was a London-based newspaper owned by William Maxwell Aitken, who at that time was Britain's Minister of Information in David Lloyd George's government. It is of course interesting but not surprising that the Minister of Information at that time was a media baron who controlled the *Daily Express* and *The Globe*. At the same time, Alfred Harmsworth, who owned the *Daily Mirror* and *The Times* and had founded the *Daily Mail* (that at that time was owned by his brother Harold Harmsworth), was the British government's Director of Propaganda. Putting the owners of large newspapers in control of propaganda and information policies constitutes a direct state-capital-nexus that undermines the freedom of the press and makes sure that there is pro-government reporting. In this particular case, the political appointments served the purpose of war propaganda and the opposition to socialism and pacifism.

This circumstance becomes evident in a piece printed in Aitken's *The Globe* on 2 May 1918, under the title "Pacifists Seek Trouble" that reported there is "every indication" that in respect to the planned "Pacifists' demonstration [...] arranged to be held in Finsbury Park [...] the British public will take the matter in their own hands and give the demonstrators a short shrift [...] unless the authorities step in and prohibit the meeting" (*The Globe*, 2 May 1918, 3). So the newspaper called on the state to prohibit the Marx meeting and on anti-socialists to violently disrupt it. Tellingly, next to this report *The Globe* featured a large call with the title "HELP to advance the British Financial Front" that calls the readers to buy National War Bonds. "YOUR COUNTRY needs £25,000,000 every week from the sale of National War Bonds. The money must be found. Are you doing your utmost to help? [...] Find out where you can cut expenses, and lend your country the money saved. [...] You are personally responsible for some part of that £25,000,000. Rich or poor – man or woman – it is to you that our sailors and soldiers look to provide the means of victory. They have faith in you. Prove that your faith is well-founded. Give them your support" (*The Globe*, 2 May 1918, 3).

Also *The Times* that was owned by the UK-government's Director of Propaganda Alfred Harmsworth reported negatively on Marx's centenary. On 2 May, it reported *The*

Times reported that "Labour's May Day will be next Sunday, the centenary of Karl Marx, when there will be a procession to Highgate Cemetery, and flowers will be placed on Marx's grave". The conservative newspaper titled this short news piece "May Day. Anti-Socialist Demonstrations at Glasgow" and wrote in it that the May Day demonstrations in Glasgow were "one of the largest of recent years", but that there were "a number of exciting incidents", including spectators shouting "go and join the Army" (*The Times*, 2 May 1918, 3). On 1 May, *The Times* ran a short news item titled "Karl Marx Unhonoured" that reported that in France, a "proposal to celebrate the centenary of Karl Marx [born 5 May 1818] has been rejected by the executive committee of the Federation of the Seine".

The *Chicago Daily Tribune* reported about a celebratory event in Chicago, writing that an "admission charge of 35 cents and a wardrobe tip of 15 cents straight assured the exclusion of many and limited the attendance of the 'Gigantic Karl Marx Celebration' to the 150 who had the price". The article spoke in its headline of the attendees as "elite Bolsheviki" and wrote that "every third tie was of crimson" (*Chicago Daily Tribune*, 6 May 1918, 3). To remind its readers of what should happen to socialists, the newspaper right next to this article printed one titled "Socialists Here Face Inquiry for Anti-War Stand".

The Scotsman reported on May 6 that the "peace demonstration, widely advertised as rank and file labour celebration of the centenary of Karl Marx [...] was prohibited by an order of the Home Secretary. Nevertheless, a crowd numbering between 500 and 1000 people assembled at half-past three, and grouped themselves around improvised stands" (*The Scotsman*, 6 May 1918, p. 7).

In Germany, the liberal *Berliner Volkszeitung* published an article about Marx's centenary that criticised "the self-indulgent overestimation of this centenarian".[12] "The number of owners has not just not continuously decreased, but has (thanks to the development of stockholding) steadily become larger. The 1,000-year Reich of the Proletarians is deferred to the distant future"[13] (Fiedler 1918, 3). "For decades to come, the idea of the International, his favourite organisational plan, seems to be buried in the abyss that the World War has ripped up between the nations"[14] (Ibid.).

Overall, we can see from this incomplete review that the reactions to Marx's centenary ranged from taking his work and life as an inspiration for the struggles of the time on the one side of the spectrum to on the other side radical dismissals of Marx's works and politics that also featured calls for the use of violence to impede celebrations.

4.5 Conclusion

The cultural forms, in which Marx's centenary was reflected in 1918, included press articles, essays, speeches, rallies, demonstrations, music, and banners. 100 years later, we can find besides all of these cultural forms of commemorating Marx's bicentenary also expressions of engagement, inspiration, interest and rejection that take on the form of memes, social media, documentaries, radio and television reports, movies, novels, exhibitions, souvenirs, books, collected volumes, etc. One should in this context not turn Marx into a depoliticised cultural spectacle (Marx for Marx's sake), but rather take the opportunity to treat him as undead and as capitalism's walking dead, who reminds us of the necessity to critically theorise and politically criticise capitalism and to struggle for alternatives (Marx for the sake of a commons-oriented society). We need to repeat Marx today.

Notes

1 Translated from German. German original: "Wie ein heller Sonnenstrahl, der durch düstere und scheinbar undurchdringliche Wolkenschichten bricht, so lenkt heute der hundertste Geburtstag von Karl Marx unseren Blick aus einer grauenvollen Gegenwart in eine hellere Zukunft [...] die rast- und ruhelose Kritik [...] ist seine wirkliche Waffe gewesen [...] So fortzuarbeiten auf den unzerstörbaren Grundlagen, die er gelegt hat, ist die würdigste Huldigung, die wir [...] [ihm] an seinem hundertsten Geburtstage darbringen können".

2 Goethe (1914, 180).

3 German original: "Das Dichterwort ‚Denn ich bin ein Mensch gewesen. Und das heißt ein Kämpfer sein' hat für das Proletariat durch Karl Marx die tiefere entwicklungsgeschichtliche Bedeutung erhalten, daß das Proletariat erst als Klassenkämpfer überhaupt zum Menschentum gelangt. Die Unmenschlichkeit des Weltkrieges hat dem Proletariat drüber einen furchtbaren Anschauungsunterricht erteilt. [...] Hier nun erst wird Marx wieder Lehrer und Führer werden. Die wirkliche Jahrhundertfeier für ihn besteht nicht in einem bloßen Gedenken seines Schaffens und Lehrens, sondern in der Lebendigerhaltung seines revolutionären Geistes".

4 German original: "Und doch, nicht einen Toten feiern wir heute, wenn wir Marxens gedenken. Sein Name ist heute noch ein Kampfruf – so gut wie damals, als der der Dreißigjährige sein Kommunistisches Manifest in die Welt schleuderte. Er ist heute noch der Wecker schlafender Seelen, heute noch Sammler und Einiger und Vorkämpfer der Proletarier aller Länder".

5 "Die Feier des hundertsten Geburtstages unseres Meisters wird seit Ausbruch des Weltkrieges die erste Handlung sein, zu der sich wieder die Proletarier aller Länder

vereinigen". Marxismus ist "zum Teil in nationale Parteien zersprengt, die nationalem Haß und nationaler Eroberungsgier ihrer Regierungen und herrschenden Klassen Vorschub leisten".

6 "ist stets getrieben durch ein weites, über die bestehende Gesellschaft hinausgehendes Ziel".

7 "Und das Einzigartige an ihm ist, daß der Forscher und der Kämpfer in ihm einander untrennbar durchdringen, daß er nur forschte, um seinem Kämpfen die Richtung zu geben und nur kämpfte, um das Resultat seiner Forschung durch die Tat zu vertreten".

8 German original: "Als ein Welteroberer auf dem Gebiet der Geistesgeschichte ragt Marx unter den Geistesgrößen der zweiten Hälfte des neunzehnten Jahrhunderts hervor, die auf die Steintafeln des Ruhmes ihren Namen eingegraben haben. [...] sein Wirken ist nicht beendet. Noch immer geht von dem Geist dieses Mannes, dessen sterbliche Hülle nun schon seit mehr als 35 Jahren der Rasen des Friedhofs von Highgate deckt, eine lebendige Kraft aus. [...] Der enorme Einfluß den Marx auf die Entwicklung der theoretisch-politischen Ökonomie wie auf die Geschichtsbetrachtung und die proletarischen Parteikämpfe in fast allen europäischen Staaten gehabt hat, beweist zur Genüge die Bedeutung des Mannes".

9 "ist die Parteispaltung vollendete Tatsache".

10 "In Deutschland muß sich die Marxfeier auf Würdigungen des Meisters in der Presse und auf Festlichkeiten in geschlossenem Kreise beschränken".

11 "So kann das geistige Werk von Karl Marx ein Maßstab sein für die Größe der Arbeiterklasse einer späteren Zeit".

12 "die maßlose Überschätzung dieses Hundertjährigen".

13 "Die Zahl der Besitzenden ist nicht nur nicht beständig kleiner, sondern sogar (dank der Entwicklung des Aktienwesens) beständig größer geworden. Das tausendjährige Reich des Proletariats rückt in weite, ungreifbare Ferne".

14 "Auf Jahrzehnte hinaus scheint der Gedanke der Internationale, sein organisatorischer Lieblingsplan, in der Kluft versunken zu sein, die der Weltkrieg zwischen den Völkern aufgerissen hat".

References

Adler, Max. 1918. Die sozialistische Idee der Befreiung bei Karl Marx. Zu seinem hundertsten Geburtstage am 5. Mai 1918. In *Max Adler: Ausgewählte Schriften*, ed. Norbert Leser and Alfred Pfabigan, 478–489. Vienna: Österreichischer Bundesverlag.

Arbeiter-Zeitung. 1918. Karl Marx. 5 May: 1–3.

Debs, Eugene V. 1918. Karl Marx the Man: An Appreciation. *St. Louis Labor* 900 (May 4, 1918): 1.

Die Neue Zeit. 1918. Karl Marx. 3 May 1918. 36: 97–103.

Fiedler, Alfred. 1918. Das tausendjährige Reich. Zum 100. Geburtstag von Karl Marx (5. Mai). *Berliner Volkszeitung*, 5 May 2018: 3.

Fitzgerald, Jack. 1918. The Centenary of Marx. *Socialist Standard*, May 1918. https://www.marxists.org/archive/fitzgerald/marxcentenary.htm

Gramsci, Antonio. 1918. Our Marx. In *The Gramsci Reader: Selected Writings, 1916-1935*, ed. David Forgacs, 36–40. New York: NYU Press.

Goethe, Johann Wolfgang von. 1914. *West-Eastern Divan*. London: Dent & Sons.

Hardt, Michael and Antonio Negri. 2017. *Assembly*. Oxford: Oxford University Press.

Kautsky, Karl. 1918. Marx über Realpolitik. *Arbeiterwille: Organ des arbeitenden Volkes für Steiermark und Kärnten*, 5 May 1918: 1–3.

Left Communists. 1918. *The Left Communists' Theses on the Current Situation*. https://libcom.org/library/theses-left-communists-russia-1918

Lenin, Vladimir I. 1918. "Left-Wing" Childishness and the Petty-Bourgeois Mentality. In *Lenin Collected Works Volume 27*, 323–354. Moscow: Progress.

Luxemburg, Rosa. 2011. *The Letters of Rosa Luxemburg*, ed. Georg Adler, Peter Hudis and Annelies Laschitza. London: Verso.

Luxemburg, Rosa. 1916. The Junius Pamphlet: The Crisis in the German Social Democracy. In *Rosa Luxemburg Speaks*, 371–477. New York: Pathfinder.

Marx, Karl. 1857/58. *Grundrisse*. London: Penguin.

Marx, Karl and Friedrich Engels. 1845/46. The German Ideology. In *Marx & Engels Collected Works (MECW) Volume 5*, 19–539, London: Lawrence & Wishart.

Mehring, Franz. 2003/1936. *Karl Marx: The Story of His Life*. Abingdon: Routledge.

Mehring, Franz. 1918. Karl Marx. In *Franz Mehring Gesammelte Schriften Band 4: Aufsätze zur Geschichte der Arbeiterbewegung*, 11–15. Berlin: Dietz.

Schumpeter, Joseph. 1918. Karl Marx, der Denker. *Arbeiterwille: Organ des arbeitenden Volkes für Steiermark und Kärnten*, 5 May 1918: 3.

Spargo, John. 1918. Today is 100th Anniversary of Marx's Birth. *New York Times*, 5 May 1918, 11–12.

Vorwärts. 1918. Zum 100. Geburtstag von Karl Marx. 5 May 2018: 1–2.

Chapter Five
Reflections on Sven-Eric Liedman's Marx-Biography
A World to Win: The Life and Works of Karl Marx

5.1. Introduction

Sven-Eric Liedman is professor emeritus of the history of ideas at the University of Gothenburg in Sweden. He published his first Swedish book on Marx in 1968. It was focused on the young Marx. Fifty years later, Verso published his Marx-biography *A World to Win: The Life and Works of Karl Marx* (Liedman 2018). The book was first released in Swedish under the title *Karl Marx: en biografi* (*Karl Marx: A Biography*) in 2015. Jeffrey N. Skinner translated it from Swedish to English.

The English version of Liedman's biography was published 18 days before a very special occasion: 5 May 2018, marks Karl Marx's bicentenary. As a consequence, lots of public attention is given to Marx's works and life in 2018, including new academic publications, novels, events, conferences, exhibitions, documentaries, films, monuments, discussions, reports on television and radio and in newspapers and magazines; memes, hashtags (#Marx200, #KarlMarx, #Marx) and postings on social media, etc. New Marx-biographies published in 2018, such as Sven-Eric Liedman's *World to Win: The Life and Thought of Karl Marx*, are therefore likely to receive significant attention.

Writings on Marx can broadly be categorised into introductions to his theory, updates of his works in respect to contemporary society, and biographies. Marx's

DOI: 10.4324/9781003199182-5

collected works amount to 50 volumes in the English *Marx & Engels Collected Works*, 44 volumes in the German *Marx-Engels-Werke*, and 114 volumes in the ongoing publication of the German *Marx-Engels-Gesamtausgabe* (MEGA^2). Given such a voluminous oeuvre, it is a challenge to write about Marx. Updates of Marx's theory for 21st-century society necessarily have to limit themselves to specific aspects. Introductory works either have to provide brief introductions to a body of works (see for example Heinrich 2012) or have to focus on more in-depth discussions of specific works such as *Capital* (see for example Harvey 2010, 2013; Fuchs 2016a) or *Grundrisse* (see for example Choat 2016; Negri 1991; Rosdolsky 1977). Given that Marx worked on a general theory of capitalism, it is possible to engage with his works without always discussing details of his life.

5.2. Jonathan Sperber's and Gareth Stedman Jones' Marx-Biographies

Writing Marx-biographies poses a different set of challenges. Given the political nature of Marx's life and works, it is not really possible to disentangle the discussion of his personal life from his writings, his political activities and the political and historical context. They need to be treated as a differentiated, dialectical unity that forms a biographical whole. Marx's works on critical political economy, society, politics and philosophy formed an integral aspect of his life. The personal situation of Marx and his family and political developments influenced his writings. But Marx-biographies do not always live up to the need of presenting Marx in such a dialectical manner, where intellectual works and personal and political life form a differentiated and integrated totality. Francis Wheen's (1999) widely acclaimed *Karl Marx* presents Marx's life without going into any detail of his works. In recent years, the two most widely read and discussed Marx-biographies have been Jonathan Sperber's (2013) *Karl Marx: A 19th-Century Life* and Gareth Stedman Jones' (2016) *Karl Marx: Greatness and Illusion*. Both books illustrate the problems of bourgeois Marx-biographies.

Sperber's (2013) goal is to put Marx in "his 19th-century context" (Ibid., xviii). He thinks that the study of Marx's ideas in themselves and Marxist theory are "useless pastimes" (Ibid., xviii). Consequentially, Sperber's book focuses much more on Marx's life than his works. And insofar as he engages with Marx's writings, the presentation remains extremely superficial and incomplete. For example, Sperber argues in Chapter 11 (titled "The Economist") that Marx's economic theory is "framed by five conceptual distinctions" (Ibid., 427): use-value/exchange-value, ex-change/accumulation, labour/labour-power, constant capital/variable capital, rate of surplus-value/rate of profit. But one can add many more dialectical relations that Marx focused on: concrete labour/abstract labour, simple form of value/expanded form of value, commodity/money, worker/means of production, necessary labour-time/surplus labour-time, single worker/collective worker, absolute/relative surplus-value production, formal/real subsumption, relations of production/productive forces, etc. (Fuchs 2016a). And these dialectics are not static, but result in sublations that constitute capitalism's dynamics and crisis-tendencies. But in Sperber's account, the dialectic is barely mentioned.

The goal of Stedman Jones' (2016) biography is to "pay as much attention to Marx's thought as to his life" because Marx's writings stand in "particular political and philosophical contexts" (Ibid., xv). But Stedman Jones' readings and interpretations of Marx are too superficial and not up to the standards of Marxian scholarship (see Fuchs 2016b for a more detailed discussion). To give just one of many examples, Stedman Jones (2016, 394) claims that the *Grundrisse*'s "[m]ention of wage labour was also sparse and unspecific". But the term "wage labour" is in the English Penguin-edition of *Grundrisse* used 163 times, Marx along with the category of surplus-value introduces the one of surplus labour, analyses capitalism's class contradiction as the one between capital on the one side and labour as "the real *not-capital*" on the other side (Marx 1857/58, 274), anticipates that in a free society the "measure of wealth is then not any longer, in any way, labour time, but rather disposable time" (Ibid., 708), etc. What remains is a biography that is much more substantial in presenting Marx's life than works. Stedman Jones fails to achieve his self-set task of presenting the unity of Marx's thought and life. The reason why his Marx-biography is relatively successful has less to do with its quality and more with the fact that Penguin-books tend to sell independent of their content because of this publisher's reputation and marketing efforts.

Sperber's and Stedman Jones' books share the approach of presenting Marx as a thinker whose influence and works are limited to the 19th century. Stedman Jones (2016, 5) writes that his aim is "to put Marx back in his 19th-century surroundings". Sperber (2013) claims that "Marx's life, his systems of thought, his political strivings and aspirations, belonged primarily to the 19th century" (Ibid., xviii), that Marx is "more a figure of the past than a prophet of the present" (Ibid., xix), and that one must see "Marx in his contemporary context, not ours" (Ibid., xx). Both authors historicise Marx based on an undialectical concept of history that conceives of history as closed and bounded process and disregards the fact that Marx simultaneously worked out an analysis of capitalism in general, capitalism's genesis and contradictory development logic, and 19th-century reality.

Sperber and Stedman Jones reproduce one of the most widely held prejudices against Marx, namely that his theory is outdated and has no relevance in 21st-century society. Terry Eagleton (2011, 1–11) argues that the claim of Marx's obsolescence is the first of ten common prejudices about Marx. He asks: "What if it were not Marxism that is outdated but capitalism itself? [...] There is thus something curiously static and re-petitive about this most dynamic of all historical regimes. The fact that its underlying logic remains pretty constant is one reason why the Marxist critique of it remains largely valid" (Ibid., 9–10). Marx's categories are not limited to 19th-century capit-alism, but invite their appropriation and development for the analysis of 21st-century capitalism based on a dialectic of historical continuity and change (Fuchs and Monticelli 2018).

5.3. Sven-Eric Liedman and Franz Mehring

By explaining "not only who Marx was in his time, but why he remains a vital source of inspiration today" (Liedman 2018, xii) and taking into account "the last few decades of intensive research concerning the *Grundrisse* and in particular *Capital*" (xi), Liedman takes an approach that is qualitatively different from Sperber and Stedman Jones. He conceives of history and biography not as closed, but open-ended, dialectical process. The book is comprised of 14 chapters on a total of 627 pages. It starts by not just setting out Marx's early years, but that he was "a child of the French Revolution 1789" and of "the Industrial Revolution" (21). And the biography does not simply end with Marx's death because Liedman is convinced that Marx's critical theory will continue to be relevant at least as long as capit-alism exists. Liedman describes Marx's death in Chapter 14, but the same chapter describes the history of Marx's theory in the 20th century by presenting both or-thodox and unorthodox Marxian approaches. Liedman's book ends by saying that Marx "lives on as the great critic of capitalism", who presents "a possible utopia for our time as well" (627) and whose "entire toolbox of critical instruments" (625) continues to "inspire topical criticism of capitalism's latest achievements, the failings of politics, and the genuflection of the contemporary world of ideas before a fetish like the market" (626) so that Marx attracts "the people of the 21st" century (626).

One of the strengths of Sven-Eric Liedman's book is that he provides thorough introductions to Marx's works that he contextualises in Marx's life and politics, history, societies' development at the time of Marx, and the contradictions of capitalism. It shares the same methodological approach as Franz Mehring (2003/1918) uses in the Marx-biography *Karl Marx: The Story of His Life* that was published on the occasion of Marx's centenary in 1918. One hundred years later, on the occasion of Marx's bicentenary, Liedman without a doubt published the 21st century's thus far best Marx-biography. Mehring's work was certainly the best Marx's biography available at the time of Marx's centenary. Mehring was together with the likes of Rosa Luxemburg and Karl Liebknecht a member of the group of people, who in 1914 in light of the Social Democratic Party of Germany's agreement to war credits founded the Gruppe Internationale that became the Spartacus League in 1916 and in December 1918 the Communist Party of Germany. Mehring knew Engels and Marx's daughter Laura. Rosa Luxemburg contributed a chapter on *Capital*'s volumes 2 and 3 to his Marx-biography. Marx's *Economic and Philosophic Manuscripts of 1844* were first published in German in 1932. His *Contribution to the Critique of Hegel's Philosophy of Law* was (except for the famous introduction that Marx published in 1844 in the *Deutsch-Französische Jahrbücher*) first released in German in 1927. In 1918, the part of the *German Ideology* that focuses on Feuerbach had not-yet been published. Marx's *Grundrisse* were first published in 1939–1941. Mehring's introduction to Marx's works and life was at the height of the time of Marx's centenary, but could not take into account important works that were unpublished at that time. One hundred years later, Sven-Eric Liedman provides a successful update that stands in the Mehring's tradition of writing Marx's biography based on a dialectic of intellectual works and personal and societal life.

Liedman devotes 28 pages to the *Economic and Philosophic Manuscripts* (Chapter 5, 133–160) and 24 pages to the *German Ideology* (172–196). He rejects Althusser's claim that there is an epistemological break between the young and the older Marx, but stresses at the same time the concepts such as alienation underwent some change in Marx's works. Marx shows in the *German Ideology* that consciousness "is inseparable from matter from the very beginning. Spirit is also directly linked to language, without which no intellectual communication or development is possible" (194). The *German Ideology* grounded the "materialist concept of history" (196). Liedman traces and documents the influence of Hegel's dialectical philosophy on Marx's works. Chapter 7

(219–266) situates the *Manifesto of the Communist Party* in the context of the revolutionary times of 1848/1849.

5.4. *Capital* and *Grundrisse*

Capital and *Grundrisse* are arguably two of Marx's most important works, which is why Liedman devotes 54 pages that form Chapter 10 to *Grundrisse* and the 72-page long Chapter 11 to *Capital*. In comparison, David McLellan (2006) in the fourth edition of *Karl Marx: A Biography* discusses the *Grundrisse* on 17 pages (Ibid., 272–288) and *Capital* on 16 pages (Ibid., 308–325).

wLiedman's focus is on the text, context and prospects of these crucial writings. The basic distinction of answers to the question how *Grundrisse* and *Capital* relate to each other is one between those who see *Grundrisse* as a mere fragment and pre-paratory work that came to fruition in *Capital* and those who treat *Grundrisse* as an original work in itself that resisted the Soviet canonisation and orthodoxy of Marx built around *Capital*. Liedman's reading dialectically mediates both positions: "The *Grundrisse* points forward to *Capital*, but also contains much else that bears witness to Marx's entire multifarious world of ideas. It is both a preparatory work and a work in itself" (394).

Liedman's presentation of the *Grundrisse* focuses especially on the dialectic of production, distribution, exchange, and consumption; the difference between the *Grundrisse* (written in 1857/58) and *A Contribution to the Critique of Political Economy* (published in 1859) ("The *Grundrisse* is an adventure in reading. *A Contribution* is a walk among a number of well-groomed concepts": 380–381), forms which precede capitalism (with a special focus on the notion of the Asiatic mode of production and the transition to capitalism), work in capitalism and the realm of freedom.

Capital's three volumes are with their more than 2,000 pages simply too extensive in order to be covered in detail in any introduction to Marx's life and works. So for example, the *Marx-Engels-Werke* edition of *Capital* consists of 2,213 pages, ex-cluding endnotes, indexes and the tables of content (Volume 1: 802 pages, Volume 2: 518 pages, Volume 3: 893 pages). Liedman provides a reasonable approach by fo-cusing besides the book's context on *Capital*'s structure, the commodity, concrete and abstract labour, money, commodity fetishism, surplus-value, constant and variable capital, the formula of capital, machinery, the circulation of capital, de-partments I and II, the transformation problem, the tendency of the rate of profit to fall, fictitious capital, crises, the trinity formula, and classes. Chapter 11 furthermore provides a brief overview of some of the interpretations of *Capital*. Liedman stresses in respect to *Capital* again the influence of Hegel's dialectics on Marx. He argues that *Capital* is based on the dialectics of essence and appearance, form and content, surface and depth.

5.5. Marx and Engels

Liedman gives special attention to the intellectual and personal relationship of Marx and Engels (125–131; 467–525). He shows that it is a mistake to assume that only Engels was interested in natural science and that Engels is to blame for the vulgar interpretation of Marxian dialectics. Marx himself engaged in in-depth studies of not just languages, philosophy, literature, economics, history, technology, and anthropology but also of the natural sciences and mathematics. The communist chemist Carl Schorlemmer was not just a friend of both Marx and Engels but also influenced both intellectually. Also the chemist August Wilhelm von Hofmann's lectures in London influenced Marx's thinking. Liedman stresses that Marx based on insights from the natural sciences thought of development as transition from quantity into new qualities and processes of emergence. But it is clear that although nature and society are linked through human production, they are not one and the same because human work constitutes the *Aufhebung* of nature in society. So there is also an emergent leap between nature and society (Fuchs 2006).

Liedman argues that the schematic, orthodox, dogmatic interpretation of the dialectic was based on a reductionist interpretation of Engels' *Dialectics of Nature* and *Anti-Dühring* that disregarded that Engels spoke of the spiral form of development as the fourth dimension of the dialectic and focused on three dialectical laws. Liedman stresses that the three dialectical laws (the contradiction, the transition from quantity to quality, the negation of the negation) became a dogma, "but it can safely be said that no one has been drawn to the tradition from Marx, or even Engels, owing to these laws. They have become an extra burden that can only be defended with all sorts of more or less sophistic reasoning" (499). Both the orthodoxies of Stalinism and the reformist strand in the Second International were built on the interpretation of society's development as deterministic natural law of history that disregarded the dialectical difference between nature and society and therefore Marx's insight into the dialectics of agency and structures and of chance and necessity in society that he summarised in *The Eighteenth Brumaire of Louis Bonaparte*: "Men make their own history, but they do not make it just as they please; they do not make it under circumstances chosen by themselves, but under circumstances directly encountered, given and transmitted from the past" (Marx 1852, 103).

Liedman does not mention that Stalin (1938) in his infamous catechism *Dialectical and Historical Materialism* that was published in the Soviet "short course" on Bolshevism does not consider the negation of the negation and sublation (*Aufhebung*) as dialectical principles operating in society, but rather presents society as governed by natural laws. The same is true of Mao's (1937) *On Contradiction*. Stalin and Mao reduced the dialectic in society to one natural law, the law of contradiction. "The law of contradiction in things, that is, the law of the unity of opposites, is the fundamental law of nature and of society and therefore also the fundamental law of thought" (Mao 1937, 311). As a consequence, it became possible to argue that the USSR and China had overcome capitalism and based on the "process of development from the lower to the higher" (Stalin 1938, 109) therefore constituted "a Socialist system" (Ibid., 119). Therefore, anyone questioning the socialist character of the Soviet or Chinese system or the authority of Stalin and Mao was considered a counter-revolutionary. The reductionist interpretation of the dialectic turned into an ideological method for justifying terror.

The dogmatic Stalinist dialectic dominated Soviet-inspired philosophy. Two examples shall illustrate this circumstance. In 1937, the Leningrad Institute of Philosophy's (1937) *Textbook of Marxist Philosophy* in line with Stalin defined "the law of unity and conflict of opposites" as "the basic law of dialectic" (1937, 152), whereas the negation of the negation was denied separate relevance by being reduced to "one of the concrete forms of manifestation of the law of the unity of opposites" (Ibid., 359). Manfred Buhr and Georg Klaus argued in the *Philosophical Dictionary* of the German Democratic Republic that the negation of the negation "is not the fundamental law of the dialectic" (1964, 381). Against orthodox interpretations of Marx, Liedman stresses the heterodox approaches of for example Rosa Luxemburg, Ernst Bloch, Antonio Gramsci, Georg Lukács, Herbert Marcuse, Theodor W. Adorno, the Praxis Group, Agnes Heller, or Karel Kosík.

We need to think of the dialectic as complex and open process. The dialectic is the absolute recoil that posits its own preconditions (Žižek 2014). Self-reference and self-constitution as processes in which something returns into itself as something different that constitutes a new positive difference that makes a difference can only occur because the dialectic is a fire that needs to burn. The dialectical fire extinguishes a contradiction and thereby itself. This extinguishment is at the same time a self-kindling of the dialectic and the kindle of a new fire, in which the old is sublated as the new and constitutes a new contradiction. The dialectic is the absolute recoil in and through being a fire that continuously extinguishes and kindles itself. In society, human praxis is the dialectical fire of social change.

5.6. The General Intellect and Nationalism

Only a reader lacking intellectual depth will completely agree with all that is written in a particular book. So the present reader also identifies some shortcomings of Liedman's *A World to Win*, of which two shall be mentioned.

Liedman discusses that Marx in the *Grundrisse* points out that in communism, work "must also become general" so that the individual becomes a "universally knowledgeable specialist" (392). But he misses to explicitly mention the concept of the general intellect and the importance of the notion of fixed capital in the *Grundrisse*. As a consequence, Liedman claims at the end of his book that "Marx underestimated the ability of capitalism to integrate new technologies" (617) and that he did not "imagine the third [technological] revolution – of electronics and biotechnology" (618). But when Marx writes in the *Grundrisse* that the "development of fixed capital indicates to what degree general social knowledge has become a direct force of production" (Marx 1857/ 58, 706), then he anticipates the emergence of a knowledge economy that is based on the technological revolution brought about by computing and microelectronics.

The Grundrisse's "Fragment on Machines" has influenced Marxist debates on technology and knowledge and should therefore form an essential part in an introduction to the *Grundrisse* (see Fuchs 2016a, 360–375). Marx sees the importance of science and knowledge in production emerging from the capitalist development of the productive forces that increases productivity in order to try to maximise profits. At a certain stage, the increasing role of science and knowledge's role in capitalism turns from quantity into the new quality of a knowledge economy as distinct mode of the organisation of labour and capital within capitalism, but at the same time creates new antagonistic forms.

Liedman argues that Marx "had not paid sufficient attention to the irrational sides of human life" (621), that "[h]e and his fellow thinkers did not see that nationalism was just as natural an element in modern society as its opposite, internationalism"

(Ibid.), and that he was "blind to the nationalist overtones in the Second French Empire" (Ibid.).

Kevin B. Anderson (2016) shows in his meticulous study *Marx at the Margins. On Nationalism, Ethnicity, and Non-Western Societies* that "Marx's critique of capitalism" is "far broader than is usually supposed. [...] he expended considerable time and energy on the analysis of non-Western societies, as well as that of race, ethnicity, and nationalism" (Ibid., 237). "Marx's theorization of nationalism, ethnicity, and class culminated in his 1869–70 writings on Ireland" (Ibid., 243). It is also not true that Marx disregarded the role of nationalism in Napoleon III's French Second Empire (1852–1870).

In *The Eighteenth Brumaire of Louis Bonaparte*, Marx (1852) uses the term *Bonapartism* for analysing Napoleon III's dictatorial rule. Napoleon III staged a coup d'état and gained power in 1851. A feature of Bonapartism is that "the state seem[s] to have made itself completely independent" (Marx 1852, 186). In *The Civil War in France*, Marx argues that nationalism forms an important feature of Bonapartism at the ideological level: Bonapartism "professed to save the working class by breaking down Parliamentarism, and, with it, the undisguised subserviency of Government to the propertied classes. It professed to save the propertied classes by upholding their economic supremacy over the working class; and, finally, it professed to unite all classes by reviving for all the chimera of national glory" (Marx 1871, 330).

Marx stresses the role of nationalism as ideology that constructs a fictive national ethnicity in order to deflect political attention from the class contradiction. In the age of Donald Trump and new nationalisms, Marx's insights into nationalism form important foundations of a critical theory of nationalism and authoritarian capitalism (Fuchs 2018). Consider the following passage, in which Marx in 1870 analysed the role of ideology in distracting attention from class struggle and benefiting the ruling class:

> Ireland is the BULWARK of the *English landed aristocracy*. The exploitation of this country is not simply one of the main sources of their material wealth; it is their greatest *moral* power. [...] And most important of all! All industrial and commercial centres in England now have a working class *divided* into two *hostile* camps, English PROLETARIANS and Irish PROLETARIANS. The ordinary English worker hates the Irish worker as a competitor who forces down the STANDARD OF LIFE. In relation to the Irish worker, he feels himself to be a member of the *ruling nation* and, therefore, makes himself a tool of his

aristocrats and capitalists *against Ireland,* thus strengthening their domination *over himself.* He harbours religious, social and national prejudices against him. [...] This antagonism is kept artificially alive and intensified by the press, the pulpit, the comic papers, in short by all the means at the disposal of the ruling class. *This antagonism* is the *secret of the English working class's impotence,* despite its organisation. It is the secret of the maintenance of power by the capitalist class. And the latter is fully aware of this.

(Marx 1870, 473; 474; 475; compare also Marx 1869)

Isn't Marx here precisely describing elements that are at the heart of today's new nationalisms? Nationalism's ideological separation of the working class into autochthonous workers and immigrant workers as two hostile camps, the strengthening of capital's power over labour through nationalism, the role of the media in the ideological spread of nationalist sentiments, nationalism as the exertion of the capitalist class' ideological power, etc.

5.7. Conclusion

Despite certain imprecisions in its conclusions, there is no doubt that Sven-Eric Liedman's (2018) *A World to Win: The Life and Works of Karl Marx* is a major achievement: it provides an excellent biographical account that dialectically integrates the presentation of (personal and societal) life and Marx's works. Two hundred years after Marx's birth, Sven-Eric Liedman renews the practice of dialectical Marx-biographies that was started on the occasion of Marx's centenary in 1918 by Franz Mehring's *Karl Marx: The Story of His Life.*

Recently, debates on Marx-biographies have often taken on the following typical form:

A: "What's the best newer Marx-biography that I should read? I heard about Gareth Stedman Jones' *Karl Marx: Greatness and Illusion* and Jonathan Sperber's *Karl Marx: A 19th-Century Life.* Can you recommend these books? Which one should I read?"

B: "They are both bourgeois crap. Don't read any of the two".

A: "But what newer Marx-biography written in the 21st century should I then read? Which one do you recommend?"

Sven-Eric Liedman's main achievement is that answering the latter question has now become possible.

References

Anderson, Kevin B. 2016. *Marx at the Margins. On Nationalism, Ethnicity, and Non-Western Societies*. Chicago, IL: The University of Chicago Press. Expanded edition.

Choat, Simon. 2016. *Marx's "Grundrisse"*. London: Bloomsbury Academic.

Eagleton, Terry. 2011. *Why Marx Was Right*. New Haven, CT: Yale University Press.

Fuchs, Christian. 2018. *Digital Demagogue: Authoritarian Capitalism in the Age of Trump and Twitter*. London: Pluto Press.

Fuchs, Christian. 2016a. *Reading Marx in the Information Age. A Media and Communication Studies Perspective on "Capital Volume I"*. New York: Routledge.

Fuchs, Christian. 2016b. Review of Gareth Stedman Jones: Karl Marx – Greatness and Illusion. *Marx & Philosophy Review of Books*, September 28, 2016. https://marxandphilosophy.org.uk/reviews/8190_karl-marx-greatness-and-illusion-review-by-christian-fuchs/

Fuchs, Christian. 2006. The Dialectic of the Nature-Society-System. *tripleC: Communication, Capitalism & Critique* 4 (1): 1–39. http://www.triple-c.at

Fuchs, Christian and Lara Monticelli, eds. 2018. Karl Marx @ 200: Debating Capitalism & Perspectives for the Future of Radical Theory (Special issue on the occasion of Marx's bicentenary on May 5, 2018). *tripleC: Communication, Capitalism & Critique* 16 (2): 406–414. http://www.triple-c.at.

Harvey, David. 2013. *A Companion to Marx's Capital Volume 2*. London: Verso.

Harvey, David. 2012. *Rebel Cities. From the Right to the City to the Urban Revolution*. London: Verso.

Harvey, David. 2010. *A Companion to Marx's Capital*. London: Verso.

Heinrich, Michael. 2012. *An Introduction to the Three Volumes of Karl Marx's Capital*. New York: Monthly Review Press.

Klaus, Georg and Manfred Buhr. 1964. *Philosophisches Wörterbuch*. Leipzig: VEB Verlag.

Leningrad Institute of Philosophy. 1937. *A Textbook of Marxist Philosophy*. London: Victor Gollancz Limited.

Liedman, Sven-Eric. 2018. *A World to Win: The Life and Works of Karl Marx*. London: Verso.

Mao, Tse-Tung. 1937. On Contradiction. In *Selected Works of Mao Tse-Tung Volume I*, 311–347. Beijing: Foreign Languages Press.

Marx, Karl. 1871. The Civil War in France. In *Marx & Engels Collected Works (MECW) Volume 22*, 307–359. New York: International Publishers.

Marx, Karl. 1870. Letter of Marx to Sigfrid Meyer and August Vogt, 9 April 1870. In *Marx Engels Collected Works Volume 43*, 471–476. London: Lawrence & Wishart.

Marx, Karl. 1869. The General Council to the Federal Council of Romance Switzerland. In *Marx Engels Collected WorksVolume 21*, 84–91. London: Lawrence & Wishart.

Marx, Karl. 1857/58. *Grundrisse*. London: Penguin.

Marx, Karl. 1852. *The Eighteenth Brumaire of Louis Bonaparte*. In *Marx & Engels Collected WorksVolume 11*, 99–197. London: Lawrence & Wishart.

McLellan, David. 2006. *Karl Marx: A Biography*. Basingstoke: Palgrave Macmillan. Fourth edition.

Mehring, Franz. 2003/1918. *Karl Marx: The Story of His Life*. Abingdon: Routledge.

Negri, Antonio. 1991. *Marx Beyond Marx. Lessons on the Grundrisse*. New York: Autonomedia.

Rosdolsky, Roman. 1977. *The Making of Marx's "Capital". Two Volumes*. London: Pluto.

Sperber, Jonathan. 2013. *Karl Marx: A 19th-Century Life*. New York: Liveright.

Stalin, Joseph. 1938. Dialectical and Historical Materialism. In *History of the Communist Party of the Soviet Union (Bolsheviks). Short Course*, 105–131. New York: International Publishers.

Stedman Jones, Gareth. 2016. *Karl Marx: Greatness and Illusion*. London: Penguin.

Wheen, Francis. 1999. *Karl Marx*. London: Fourth Estate.

Žižek, Slavoj. 2014. *Absolute Recoil. Towards a New Foundation of Dialectical Materialism*. London: Verso.

References

Chapter Six

Universal Alienation, Formal and Real Subsumption of Society Under Capital, Ongoing Primitive Accumulation by Dispossession: Reflections on the Marx@200-Debate Between David Harvey and Michael Hardt/Toni Negri

6.1 Introduction

On the occasion of Marx's bicentenary in 2018, the journal *tripleC: Communication, Capitalism & Critique* published a special issue dedicated to the discussion of Marx's relevance today under the title "Karl Marx @ 200. Debating Capitalism & Perspectives for the Future of Radical Theory" (Fuchs and Monticelli 2018).

It asked: how can we "repeat" Marx today? The editors of the special issue invited David Harvey, Michael Hardt, and Toni Negri to contribute and to discuss the relevance of Marx with each other. The starting point were the following two questions: 200 years after Marx's birth, in what type of capitalism do we live today? What elements of Marx's theory and the 200-year history of Marxian theory can we best draw from in order to advance radical theory, the analysis of capitalism and struggles for alternatives to capitalism today?

The resulting debate between Harvey and Hardt/Negri consists of four parts (Hardt and Negri 2018a; Harvey 2018a; Hardt and Negri 2018b; Harvey 2018b). In their analysis, Michael Hardt and Toni Negri stress, among other elements, that Marx's notions of formal and real subsumption can be extended in order to understand contemporary capitalism and inform political praxis. David Harvey finds Marx's concept of alienation

DOI: 10.4324/9781003199182-6

an important intellectual means that can be generalised into the notion of universal alienation for understanding capitalism today and informing social struggles.

The interventions, reflections and mutual comments on each other by Harvey and Hardt/Negri show that Marx is not a "dead dog" but remains very much alive today as his theory informs our struggles in 21st-century capitalism. Marx is a historical, materialist, and dialectical thinker. The implication is that with the development of capitalism, also Marxian categories develop based on a dialectic of continuity and change. Harvey, Hardt and Negri show that in order to critically theorise 21st-century capitalism, it is feasible to simultaneously ground the analysis in Marx's original works and further develop his categories.

It is not the first time that Harvey, Hardt, and Negri engage in dialogue. In 2009, David Harvey reviewed Michael Hardt and Toni Negri's book *Commonwealth* in the journal *ArtForum* and Hardt and Negri responded (Harvey, Hardt and Negri 2009). The *tripleC* and *ArtForum* dialogues are not just theoretically inspiring but also exemplary for constructive, critical debate in radical theory. The tone and style of these debates is respectful, appreciative, and constructive, which has enabled clarifying theoretical commonalities and differences. One problem of lots of debates in Marxist theory is the repetition of political sectarianism at the level of theory. To put it bluntly: Marxist theorists often do not see the forest beyond the trees and instead of focusing on the critique of bourgeois, conservative and right-wing theories invest much time and energy into internal theoretical infighting that takes on the form of theoretical Stalinism: those who should act as comrades and allies in order to collectively challenge bourgeois theory and instrumental research that support domination and the commodification of everything accuse each other of false interpretations of Marx, of not being "Marxists", advancing reactionary politics, of imperialism, racism, fascism, etc. As a consequence, political comrades are treated as enemies in the world of theory. Harvey, Hardt, and Negri exemplify a different way of engaging in theoretical discussion. They also show how Marxian categories – such as alienation, formal/real subsumption, and primitive accumulation – matter today.

6.2 Alienation

Marx develops and uses the term "alienation" in respect to political economy the first time in the essay *The Jewish Question* that he wrote in autumn 1843 and that was published in February 1844: "Money is the estranged essence of man's work and man's existence, and this alien essence dominates him, and he worships it" (Marx 1844b, 172). In his doctoral dissertation, Marx (1841, 64) spoke in the context of Epicurus' philosophy of the "alienation of the essence".

In 1843, in a reading of Hegel in the *Contribution to the Critique of Hegel's Philosophy of Law*, Marx argues that there is also political and ideological alienation: "It is indeed *estrangement* which matters in the so-called Christian state, but not *man*. The only man who counts, the *king,* is a being specifically different from other men, and is moreover a religious being, directly linked with heaven, with God. The relationships which prevail here are still relationships dependent on *faith*" (Marx 1843, 158). "Political emancipation is at the same time the *dissolution* of the old society on which the state alienated from the people, the sovereign power, is based" (Marx 1843, 165).

In the *Economic and Philosophic Manuscripts of 1844*, Marx specifies that capitalism results in the alienation of labour, which means a fourfold form of alienation (Marx 1844a, 276–277): 1) the alienation of humans from nature, 2) from their activities and species-being, 3) from their bodies and mind that form the human essence, 4) from the "product of his [the worker's] labour, from his life activity" (Marx 1844a, 276–277) and as a consequence from other humans and society. In the *Grundrisse*, Marx presents economic alienation as the class relation between capital and labour:

> The emphasis comes to be placed not on the state of being objected, but on the state of being alienated, dispossessed, sold [Der Ton wird gelegt nicht auf das *Vergegenständlichtsein*, sondern das *Entfremdet-*, Entäußert-, Veräußertsein]; on the condition that the monstrous objective power which social labour itself erected opposite itself as one of its moments belongs not to the worker, but to the personified conditions of production, i.e. to capital. (Marx 1857/58, 831)

In *Capital Volume 1*, Marx argues that capital is an "alien power that dominates and exploits" workers and that in capitalism labour is "separated from its own means of objectification and realization" (Marx 1867, 716). In *Capital Volume 3*, Marx (1894) talks about alienation in Chapters 5, 23, 27, 36, and 48. He argues in Chapter 23 that interest means the transfer of alienation from the realm of labour's exploitation into the realm of interest-bearing capital. In Chapter 48, he writes that alienation not just exists in the relationship of capital and labour but that also rent and interest are expressions of economic alienation.

Taken together, we see that alienation for Marx on the one hand is the particular form of domination and exploitation that shapes the capitalist mode of production, in which labour creates commodities without owning the means of production and without controlling the conditions and the results of production. On the other hand, Marx sees alienation also as the universal form of domination, in which humans are not in control of the structures that affect their everyday lives. All class relations are economic forms of alienation. But alienation extends beyond the economy so that also the state and ideology alienate humans from the conditions of collective political decision-making and cultural meaning-making.

In his essay *Universal Alienation*, David Harvey (2018a) defines alienation as universal in three respects:

1) Alienation in the economy not just entails capital's exploitation of labour but also the realms of realisation, distribution and consumption, which means it extends to phenomena such as unemployment, consumerism, land seizure, deindustrialisation, debt peonage, financial scams, unaffordable housing, high food prices, etc.

2) Alienation entails processes beyond the economy, such as frustrations with politics, unaffordable public services, nationalist ideology, racism, police violence, militarism, warfare, alcoholism, suicide, depression, bureaucracy, pollution, gentrification, or climate change.

3) Alienation entails the geographic and social expansion of capital accumulation so that capital relations "dominate pretty much everywhere" (Harvey 2018a, 427). "Alienation is everywhere. It exists at work in production, at home in consumption, and it dominates much of politics and daily life" (Harvey 2018a, 429).

So, the universalisation of alienation means its extension beyond production, the economy and bounded spaces. Capital and capitalist society overcome and break down their own barriers in order to expand. In *Marx, Capital and the Madness of Economic Reason*, Harvey (2017, 47) argues that "a great deal of appropriation of value through predation occurs at the point of realization", which results in "[a]lienation upon realization" (Harvey 2017, 196).

In all forms of alienation, humans face asymmetric power relations and conditions that hinder their control over certain objects, structures or products (external nature, the means of production, the means of communication, the political system, the cultural system, etc.) so that aspects of their subjectivity are damaged (concerning human activities, well-being, consciousness, mind/psyche, body, worldviews, social relations). Alienation is neither purely objective nor purely subjective, but a negative relationship between social structures and humans in heteronomous societies.

In *Seventeen Contradictions and the End of Capitalism*, David Harvey (2014) devotes Chapter 17 to the topic of "The Revolt of Human Nature: Universal Alienation". He argues that Marxists have often excluded alienation from consideration and have cancelled it off as "non-scientific concept" (Harvey 2014, 269). But the "scientistic stance failed to capture the political imagination of viable alternatives" and "could not even confront the madness of the prevailing economic and political reason" (Harvey 2014, 269). Universal alienation is therefore a concept that in light of the danger that we may face "a less-than-human humanity" (Harvey 2014, 264) can provide prospects for alternatives. Alienation has always been a prominent concept in Socialist/Marxist Humanism (Fromm 1966; Alderson and Spencer 2017). Radical Socialist Humanism is the best way of opposing authoritarian capitalism's and neoliberalism's anti-humanism (Fuchs 2018).

Consequently, Harvey argues for both the use of the concept of universal alienation and for revolutionary humanism (Harvey 2014, 282–293 [Conclusion]). Humanism argues that "[w]e can through conscious thought and action change both the world we live in and ourselves for the better" (Harvey 2014, 282) and "that measures its achievements in terms of the liberation of human potentialities, capacities and powers" (Harvey 2014, 283). Harvey notes that humanism has been perverted and turned into a particularism that disguises itself as universalism but advances "imperialist and colonial cultural domination" (Harvey 2014, 285). He therefore argues for a "secular *revolutionary* humanism" that counters "alienation in its many forms and to radically change the world from its capitalist ways" (Harvey 2014, 287). Hardt and Negri (2017, 72–76) argue that there are parallels between autonomist and humanist Marxism: both take subjectivity, social struggles and social change serious and oppose dogmatic Marxism and Stalinism.

6.3 Formal and Real Subsumption

In their article *The Powers of the Exploited and the Social Ontology of Praxis* that is part of the debate with David Harvey, Michael Hardt and Toni Negri (2018a) argue that neoliberalism has advanced the formal and real subsumption of society under capital, which means that ever more spaces that were autonomous from capital have come under its influence and control and have been turned into spheres of capital accumulation, commodity production, and the exploitation of labour. The commons that are available to all and produced as gift by nature or society have thereby become commodified. The subsumption of society under capital affects "muscles, languages, affects, codes" (Hardt and Negri 2018a, 416), "images" (416), "social intelligence, social relations" (419), "the cognitive, social, and cooperative components of living labour" (419), etc.

In the *Economic Manuscripts of 1861-63*, Marx introduces the concepts of the formal and real subsumption of labour under capital:

> Historically, in fact, at the start of its formation, we see capital take under its control (subsume under itself) not only the labour process in general but the specific actual labour processes as it finds them available in the existing technology, and in the form in which they have developed on the basis of non-capitalist relations of production. It finds in existence the actual production process – the particular mode of production – and at the beginning it only subsumes it *formally*, without making any changes in its specific technological character. Only in the course of its development does capital not only formally subsume the labour process but transform it, give the very mode of production a new shape and thus first create the mode of production peculiar to it. [...] This *formal* subsumption of the labour process, the assumption of control over it by capital, consists in the worker's subjection as worker to the supervision and therefore to the command of capital or the capitalist. Capital becomes command over labour.
>
> (MECW 30, 92–93, emphasis in original)

Formal subsumption means that wage-labour relations are imposed on particular forms of labour without transforming the mode of production. Real subsumption in contrast means a qualitative change of the mode of production so that more radical organisational and technological changes take place. Marx speaks of formal and real subsumption as "*two separate forms of capitalist production*" (MECW 34, 95, emphasis in original). Formal and real subsumption for Marx correspond to forms of capitalist production that are based on absolute and relative surplus-value production: "I call the form which rests on absolute surplus value the *formal subsumption of labour under capital*. [...] The real subsumption of labour under capital is developed in all the forms which produce relative, as opposed to absolute, surplus value" (MECW 34, 95, 105, emphasis in original).

In real subsumption, science and technology transform the production process qualitatively:

> With the real subsumption of labour under capital, all the CHANGES we have discussed take place in the technological process, the labour process, and at the same time there are changes in the relation of the worker to his own production and to capital – and finally, the development of the productive power of labour takes place, in that the productive forces of social labour are developed, and only at that point does the application of natural forces on a large scale, of science and of machinery, to direct production become possible.
>
> (MECW 34, 106)

The *Results of the Immediate Process of Production* is a text of 130 printed pages that Marx wrote sometime between June 1863 and December 1866 (Ernest Mandel, in Marx 1867, 944). It is printed as appendix in the Penguin-edition of *Capital Volume 1* (Marx 1867, 948–1084), but is not contained in the German Marx-Engels-Werke (MEW). In the *Results*, Marx again takes up the question of the formal and real subsumption of labour under capital and points out the importance of machinery as method of relative surplus-value production in the real subsumption of labour under capital:

> The general features of the *formal subsumption* remain, viz. the *direct subordination of the labour process to capital*, irrespective of the state of its technological development. But on this foundation there now arises a technologically and otherwise *specific mode of production – capitalist production* – which transforms the nature *of the labour process and its actual conditions*. Only when that happens do we witness the *real subsumption of labour under capital*. [...] The real subsumption of labour under capital is developed in all the forms evolved by relative, as opposed to absolute surplus-value. With the real subsumption of labour under capital a complete (and constantly repeated) revolution takes place in the mode of production, in the productivity of the workers and in the relations between workers and capitalists.
>
> (Marx 1867, 1034–1035)

Hardt and Negri have further developed Marx's notions of formal and real subsumption by extending them from the realm of labour to society as totality and all of society's moments. In *Marx Beyond Marx: Lessons on the Grundrisse,* Negri (1991, 121) speaks of "the real subsumption of world society under capital" and says that in the passage

Formal and Real Subsumption

from formal to real subsumption, capital becomes "a real subject" (Negri 1991, 123). In *Labor of Dionysus*, Hardt and Negri (1994) characterise real subsumption as the postmodern phase of capitalist development:

> Postmodern capitalism should be understood first, or as a first approximation, in terms of what Marx called the phase of the real subsumption of society under capital. In the previous phase (that of the formal subsumption), capital operated a hegemony over social production, but there still remained numerous production processes that originated outside of capital as leftovers from the pre-capitalist era. Capital subsumes these foreign processes formally, bringing them under the reign of capitalist relations. In the phase of the real subsumption, capital no longer has an outside in the sense that these foreign processes of production have disappeared. All productive processes arise within capital itself and thus the production and reproduction of the entire social world take place within capital. The specifically capitalist rules of productive relations and capitalist exploitation that were developed in the factory have now seeped outside the factory walls to permeate and define all social relations – this is the sense in which we insist that contemporary society should now be recognized as a factory-society.
>
> (Hardt and Negri 1994, 15)

In *Commonwealth*, Hardt and Negri argue that formal subsumption means the creation of "circuits of capitalist production" and the passage from formal to real subsumption results in the production of "severe divisions and hierarchies within the capitalist globe" (Hardt and Negri 2009, 230). Real subsumption creates "new, properly capitalist forms", whereas formal subsumption merely instrumentalises non-capitalist practices and relations (Hardt and Negri 2009, 142). In their latest book *Assembly*, Hardt and Negri write that *"the richness of the category of formal subsumption is indeed that it reveals the economic and cultural differences of labor, land, society, and community that have been subsumed within capitalist production but maintain their connection to the territory and the past"* (Hardt and Negri 2017, 182; emphasis in original).

In *Assembly*, Hardt and Negri (2017, xix) argue that we have experienced the rise of what they term "the capitalist extraction of value [...] from the common". We can say that subsumption has two aspects: it is on the one hand the starting point and en-ablement of the application of the logic of capital and commodities to a space, system, realm, practice, structure, or resource. On the other hand, there can be potential re-sistance to subsumption – struggles for decommodification and the appropriation of the commons – so that capital needs to reproduce subsumption by means of, e.g., law, ideology, corruption, the dull compulsion of the market, or physical violence (including warfare). Contemporary capitalism's class structure is for Hardt and Negri (2017, 166–171) based on the extraction of the common, which includes the extraction of natural resources; data mining/data extraction; the extraction of the social from the urban spaces on real estate markets; and finance as extractive industry.

Hardt and Negri (2017, 166) discern among two main forms of the common: the natural and the social commons. These two types are further subdivided into five forms (Hardt and Negri 2017, 166):

1) The earth and its ecosystems;

2) The "immaterial" common of ideas, codes, images, and cultural products;

3) Tangible goods produced by co-operative work;

4) Metropolitan and rural spaces that are realms of communication, cultural interaction, and co-operation;

5) Social institutions and services that organise housing, welfare, health, and education.

In his second contribution to the debate with Hardt/Negri, David Harvey (2018b) in the article titled *Universal Alienation and the Real Subsumption of Daily Life Under Capital: A Response to Hardt and Negri* welcomes Michael Hardt and Toni Negri's interpretation of Marx's concepts of formal and real subsumption and points out parallels to his notion of universal alienation. He stresses that it is important to be "explicit about what it is that is being subsumed into what" (Harvey 2018b, 450) and about the "many different forms that real subsumption under the power of capital in general takes in our times" (Harvey 2018b, 452).

6.4 Primitive Accumulation

Marx (1867) dedicated a long chapter of *Capital Volume I* to primitive accumulation – Chapter 24 in the German edition. In the English edition, Chapter 24's seven sub-sections were turned into seven separate chapters (Chapters 26–32). Together with the concluding chapter on the modern theory of colonisation, they form part eight that is titled "So-Called Primitive Accumulation".

For Marx, primitive accumulation is the phase that "precedes capitalist accumulation" (1867, 873), "the pre-history of capital" (875), and capitalism's "point of departure"

(873), where "conquest, enslavement, robbery, murder, in short, force, play the greatest part" (874). During this phase, resources are transformed into capital and humans into proletarians. Primitive accumulation is "the historical process of divorcing the producer from the means of production" (875). Marx shows that small landowners have been robbed of their land and how communal land was turned into private property. As a consequence, feudalism turned into capitalism. The history of expropriation "is written in the annals of mankind in letters of blood and fire" (875).

In the report (to the Central Council of the International) *Value, Price and Profit*, Marx (1865, 129) argues that primitive accumulation should in fact be called primitive expropriation because it means the separation of the producers from the means of production. "*Separation* between the Man of Labour and the Instruments of Labour once established, such a state of things will maintain itself and reproduce itself upon a constantly increasing scale, until a new and fundamental revolution in the mode of production should again overturn it, and restore the original union in a new historical form" (Marx 1865, 129).

Rosa Luxemburg interpreted primitive accumulation not just as the early, violent stage of capitalism, but as an ongoing process. Marx hinted at such an understanding by saying that primitive accumulation has to "maintain itself and reproduce itself" (Marx 1865, 129). "The accumulation of capital, seen as an historical process, employs force as a permanent weapon, not only at its genesis, but further on down to the present day" (Luxemburg 1913, 351). Luxemburg argues that capital creates milieus of primitive accumulation that "provide a fertile soil for capitalism" (Luxemburg 1913, 397).

David Harvey (2003) has interpreted Luxemburg's concept of ongoing primitive accumulation as accumulation by dispossession, the central feature of neoliberal capitalism. "A general re-evaluation of the continuous role and persistence of the predatory practices of 'primitive' or 'original' accumulation within the long historical geography of capital accumulation is, therefore, very much in order, as several commentators have recently observed. Since it seems peculiar to call an ongoing process 'primitive' or 'original' I shall, in what follows, substitute these terms by the concept of 'accumulation by dispossession'" (Harvey 2003, 144). Methods of accumulation by dispossession include e.g. privatisation, commodification, financialisation, the management and manipulation of crises, and state redistribution (Harvey 2005a, 160–165). Through accumulation by dispossession, "predatory activity has become internalized within capitalism (through, for example, privatization, deindustrialization or the erosion of pension and welfare rights orchestrated largely through the credit system and the deployment of state powers)" (Harvey 2006, xvii). "Capitalism would long ago have ceased to exist had it not engaged in fresh rounds of primitive accumulation, chiefly through the violence of imperialism" (Harvey 2010, 306).

Hardt and Negri (2018a) in their article *The Powers of the Exploited and the Social Ontology of Praxis* argue that the subsumption of society under capital is the "new primitive accumulation of the socially produced commons by capital" (418). They write that this process resembles what David Harvey describes as accumulation by dispossession, which he conceives as ongoing primitive accumulation. Subsumption does not necessarily operate only "by brute force" (Hardt and Negri 2018a, 418) (as in warfare), although physical violence can also be involved. Other methods used can include the law, illegal practices tolerated by the state, corruption, the neoliberal ideology of entrepreneurship, ideologies that create and reproduce capitalist hegemony, financial markets, and other forms of violence.

Hardt and Negri prefer to define primitive accumulation as a phase in capitalist development and to use the term (formal and real) subsumption for what Luxemburg and Harvey characterise as ongoing primitive accumulation. In *Assembly*, they discern among "three broad phases of capital: the phase of so-called primitive accumulation, by which we mean here simply the period in which capital was accumulated primarily through the expropriation and enclosures of the commons in Europe and elsewhere through the various forms of theft that accompanied European conquest and colonization; the phase that stretches from the birth of manufacture through the dominance of large-scale industry over the global economy; and, finally, the contemporary, post-Fordist phase characterized by the realization of the world market and the forms of extraction typical of finance" (Hardt and Negri 2017, 184–185).

As part of the debate with Harvey, Hardt and Negri (2018b) argue in their essay *The Multiplicities within Capitalist Rule and the Articulation of Struggles* that they prefer to use the concepts of formal/real subsumption over the use of (ongoing primitive) accumulation and universal alienation. They say that the concepts of formal and real subsumption allow to best capture the inner and outer dynamics of capitalism: formal subsumption subsumes something from the outside into capital, whereas real subsumption qualitatively transforms capital's inner dynamics. Hardt and Negri write that the concept of subsumption allows the argument that racism and patriarchy are older than capital and relatively autonomous, but have become subsumed under capitalism, creating racial capitalism and patriarchal capitalism so that capitalism, racism, and patriarchy have become "intimately intertwined" (Hardt and Negri 2018b, 443).

Primitive Accumulation

Patriarchy and racism are relatively autonomous and therefore only formally subsumed. At the same time, they have transformed capitalist production and so have also become really subsumed under capital. Capitalism as form of exploitation and other forms of domination are identical and different at the same time, they form a dynamic dialectic, a totality with open and overgrasping moments that are mutually producing each other.

The notion of ongoing primitive accumulation – that goes back to Rosa Luxemburg and has, among others, been used by Harvey and Marxist feminists such as the "Bielefeld School of Feminism" (Veronika Bennholdt-Thomsen, Maria Mies, Claudia von Werlhof) – can be employed in a manner comparable to Hardt and Negri's use of the notions of the formal and real subsumption of society under capital (see Fuchs 2016, Chapter 26 for a detailed interpretation of the concept of primitive accumulation based on Marx, Luxemburg, Marxist feminism and Harvey). Mies, Bennholdt-Thomsen and Werlhof (1988) argue from a feminist perspective that capitalism requires milieus of primitive accumulation for its reproduction. Capital cannot exist without making use of unpaid resources stemming from nature, nonwage/unremunerated labour (such as housework), and the periphery. "Women, colonies and nature" are "the main targets of this process of ongoing primitive accumulation" (Mies, Bennholdt-Thomsen and Werlhof 1988, 6). They form inner colonies of capitalism. This process corresponds to what Hardt/Negri term formal subsumption of society under capital. In neoliberal capitalism, the inner colonies transform the very nature of capitalist production so that housewifised labour that is "a source of unchecked, unlimited exploitation" emerges (Mies 1986, 16). This process corresponds to what Hardt/Negri term the real subsumption of society under labour: the precarious reality of the houseworker, the unemployed, and the Global South is taken as model for qualitatively transforming capitalism into neoliberal capitalism. Primitive accumulation thereby not just forms inner colonies of capitalism but also qualitatively transforms wage-labour and capitalism's core relations. Primitive accumulation and formal/real subsumption are both suited means for the Marxian explanation of the role of domination in capitalism and the relationship of class and domination.

The notion of primitive accumulation in Luxemburg's meaning of the term helps to grasp capitalism's "'inside-outside' dialectic" (Harvey 2003, 141). Not everything is subsumed under capital accumulation. For hope, resistance and potentials for alternatives to thrive, outside spaces that transcend the logic of capital are important. The potential for the creation of such spaces of hope (Harvey 2000) and resources of hope (Williams 1989) always remain and constitute material foundations of the principle of hope. "Hope is thus ultimately a practical, a militant emotion, it unfurls banners. If confidence emerges from hope as well, then the expectant emotion which has become absolutely positive is present or as good as present, the opposite pole to despair" (Bloch 1986, 112).

Within capitalist society, we find experienced spaces, conceptualised spaces and lived spaces (Harvey 2005b, 105–106) in which hope and struggles for alternatives to capitalism can develop. But capitalism is a totality, which means that everything that exists in contemporary society is related to capital. Capital accumulation implies an imperialistic character: it tries to subsume social relations into its inner dynamic in processes of original primitive accumulation (that can also be termed processes of formal subsumption) in order to create inner colonies of accumulation that are cheap or gratis resources instrumentalised in capital accumulation. Capitalism through crises and destruction also wrecks parts of its inner dynamics, which requires to create new spheres of accumulation and instrumentalisation. At the same time, existing inner milieus also need to be economically, politically and ideologically reproduced in order to hinder resistance and alternatives. Original primitive accumulation is thereby constantly repeated and reproduced as an ongoing process. At certain moments, capitalism's inner colonies can become models for the qualitative transformation of capitalist production, distribution, circulation, and consumption into a new capitalist regime of accumulation. In such cases, spheres of ongoing primitive accumulation and formal subsumption can become models for a new regime of accumulation (corresponding to the real subsumption of society under capital). Social struggles resist original and ongoing primitive accumulation, formal and real subsumption, by trying to create spaces that stand outside the logic and influence of capital.

The capitalist welfare state and the public university are good examples: they are funded out of general taxation and do not follow the logic of capital accumulation. But they create resources that capital requires and subsumes: skilled workers, skilled managers, reproduced labour-power, scientific knowledge, and technological innovations that take on the form of fixed capital, etc. The welfare state and the public university are therefore within capitalism always formally subsumed, at the same time inside and outside of capital. The rise of neoliberal capitalism has brought a qualitative shift: many public institutions have become directly spheres shaped by the logic of capital. Education, health care, and other public services have become commodities, public institutions define profit goals, public service employees have constant pressure

Primitive Accumulation

to increase efficiency and face the threat of being laid off due to cuts and austerity, etc. The model of precarious life and labour that has shaped the lives of houseworkers, the poor, the unemployed and the Global South for a long time, has become capitalism's regime of accumulation that shapes and qualitatively transforms social relations, including the welfare state and the public university.

Although the theoretical perspectives of Harvey and Hardt/Negri are highly compatible, one can identify certain differences and nuances, for example in respect to the relationship of capital, racism, and patriarchy. Hardt and Negri argue that capitalism, patriarchy, and racism have "equal weight" (Hardt and Negri 2018b, 443) and are "on equal terms" (Hardt and Negri 2018b, 445). They form a multiplicity of contradictions with relative autonomy. David Harvey (2014, 8) argues for the existence of a unity within the diversity of such contradictions and therefore says that the contradictions of capital form the "economic engine of capitalism".

> Racialisation and gender discriminations have been around for a very long time and there is no question that the history of capitalism is an intensely racialised and gendered history. [...] Contemporary capitalism plainly feeds of gender discriminations and violence as well as upon the frequent dehumanisation of people of colour. The intersections and interactions between racialisation and capital accumulation are both highly visible and powerfully present. But an examination of these tells me nothing particular about how the economic engine of capital works, even as it identifies one source from where it plainly draws its energy. [...] wars, nationalism, geopolitical struggles, disasters of various kinds all enter into the dynamics of capitalism, along with heavy doses of racism and gender, sexual, religious and ethnic hatreds and discriminations.
>
> (Harvey 2014, 7–8)

As an implicit critique of postmodernism – that David Harvey (1990) sees as the ideology corresponding to the flexible regime of capitalist accumulation – Harvey (2014, 10) argues that it is "surely myopic, if not dangerous and ridiculous, to dismiss as 'capitalo-centric' interpretations and theories of how the economic engine of capital accumulation works in relation to the present conjuncture. Without such studies we will likely misread and misinterpret the events that are occurring around us. Erroneous interpretations will almost certainly lead to erroneous politics whose likely outcome will be to deepen rather than to alleviate crises of accumulation and the social misery that derives from them".

The economic and the non-economic are at the same time identical and different: they are all realms of social production, which is the economic moment of the social that binds together all human existence. All social spaces and systems have their relative autonomy from the economy and not just overgrasp into but also shape the economy. In capitalism, the economic moment takes on the form of the logic of capital accumulation and general commodity production, circulation, distribution, and consumption. In capitalism, society's moments are as a consequence at the same time shaped by and shaping the logic of capital and to specific, variable degrees more or less autonomous from it. Capital's imperialist logic aims to subsume as many social relations as possible directly and indirectly under the logic of capital. Progressive social struggles have concrete goals but can only be emancipatory if they are struggles against capital.

6.5 Conclusion: Anti-Value Struggles and Self-Valorisation

The discussion between David Harvey and Michael Hardt/Toni Negri shows that 200 years after Karl Marx's birth, his theory and politics remain of key importance for critiquing capitalism and envisioning and informing struggles for alternatives. Hardt, Harvey and Negri have consistently shown that Marxian categories, such as capitalism, labour, class, class struggles, etc. remain vital for interpreting and changing contemporary society. In their debate, they show that this is also true for the categories of alienation and formal/real subsumption.

We can summarise some key results of the present chapter:

- **Alienation as Marx's most universal critical category:**
  For Marx, alienation is both the specific form of the object–subject dialectic that constitutes capitalism as well as the general process of domination, by which humans are continuously put out of control of the structures that constitute their lives. Alienation is a particular Marxian category as well as the most universal critical category he uses for characterising domination.
- **Three aspects of universal alienation:**
  David Harvey shows that alienation is universal in three respects:

    1) Alienation extends beyond production into the realms of realisation distribution and consumption;

    2) It extends beyond the economy into politics, culture, social relations, and subjectivity;

3) It has in neoliberal capitalism been generalised as the commodification of (almost) everything and accumulation by dispossession, which has resulted in far-right phenomena such as Donald Trump (for a detailed analysis of the rise of Trump's political economy and ideology and the associated transformation of capitalism, see Fuchs 2018).

- **The relationship of capital and its outside:**
  Capitalism has always lived from economically instrumentalising non-capitalist milieus, practices, structures, and social systems. The subsumption of non-capitalist social relations into capitalism again and again also transforms the capitalist modes of production, reproduction, circulation, distribution, and consumption. These two processes can be explained both with the help of Marx's notion of primitive accumulation and his notions of formal and real subsumption.

- **Original/ongoing primitive accumulation, formal/real subsumption:**
  Whereas Hardt/Negri interpret primitive accumulation as the original phase of capitalism, Harvey sees it as an ongoing process of accumulation by dispossession. The distinction between original and ongoing primitive accumulation corresponds to the notions of formal and real subsumption of society under capital.

- **The reproduction of capitalism:**
  For capitalism to continue to exist, it needs to again and again subsume social relations under capital. Subsumed social relations can subsequently also qualitatively transform capitalism itself. There are certain initial processes that start off specific forms of alienation and accumulation within capitalist society. Formal subsumption and original primitive accumulation (by dispossession) are categories characterising this point of subsumption. But capitalism needs to be reproduced, otherwise it enters a crisis phase and its potential demise. As a consequence, capitalist practices aim at the ongoing reproduction of alienation, primitive accumulation, and the subsumption of society under capital. Marx identified both original and ongoing aspects of alienation, subsumption, and primitive accumulation. Capitalism reproduces itself through the dialectic of ongoing and primitive accumulation and the dialectic of formal and real subsumption.

The approaches of Toni Negri/Michael Hardt and David Harvey share the political perspective of a commons-based, participatory-democratic society as alternative to capitalism – democratic communism. As the means to this end, they propagate radical reformism, the dialectic of reform and revolution, or what Rosa Luxemburg terms "*revolutionary Realpolitik*" (Luxemburg 1903/2018, 732). The political question is how political praxis can turn the contradictions of capital and value into alternatives to capitalism. These alternatives are not sufficiently characterised as "post-capitalism" because one thereby only names a later stage of society but not its desirable quality as democratic commons-based society.

David Harvey (2017, Chapter 4) distinguishes between anti-value arising from debt and devaluation in crises from "the active anti-value of political resistance to commodification and privatisation" that defines "an active field of anti-capitalist struggle" (Harvey 2017, 76). He argues that such struggles include consumer boycotts and "struggles over realization" (Harvey 2017, 200) for example over telephone bills, credit card fees, etc. (Harvey 2017, 199) and anti-debt struggles as struggles over distribution.

The category of anti-value can both mean *Nicht-Wert* (not-value) and *Gegenwert* (opposition to value). These are two moments of a dialectic of struggle: the opposition to value constitutes struggles that aim at a society based on not-value, i.e. goods and social relations that are defined by their meaningfulness for human use and not by the logic of exchange and capital accumulation.

Marx uses the notion of "not-value" (*Nicht-Wert* in German) in a passage in the *Grundrisse* (Marx 1857/58, 295–297), where he discusses the dialectic of capital as not-labour and labour as not-value and not-capital. Not-value is "purely objective use value" (Marx 1857/58, 296). Under capitalism's dull compulsions, labour is "*absolute poverty*" (Marx 1857/58, 296). But at the same time, work is the "the general possibility of wealth as subject and as activity" (Marx 1857/58, 296) and therefore the source of commodities, capital, and value. Not-value is also the determinate negation of capital, commodities, and value. Not-value is the revolutionary sublation of capital and capitalism, the moment of political praxis.

David Harvey's stress on anti-value as moment of political praxis has clear parallels to autonomist Marxism's notion of self-valorisation. Marxists do not agree on the theoretical question of whether the alternative to value is another form of value or the abolition of value, which relates to the question of whether value is a capitalist or a more general phenomenon. But notwithstanding pure terminology, there are parallels between Harvey's notion of anti-value and Hardt/Negri's concept of self-valorisation.

Capital "consists solely in its own motion as self-valorizing value" (Marx 1867, 425). Toni Negri opposes capital's self-referential character by the working class' potential for self-referential autonomy, in which work does not produce capital and commodities, but an end-in-and-for-itself, i.e. products that satisfy humanity's need and thereby do not serve class distinctions.

Negri (1991, 148) contrasts the concept of capital's self-valorisation to worker self-valorisation. Self-valorisation means the "independence of the worker-subject" (Negri 1991, 135), "non-work" (Negri 1991, 149). Negri (1991, 148) writes that proletarian self-valorisation starts with the refusal of work in capitalism and comes to full effect in communism. Michael Ryan says in the introduction to the English translation of Negri's (1991) *Marx Beyond Marx* that Negri defines self-valorisation as "working for oneself as a class, asserting one's own needs as primary to capital's need for value" (Negri 1991, xxx). Harry Cleaver (1992, 129) defines self-valorisation as "a process of valorisation which is autonomous from capitalist valorisation – a self-defining, self-determining process which goes beyond the mere resistance to capitalist valorisation to a positive project of self-constitution" that constitutes a "working class for-itself". "Auto-valorisation and sabotage are the double figure of one and the same object – or, better, they are the two faces of Janus, the gateway to the constitution of the subject" (Negri 1992, 82). In *Assembly*, Hardt and Negri re-affirm self-valorisation as struggle against digital capital(ism): "Exploit yourself, capital tells productive subjectivities, and they respond, we want to valorize ourselves, governing the common that we produce" (Hardt and Negri 2017, 123).

David Harvey (2017, 77) points out the parallels between his concept of anti-value and the autonomist notion of self-valorisation: "The working class (however defined) is the embodiment of anti-value. It is on the basis of this conception of alienated labour that Tronti, Negri and the Italian autonomistas build their theory of labour resistance and class struggle at the point of production. The act of refusal to work is anti-value personified. This class struggle occurs in the hidden abode of production". Harvey stresses in the debate with Hardt and Negri that "[w]e can debate and disagree on this or that but the spirit of our endeavours is similar" (Harvey 2018b, 452). It is only out of the opposition to "nihilistic forms of protest and fascistic accommodations", as Harvey (2018b, 452) stresses, that "anti-capitalist movements" can arise that create, as Hardt and Negri (2018a, 423) say at the end of their first contribution to the debate with Harvey, a new foundation of production. Only then will real subsumption be reversed so that capital becomes subsumed under society in a process of political sublation of capital that abolishes exploited labour and necessity and establishes the realm of human freedom.

References

Alderson, David and Robert Spencer. 2017. *For Humanism: Explorations in Theory and Politics.* London: Pluto Press.

Bloch, Ernst. 1986. *The Principle of Hope Volume 1.* Cambridge, MA: The MIT Press.

Cleaver, Harry. 1992. The Inversion of Class Perspective in Marxian Theory: From Valorisation to Self-Valorisation. In *Open Marxism*, ed. Werner Bonefeld, Richard Gunn and Kosmos Psychopedis *Volume 2*, 106–144. London: Pluto Press.

Fromm, Erich, ed. 1966. *Socialist Humanism. An International Symposium.* Garden City, NY: Doubleday.

Fuchs, Christian. 2018. *Digital Demagogue: Authoritarian Capitalism in the Age of Trump and Twitter.* London: Pluto Press.

Fuchs, Christian. 2016. *Reading Marx in the Information Age. A Media and Communication Studies Perspective on "Capital Volume I".* New York: Routledge.

Fuchs, Christian and Lara Monticelli, eds. 2018. Karl Marx @ 200. Debating Capitalism & Perspectives for the Future of Radical Theory. *tripleC: Communication, Capitalism & Critique* 16 (2): 406–741. https://doi.org/10.31269/triplec.v16i2.1040

Hardt, Michael and Antonio Negri. 2018a. The Powers of the Exploited and the Social Ontology of Praxis. *tripleC: Communication, Capitalism & Critique* 18 (2): 415–423. https://doi.org/10.31269/triplec.v16i2.1024

Hardt, Michael and Antonio Negri. 2018b. The Multiplicities Within Capitalist Rule and the Articulation of Struggles. *tripleC: Communication, Capitalism & Critique* 18 (2): 440–448. https://doi.org/10.31269/triplec.v16i2.1025

Hardt, Michael and Antonio Negri. 2017. *Assembly.* Oxford: Oxford University Press.

Hardt, Michael and Antonio Negri. 2009. *Commonwealth.* Cambridge, MA: Harvard University Press.

Hardt, Michael and Antonio Negri. 1994. *Labor of Dionysus. A Critique of the State-Form.* Minneapolis, MN: University of Minnesota Press.

Harvey, David. 2018a. Universal Alienation. *tripleC: Communication, Capitalism & Critique* 18 (2): 424–439. https://doi.org/10.31269/triplec.v16i2.1026

Harvey, David. 2018b. Universal Alienation and the Real Subsumption of Daily Life under Capital: A Response to Hardt and Negri. *tripleC: Communication, Capitalism & Critique* 18 (2): 449–453. https://doi.org/10.31269/triplec.v16i2.1027

Harvey, David. 2017. *Marx, Capital and the Madness of Economic Reason.* London: Profile.

Harvey, David. 2014. *Seventeen Contradictions and the End of Capitalism.* London: Profile.

Harvey, David. 2010. *A Companion to Marx's Capital.* London: Verso.

Harvey, David. 2006. *The Limits to Capital.* London: Verso.

Harvey, David. 2005a. *A Brief History of Neoliberalism.* Oxford: Oxford University Press.

Harvey, David. 2005b. *Spaces of Neoliberalization.* Stuttgart: Franz Steiner Verlag.

Harvey, David. 2003. *The New Imperialism.* Oxford: Oxford University Press.

Harvey, David. 2000. *Spaces of Hope*. Berkeley, CA: University of California Press.

Harvey, David. 1990. *The Condition of Postmodernity*. Cambridge, MA: Blackwell.

Harvey, David, Michael Hardt and Antonio Negri. 2009. *Commonwealth*: An Exchange. *Artforum* 48 (3): 210–221.

Luxemburg, Rosa. 1903/2018. Karl Marx. Translated from German by Christian Fuchs. *tripleC: Communication, Capitalism & Critique* 16 (2): 729–741. https://doi.org/10.31269/triplec.v16i2 .1040

Luxemburg, Rosa. 1913. *The Accumulation of Capital*. New York: Routledge.

Marx, Karl. 1894. *Capital. A Critique of Political Economy Volume 3*. London: Penguin.

Marx, Karl. 1867. *Capital. A Critique of Political Economy Volume 1*. London: Penguin.

Marx, Karl. 1865. Value, Price and Profit. In *Marx & Engels Collected Works Volume 20*, 101–149. London: Lawrence & Wishart.

Marx, Karl. 1857/58. *Grundrisse*. London: Penguin.

Marx, Karl. 1844a. Economic and Philosophic Manuscripts of 1844. In *Marx & Engels Collected Works (MECW)Volume 3*, 229–346. London: Lawrence & Wishart.

Marx, Karl. 1844b. On the Jewish Question. In *Marx & Engels Collected Works (MECW) Volume 3*, 146–174. London: Lawrence & Wishart.

Marx, Karl. 1843. Contribution to the Critique of Hegel's Philosophy of Law. In *Marx & Engels Collected Works (MECW)Volume 3*, 3–129. London: Lawrence & Wishart.

Marx, Karl. 1841. Difference Between the Democritean and Epicurean Philosophy of Nature. In *Marx & Engels Collected Works (MECW)Volume 1*, 25–107. London: Lawrence & Wishart.

MECW: Marx, Karl and Friedrich Engels: *Marx & Engels Collected Works (MECW)*. 50 Volumes. London: Lawrence & Wishart.

Mies, Maria. 1986. *Patriarchy & Accumulation on a World Scale: Women in the International Division of Labour*. London: Zed Books.

Mies, Maria, Veronika Bennholdt-Thomsen, and Claudia von Werlhof. 1988. *Women: The Last Colony*. London: Zed Books.

Negri, Antonio. 1992. Interpretation of the Class Situation Today: Methodological Aspects. In *Open Marxism. Volume II: Theory and Practice*, ed. Werner Bonefeld, Richard Gunn and Kosmas Psychopedis, 69–105. London: Pluto Press.

Negri, Antonio. 1991. *Marx Beyond Marx: Lessons On The Grundrisse*. New York: Autonomedia.

Williams, Raymond. 1989. *Resources of Hope: Culture, Democracy, Socialism*. London: Verso.

Chapter Seven

Critical Social Theory and Sustainable Development:
The Role of Class, Capitalism, and Domination in a
Dialectical Analysis of Un/Sustainability

7.1 Introduction

The sustainability concept has a strong policy background in institutions such as the United Nations and the European Union. Its links to social theory are fairly weak. It is still a relatively open question how sustainability fits into a theory of society. Sustainability has not been a very popular concept in sociological theory. One of the reasons may be that sociology has a strongly critical tradition focusing on the analysis and critique of power structures in modern society. It is therefore often sceptical of ideas coming from the policy world that are susceptible to have an administrative character so that they do not question the main power inequalities of bureaucracies and capitalism. It is for example telling that since 2008, we have experienced the largest crisis of capitalism since 80 years that has also resulted in political crises, but sustainability discourses tend to ignore speaking of capitalism and class.

Based on this background, this paper asks the question: How can we integrate sustainability into a critical social theory framework? Section 7.2 re-visits the Brundtland Report's account of sustainability. Section 7.3 frames the sustainability discussion in terms of class and capitalism. Section 7.4 discusses multidimensional sustainability concepts. Section 7.5 introduces the notion of critical theory. Section 7.6 discusses how to use critical social theory for thinking about sustainability.

DOI: 10.4324/9781003199182-7

7.2 The Environmental Understanding of Sustainability

The United Nations World Commission on Environment and Development (WCED) in the years 1983–1987 conducted an investigation of possible solutions to the environmental crisis. Gro Harlem Brundtland, who then was Norway's prime minister, chaired the Commission that in 1987 published its report "Our Common Future" (WCED 1987). The Brundtland Report provided the most widely adopted and cited definition of sustainable development:

> Sustainable development is development that meets the needs of the present without compromising the ability of future generations to meet their own needs. It contains within it two key concepts:

> - the concept of 'needs', in particular the essential needs of the world's poor, to which overriding priority should be given; and
> - the idea of limitations imposed by the state of technology and social organization on the environment's ability to meet present and future needs.

> Thus the goals of economic and social development must be defined in terms of sustainability in all countries – developed or developing, market-oriented or centrally planned.

> (WCED 1987, 41)

Sustainability is the basic survival capacity of humans in society. It means an institutional, social, economic, political, environmental, technological, and cultural design of society that allows future generations to survive and to satisfy basic human needs for all. The Report was primarily concerned with the relationship of nature and society, i.e. the environmental crisis. The identified scope of global problems was centred on the nature–society relationship, whereas the solution was seen as having to be multi-dimensional. Other global problems – such as global conflicts, wars and violence, right-wing and religious extremism, precarious living and working conditions, the continued existence of slavery; social, income, and wealth inequalities; illiteracy and educational inequalities, gender inequalities, racism and xenophobia, displacement and forced migration, human rights violations, etc. – only played a subordinated role in the Report.

The Reports' somewhat limited understanding of society's problems also becomes evident in its definition of human needs (WCED 1987, 49–50). It mentions livelihood (employment), energy, housing, water supply, sanitation, and health care as the basic human needs that development needs to ensure. Needs that are missing in this list are cultural ones (such as education, communication possibilities for ensuring communication and social relations, recognition by others), political ones (the participation in collective decision-making [democracy], the guarantee of and realisation of human rights), and social ones (the protection from poverty, the social security of a population that has an increasing average age via publicly provided insurance, pension, and care systems).

"The most basic of all needs is for a livelihood: that is, employment" (WCED 1987, 49). The Brundtland Report here reduces human needs to employment, i.e. wage-labour, which is the main organisation of labour in modern societies. In 2015, only half of the world's eco-nomically active population were wage and salaried employees, whereas the other half was working on its own account, in households or families (ILO 2015, 13). The critical analysis of class, labour, and capitalism has often been ignored in discussions of sustainability.

7.3 Unsustainability, Class, Capitalism

Class is not an issue in the Brundtland Report and many other sustainability-reports and -studies (Deutz 2014). Although Western capitalism and the Soviet and Chinese versions of state command economies certainly had differences, they also shared the feature of being class societies: In Western capitalism, a capitalist class controls wealth and ownership of resources, from which everyday people are excluded. In the Soviet and Chinese model, a class of party bureaucrats, who enjoyed social privileges inaccessible to everyday people, controlled the economy and politics. Both models of society share the feature that the mass of everyday people produces use-values that they do not directly control in terms of ownership and decision-making. They are models of class society.

In class societies, those who are rich in terms of the amounts of the wealth, income, and power they control, are likely to be less affected by unsustainability because a) resource inequality is itself a form of unsustainable development: Sustainability not just means that a social system can reproduce itself, but does so in a fair and just way. Wealth and abundance on one side and poverty and lack on the other side are an expression of a fundamental social mismatch in society. And b), those controlling significant amounts of money, influence, reputation, and social relations can more easily escape unsustainable living conditions by changing their places, contexts, and forms of work and life in the case of risks and crises. Unsustainability is class-structured and tends to affect those with the least power in society most drastically.

The disregard of class was certainly a tendency that strongly shaped the analysis of society in the 1980s. A prototypical example is the work of the popular German sociologist Ulrich Beck, who in 1986 published his most well-known book *Risikogesellschaft: Auf dem Weg in eine andere Moderne* (released in English in 1992 as *Risk Society: Towards a New Modernity*). Individualisation, education, mobility, and competition would have brought about an individualised, self-reflexive risk society. "Race, skin color, gender, ethnicity, age, homosexuality, physical disabilities" (Beck 1992, 101) would have become more important than class. In the risk society, "risks, risk perception and risk management in all sectors of society become a new source of conflict and social formation" (Beck 1992, 99). "At the centre lie the risks and consequences of modernization, which are revealed as irreversible threats to the life of plants, animals, and human beings" (Beck 1992, 13). There is a striking parallel between Beck's dismissal of class and the class- and capitalism-blindness of sustainability concepts.

It is inappropriate to neglect class in the analysis of sustainability and society. According to estimations, the world's richest 10% in 2014 owned 87% of the global wealth, the richest 1% 48.2%, and the bottom half less than 1% (CSRI 2014, 11). In 2014, 69.8% of the world's population owned a wealth of less than US $10,000 and 0.7% more than US $1 million (CSRI 2014, 23–24). In 2015, the share of those owning less than US $10,000 increased to 71.0% and the share of those having more than US $1 million remained constant (CSRI 2015, 104). The worldwide Gini coefficient (a measure of inequality) was 0.915, which is a very high level (CSRI 2015, 104). The same study also found that the financial crisis and the neoliberal responses to it in the form of austerity measures resulted in an increase of wealth inequality: In the years 2007–2014, "wealth inequality rose in 35 countries and fell in only 11" (CSRI 2014, 32). For example, the share of the richest decile increased in China from 56.1% in 2007 to 64.0% in 2014, from 65.3% to 73.3% in Egypt, from 72.3% to 74.0% in India, from 75.4% to 84.8% in Russia, from 52.0% to 54.0% in the UK, from 52.0% to 55.6% in Spain, from 48.6% to 56.1% in Greece, from 56.0% to 58.3% in Ireland, from 69.0% to 71.7% in South Africa, from 47.9% to 51.5% in Italy, from 62.6% to 67.5% in Denmark, from 51.1% to 53.1% in France (CSRI 2014, 33: Table 2).

The labour share is the share of wages in the global GDP. Karabarbounis and Neiman (2014) created a model that analyses the development of the labour share in 59 (developing and developed) countries from 1975 until 2012. They found "a 5 percentage point decline in the share of global corporate gross value added paid to labour over the past 35 years" (61). "Of the 59 countries with at least 15 years of data between 1975 and 2012, 42 exhibited downward trends in their labour shares" (62). "From a level of roughly 64%, the global corporate labour share has [in the period from 1975 until 2012] exhibited a relatively steady downward trend, reaching about 59% at the end of the sample" (Karabarbounis and Neiman 2014, 69). The share of the world's 2,000 largest corporations revenues' in the world GDP increased from 50.8% in 2004 to 51.4% in 2014 (Fuchs 2016c).

Moris Triventi (2013) analysed data on educational achievement from 11 European countries. "Individuals with more educated parents have the highest likelihood of graduating from the best institutions, and differences with individuals with less educated parents are significant in all the countries except Germany. [...] parental education is strongly associated with the probability of attaining different types of qualifications in tertiary education. In particular, students from culturally advantaged families have a higher probability of graduating from the best educational paths in terms of quality and future occupational outcomes" (Triventi 2013, 495, 499).

Barro and Lee (2013) provide data for 146 states that shows that the share of the combined population in these countries, who have completed tertiary education, has increased from 1.1% in 1950 to 7.8% in 2010. There are, however, significant inequalities between developed and developing countries: Whereas the share was 17.9% in developed countries (N = 24), it was only 5.7% in developing countries (N = 2,010), which indicates that wealth differences play a role in possibilities for educational attainment.

Bukodi and Goldthorpe (2013) analysed how parents' occupational groups, occupational status, and education influence the educational attainment of children born in 1946, 1958, and 1970. Children of "parents in Classes 6 and 7 [semi-routine and routine workers], which can be equated with the working class, tend to do worst" (Bukodi and Goldthorpe 2013, 1030). "We find that level of family income does itself have an independent – positive – effect on children's educational attainment" (1030). "[L]ittle change is evident in the tendency for children from relatively disadvantaged class backgrounds to be less ready than children from more advantaged backgrounds to take a given standard of secondary school performance as a basis for seeking tertiary level qualifications" (1036).

It is a consistent pattern that children from households, where the parents have low income, low skills, and low educational attainments are more unlikely to attain a university degree than those who come from more privileged backgrounds.

Unsustainability, Class, Capitalism

The ND-GAIN Vulnerability Index measures countries' vulnerability to climate change by considering six aspects, namely how climate change affects ecological resources that support livelihood, food provision, public health, human habitat, costal and energy infrastructure, and fresh water supplies. In 2018, 38 of the 50 countries most vulnerable to climate change were located in Africa (data source: http://index.gain.org). Most highly vulnerable countries are poor and have low human development. Two of the countries most at risk of climate change, Sudan and Eritrea, were in 2015 ranked on position 167 and 186 out of 188 countries in the inequality-adjusted Human Development Index (UNHDR 2015).[1] Whereas Africa in contrast to the two largest carbon dioxide-emitting countries China (25%) and the USA (16%), as a whole produces only around 4% of global carbon dioxide emissions, it is the part of the world that is most at risk of climate change's negative impacts.

In 2015, 10 of the world's largest 100 companies were oil and gas producers (data sources: Forbes 2000, 2015 list): Exxon Mobil (#7), PetroChina (#8), Royal Dutch Shell (#13), Chevron (#16), Sinopec (#24), Gazprom (#27), Total (#35), BP (#41), Rosneft (#59), ConocoPhillips (#89). In addition, there were nine companies producing cars, trucks and airplanes in the top 100: Toyota (#11), VW (#14), Daimler (#26), BMW (#45), Honda (#63), General Motors (#64), Ford (#69), Boeing (#72), Nissan (#96). These data indicate that the mobility industry that generates vast amounts of carbon dioxide is one of the world's most profitable industries. The global environmental crisis has been created and sustained by profitable businesses.

Waste is another environmental problem that disproportionally affects the poor. "Waste, including highly toxic industrial waste, is frequently exported to poor countries for disposal or supposed recycling. Beginning in the 1970s, African countries – such as Nigeria, Ghana, and Ivory Coast – have been prime recipients of the industrial and sewage wastes of developed countries" (Magdoff and Foster 2011, 86). In 2014, 41.8 million tonnes of e-waste were produced in the world (UNU 2014, 22). In 2015, it was 43.8 million tonnes (24). Whereas in Africa the e-waste generated per person was just 1.7 kg, it was 12.2 kg in the Americas and 15.6 kg in Europe (25). Africa is hardly a source, but the world's largest dumping ground for e-waste (UNU 2014, 38).

The discussed examples of the inequality of wages and profits, educational achievements, climate change, and waste show that class is an important factor in all forms of unsustainable development. Sociologists like Ulrich Beck are mistaken in dismissing and ignoring class and capitalism in the analysis of contemporary society. The implication for theorising un/sustainable development is that they need to take issues of class and capitalism serious. A critical concept of un/sustainability is needed.

The rich form an elite that owns large shares of the world's wealth that the mass of the world population creates, but that everyday people do not own. The unequal distribution of the world's income between capital and labour has in the past forty years significantly increased globally. Wealth inequality has increased. Children from elite and upper class families that control large amounts of economic, cultural, and social capital are more likely to obtain a university degree and attend elite universities. There are much fewer university graduates in poor than in rich countries. Children with parents belonging to the elite are very likely to themselves be part of the elite, whereas working class children are unlikely to attain such a status in society. The world's poor are most hit by the negative impacts of global environmental problems such as pollution and climate change, whereas transnational corporations are turning environmental devastation into profit by fostering carbon dioxide emissions and polluting nature as a negative externality. These are just some examples that indicate that class inequalities form a crucial factor in the advancement of unsustainability.

It is paradoxical that at the time of the rise of neoliberal capitalism that has brought about a massive increase of inequalities, claims that we are witnessing the end of class structures and capitalism intensified.

In the *Grundrisse*, Marx (1857/1858) conceptualises class as a relationship between those who own and control resources and those who do not. The poor are for Marx the dominated class because they produce society's wealth, but do not own and control it:

Labour posited as not-capital as such is [...] not-rawmaterial, not-instrument of labour, not-raw-product: labour separated from all means and objects of labour, from its entire objectivity. [...] Labour as absolute poverty: poverty not as shortage, but as total exclusion of objective wealth. [...] Labour [is] the living source of value. [Namely, it is] general wealth (in contrast to capital in which it exists objectively, as reality) as the general possibility of the same, which proves itself as such in action. Thus, it is not at all contradictory, or, rather, the in-every-way mutually contradictory statements that labour is absolute poverty as object, on one side, and is, on the other side, the general possibility of wealth as subject and as activity, are reciprocally determined and follow from the essence of labour, such as it is presupposed by capital as its contradiction and as its contradictory being, and such as it, in turn, presupposes capital.

(Marx 1857/1858, 295–296)

The mass of everyday people produces the goods that sustain the existence of humans and society and the social relations that enable, govern and reproduce everyday life in society. But it is just an elite that controls and accumulates vast amounts of money (economic capital), decision-power (political capital), influence and reputation (cultural capital). Modern society's logic of accumulation creates a class structure, in which the mass of the producers of (economic, political, cultural) capital are kept poor by not being able to control the structures they create and that enable society's reproduction. Inequalities are built into the logic of accumulation on which modern society is built.

The sustainability concept has developed from an initial environmental focus towards multidimensionality. Has this multidimensionality also resulted in a focus on class and capitalism?

7.4 The Emergence of a Multidimensional Concept of Sustainability

In 1992, the UN Conference on Environment and Development ("Earth Summit") took place in Rio de Janeiro, Brazil. It passed the Rio Declaration on Environment and Development (UNCED 1992, principle 1). Although the Rio Declaration covers a wide range of issues such as the environment, poverty, demography, the economy, gender, youth, indigenous people, or peace, its primary focus is still the natural environment, which becomes evident by the fact that it contains the keywords "environment" and "environmental" 40 times and the keywords "society" and "societies" just twice. Whereas the Earth Summit focused on the environmental issues of sustainability, the 2002 World Summit on Sustainable Development (WSSD) conference more effectively integrated economic and equity issues into the discussion.

In the discourse on sustainability, there has been a shift from a focus on ecological issues towards the inclusion of broader societal issues. "Sustainability discourse shifted from an emphasis on pollution and availability of natural resources to [...] more complex and integrated frameworks" (Quental, Lourenço and Nunes da Silva 2011, 27). The "triangle of sustainability" introduced by the World Bank has been important in shifting the sustainability discussion from purely ecological aspects towards more integrative concepts (Serageldin 1995). By 2002, it had become common to identify an ecological, an economic, a social, and an institutional dimension of sustainability (Heinrich Böll Foundation 2002, 22; WSSD 2002, principle 5).

Also the 2012 Rio+20 Conference's outcome document *The Future We Want* foregrounds the importance of the three pillars of sustainability that the Johannesburg Conference stressed (UNCSD 2012, principle 1). It accentuates the importance of institutions that foster these three pillars of sustainable development (UNCSD 2012, 75). As a follow-up to Rio+20, the *2030 Agenda for Sustainable Development* (United Nations 2015) contains 17 goals.

There is certainly a multidimensional understanding of sustainability as social, environmental, and economic underlying these objectives. But there are two problems that are characteristic for all the mentioned policy documents:

1) Communication and culture are not mentioned as realms of sustainability (except for education);
2) Class and capitalism are not mentioned a single time as problems negatively impacting sustainability. This is particularly striking in the 2012 and 2015 documents because they were written in the course of the global capitalist crisis that started in 2008.

Whereas these declarations are silent on class and capitalism, they express the need of economic sustainability, a term that has no straightforward meaning. It would be a meaningful general term if conceived as the satisfaction of basic human needs for all humans on the planet in ways that guarantee equality and the protection of the environment. But the understanding of economic sustainability tends to be much more fetishistic and focused on GDP growth, which mainly means the growth of private businesses' profits. The Rio+20 outcome document speaks of the need for "sustained economic growth" (UNCSD 2012, 2) and "sustained, inclusive and equitable economic growth" (UNCSD 2012, 19). Similar formulations can be found in the *2030 Agenda for Sustainable Development*: "We envisage a world in which every country enjoys sustained, inclusive and sustainable economic growth and decent work for all. [...] Sustained, inclusive and sustainable economic growth is essential for prosperity. This will only be possible if wealth is shared and income inequality is addressed. [...] Sustain per capita economic growth in accordance with national circumstances and, in particular, at least 7% gross domestic product growth per annum in the least developed countries" (United Nations 2015, 4, 8, 19).

The GDP is a peculiar variable that lumps together labour costs, the costs for new means of production, and profits, i.e. labour and capital. GDP growth is no guarantee at all for socio-economic equality because profits can grow faster than labour income, which, as we saw earlier, has been an important tendency in neoliberal capitalism since the 1970s. "[M]ost people have not benefited from the growth of GDP as quality of life has become separated from economic growth" (Giddings, Hopwood, and O'Brien 2002, 190). Should "progress be purely a growth-only (economic) phenomenon and be measured mainly in GDP terms; should we not rather be treating economy as a means and target to achieve what we term 'good society' as our end goal?" (Khan 2015, 69). Joseph Stiglitz, Amartya Sen, and Jean-Paul Fitoussi (2010) argue that the GDP is of limited use for measuring social progress and that it is "an inadequate metric to gauge well-being over time" (Stiglitz, Sen, and Fitoussi 2010, 8). Measuring well-being by the GDP could for example "send the aberrant message that a natural catastrophe is a blessing for the economy, because of the additional economic activity generated by repairs" (Stiglitz, Sen, and Fitoussi 2010, 265). "If inequality increases enough relative to the increase in average [...] GDP, most people can be worse off even though average income is increasing" (8). They call for a shift of emphasis "*from measuring economic production to measuring people's well-being*" (12) in policymaking and research in the context of sustainability.

We saw that the mobility industry that is based on non-renewable energy resources and produces large amounts of carbon dioxide is among capitalism's most profitable industries. Approaches calling for GDP growth without questioning capitalist interest therefore leave an important factor contributing to environmental and social unsustainability untouched. They also act as a legitimating ideology that supports neoliberalism. Such ideologies are dualistic in character: They want to develop capitalist profits and formulate at the same time a list of desirable social and environmental moral values without considering that capitalism and capitalist expansion may negatively impact society.

The sustainability concept's ideological character has to do with the fact that just like the concept of the network society it sounds immensely positive and allows diverse groups that have opposing interests to project their political goals into it. "Who in his or her right mind would be against 'sustainability'?" (O'Connor 1994, 152). Does this mean we have to drop the sustainability concept in a critical theory of society because of its ideological character? Or is it possible to ground a critical theory concept of sustainability?

7.5 What is Critical Theory?

Critical theory is a term that theorists based at the Frankfurt Institute for Social Research introduced in the 1920s and 1930s. They became also known as the Frankfurt School. Their most important representatives include Theodor W. Adorno, Max Horkheimer, Herbert Marcuse, Jürgen Habermas, and Axel Honneth. Whereas some observers argue that critical theory are the works of these authors, another interpretation that the present author follows is that many of their works foregrounded principles of social theory that are more general characteristics of approaches that critically scrutinise society (Fuchs 2016a, 2016b). In a general understanding, critical theory has been influenced by the works of Karl Marx (Fuchs 2016c) and tries to understand the role of power, domination, and exploitation in society by investigating contradictions, structures, practices, ideologies, relations, and political praxis.

One can now ask: Is not all science critical of other approaches, theories, methods, and paradigms? Does the term critical theory therefore make sense? This question was at the heart of the *Positivist Dispute in German Sociology* (Adorno et al. 1976). Karl Popper argued that criticism means the testing of scientific assumptions by empirical research, falsification, and deduction. He understood critique as epistemological and methodological criticism. Theodor W. Adorno in contrast argued for a critique of society, societal problems, domination, and power. He spoke of the need for a critical theory of society.

Based on Popper, any study of sustainability is critical in so far as it is based on and goes beyond other studies. Such a general understanding of critique makes it impossible to give special attention to the role of power asymmetries having to do with class inequalities, gender inequalities, racism, nationalism, etc. in the analysis of sustainability. Adorno's notion of a critical theory of society is therefore more suited and implies the need for a critical theory of sustainability.

An important aspect of critical theory is the critique of instrumental reason. This notion is grounded in Karl Marx's (1867) concept of fetishism and Georg Lukács' (1971) concept of reification (Fuchs 2016b). Instrumental reason is a logic that treats humans and society like things so that specific groups benefit at the expense of others. Instrumental logic instrumentalises humans, society, and nature in processes of domination. In the form of ideology, instrumental reason tries to instrumentalise human consciousness, i.e. it tries to justify and rationalise structures of domination and exploitation. We can on the one hand say that unsustainability is always based on instrumental reason. On the other hand, we saw in the previous sections that sustainability concepts often disregard aspects of class and capitalism. Critical theory could therefore also argue that sustainability is an ideology that justifies capitalism and class societies. The question that arises as a consequence of this analysis is whether the sustainability concept should then be dropped in a critical theory of society or whether it can be reconstructed in the form of the notion of critical sustainability.

It is in this context interesting that Karl Marx in his works provided an understanding of society's development that in a striking manner parallels the Brundtland Commission's definition of sustainable development as "development that meets the needs of the present without compromising the ability of future generations to meet their own needs" (WCED 1987, 43):

> From the standpoint of a higher economic form of society, private ownership of the globe by single individuals will appear quite as absurd as private ownership of one man by another. Even a whole society, a nation, or even all simultaneously existing societies taken together, are not the owners of the globe. They are only its possessors, its usufructuaries, and, like *boni patres familias,* they must hand it down to succeeding generations in an improved condition.
>
> (Marx 1894, 784)

We can therefore say that Marx was an early theorist of sustainability. Marx just like the Brundtland Commission understands sustainability as the organisation of society in a manner that allows future generations to satisfy their needs and that improves society. For Marx, the "improved condition" of society implied the quest for participatory democracy and Democratic Socialism. Given that Marx, who is one of the most important critical theories, was an early theorist of sustainability, the quest for a critical theory of un/sustainability is certainly feasible.

Critical theory is also interested in how economic and non-economic forms of domination are related. It investigates the relationship of capitalism and domination, class and exclusion, the economic and the non-economic. Just like it opposes ignoring class and capitalism, critical theory also opposes reducing all societal problems to the economy. It sees capitalism and class as conditioning, but not determining society's problems. Capitalism exerts pressure on and interacts with all realms of contemporary society. Societal problems therefore simultaneously have aspects of class and go beyond class in specific ways. The implication of this insight for a critical theory of sustainability is that societies' unsustainability is grounded in global capitalism's destructive, dominative, exploitative and exclusionary character that interacts with specific forms of domination such as patriarchy, racism, nationalism, bureaucracy, destructive industrialism, etc. What all these is that they are forms of instrumental reason.

Critical theory analyses society based on dialectical reason (Fuchs 2011, 2016b). Dialectical reason is opposed to instrumental reason that it sees as reducing the complexity of the world and society to one dimension only. A dialectic is a contradictory relationship between two entities (Fuchs 2014). They simultaneously are identical and different. They require and exclude each other. Dialectical logic challenges classical binary and reductionist thought. It questions the reduction of the world to just one dimension. It is, however, not just relational and multidimensional but also sees the world as being in flux and development. Development potentialities emerge out of poles that contradict each other. At a certain level of organisation, everything constantly develops. There are, however, also more continuous processes that only change at specific critical points. Dialectical development includes situations of crisis and change and the emergence of novelty at such critical points. In society, there are two basic forms of the dialectic: One has to do with the very basic conditions and the basic development of society. So for example there is a social dialectic between human beings: In order to exist, humans have to communicate with each other. They are different individuals, but can only inform themselves by mutual symbolic interaction. The second form of societal dialectic has to do with power relations. In a power dialectic, we find conflicting interests and conflicting structures.

A critical, dialectical theory of society is well suited as a framework for theorising un/sustainability. Critical theory has, however, thus far not played a major role in the discourse on sustainability. But some work has been done on it.

First, some authors have acknowledged the importance of Marx's works. Harlow, Golub, and Braden (2011, 278) argue that the critical tradition that goes back to Marx allows to "address the structures in which conventional sustainable development discourse takes place, and question the opening of countless local communities to global markets and the modern vision of a one-world system based on the expansion of western culture and capitalism". Hopwood, Mellor, and O'Brien (2005, 46) argue that in the sustainability discourse, Marx and Engels' works have had influence on ecosocialist thinking, which is a specific form of a transformatory approach on sustainable development. O'Connor (1998), Foster (2002), and Fuchs (2006) are among those authors who have based on Marx explored the relationship of capitalism and nature.

What is Critical Theory?

Second, there have been authors, who in the tradition of Frankfurt School ideology critique have argued that sustainability is an ideology. Luke (2005, 235) says based on Herbert Marcuse that "sustainability is the dominant ideological guise of the capitalist mode of production". Redclift and Woodgate (2013, 99) argue in a similar vain that sustainable development "has turned into a thinly disguised mantra for economic growth, and this growth has proved, in turn, something of a chimera".

Third, there have been approaches on sustainability that have used Habermas's theory. Redclift (2005) argues that Habermas's theory allows us to understand how capitalism colonises nature and society so that "much wealth is created in ways that undermine sustainability" (215). Habermas would also allow understanding how sustainability discourses "hid, or marginalized, the inequalities and cultural distinctions that had driven the 'environmental' agenda internationally" (224). O'Mahony and Skillington (1996) argue that combining the sustainability discourse with Habermas's concept of discursive and deliberative democracy allows exploring foundations of an alternative model of democracy.

What is missing is a systematic framework that allows grounding theoretical foundations of a critical theory of un/sustainability.

7.6 Towards a Critical, Dialectical Understanding of Sustainability

The three dimensions of sustainability seem to have been relatively arbitrary chosen. They are not underpinned by a theory of society. "While the use of the term 'sustainability' has become almost inflationary in both science and society, the work on theories of sustainable development has received much less attention" (Enders and Remig 2015, 1). Giddings, Hopwood, and O'Brien (2002) argue that the three dimension model sees the economy, society and nature as autonomous and encourages "a technical fix approach to sustainable development issues" (189), focuses on parts instead of the whole (190), and provide an ideology that allows to reduce society and the environment to capitalist resources (191). They instead of the three-ring model suggest a nested model of sustainability.

In Figure 7.1, models 1 (M1) and 2 (M2) visualise the two models of sustainability that Giddings, Hopwood, and O'Brien discern. I argue for a third model (M3) that is a further development of M2. It besides the economy also foregrounds the political and the cultural system as parts of society and is based on a dialectic of nature/society and a

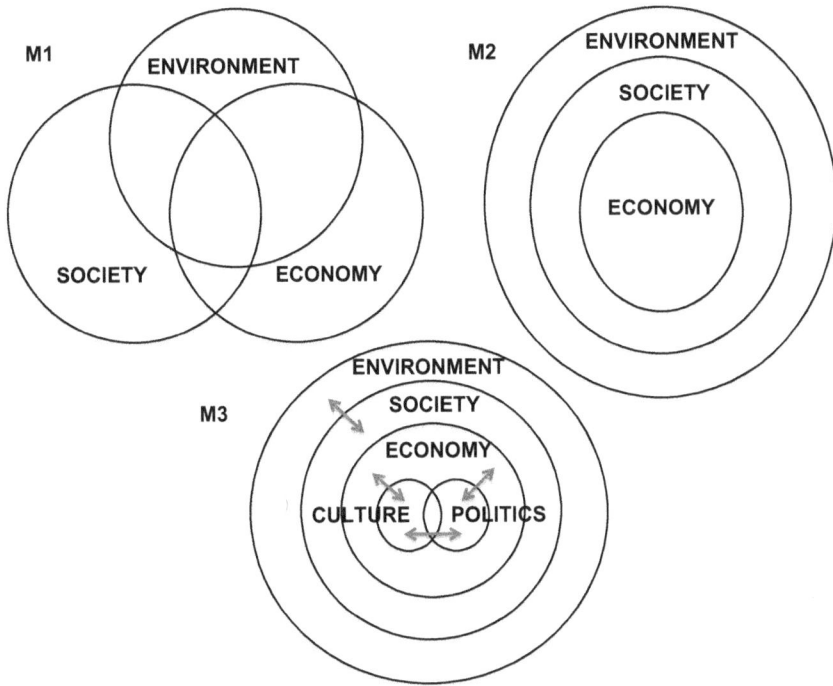

FIGURE 7.1 Three models of sustainability

dialectic of the economy/the non-economic (the political and the cultural). In model M3, society is made up of the economy, politics, and culture and these three inter-acting realms of society are grounded in nature, with which society interacts.

A distinction of three subsystems of society (economy, polity, culture) can be found in several widely adopted social theories: Giddens (1984, 28–34) distinguishes between economic institutions, political institutions and symbolic orders/modes of discourse as the three types of institutions in society. Bourdieu (1986) speaks of economic, political, and cultural capital as the three types of structures in society. Jürgen Habermas (1987) differentiates between the lifeworld, the economic system and the political system. Daniel Bell (1974) discerns between society's social structure (economy, technology, occupational system), polity, and culture.

These social theories have different theory backgrounds and implications for society. They do however broadly share a distinction between economy, politics, and culture as the three main domains of society (Fuchs 2008, 2011): The economy is the realm of society, where humans enter a metabolism with nature so that work organises nature and culture in such a way that use-values that satisfy human needs emerge. Given that it is the economy, where the man–nature relationship is established and that the ecological system is closely linked to the economy, one could treat the ecological system as part of the economy. But the circumstance that society is part of nature, but at the same time a sublation of nature, allows giving specific analytical attention to the ecological system as part of society. Nature is larger than society and there are vast parts of it that are unknown to humans. But the part of nature that stands in a metabolism with humans is part of society. Nature is at the same time part and no-part of society. The political system is the realm of society, where humans deliberate on or struggle about the distribution of decision power in society. Culture is the realm of the recreation of the human body and mind in such ways that meanings, identities and values emerge and are renegotiated in everyday life. It includes aspects of society such as the mass media, science, education, the arts, ethics, health care and medicine, sports, entertainment, and personal relations.

Society is an interconnection of social systems. In a social system, humans enter into social relations, in which they make meaning of each other and in their practices produce and reproduce specific social structures that enable and constrain individual thought, individual action, and further social practices that again produce and reproduce social structures, and so on ad infinitum. A social system is a dialectic of social practices and social structures (Fuchs 2003a, 2003b). Marx (1988, 104) described society's dialectic when writing that "just as society itself produces man as man, so is society produced by him". Communication plays a very basic role in social systems: It is the means, by which humans relate to each other symbolically (either in linguistic and non-linguistic ways) and establish and produce social relations. A social system exists as long as the structure-agency dialectic is organised regularly via communication in time and space. Without communication and the social dialectic there can be no social system. A social system therefore ceases to exist when its dynamic comes to an end. Figure 7.2 illustrates society's social dialectic.

All social systems have an economic, a political, and a cultural dimension: Humans in all social systems use resources, take decisions, and produce meanings. Depending on the social system and the social role that humans have in it, one of these dimensions can be primary, which allows us to distinguish between economic, political, and cultural social systems. So for example in modern society, companies and markets

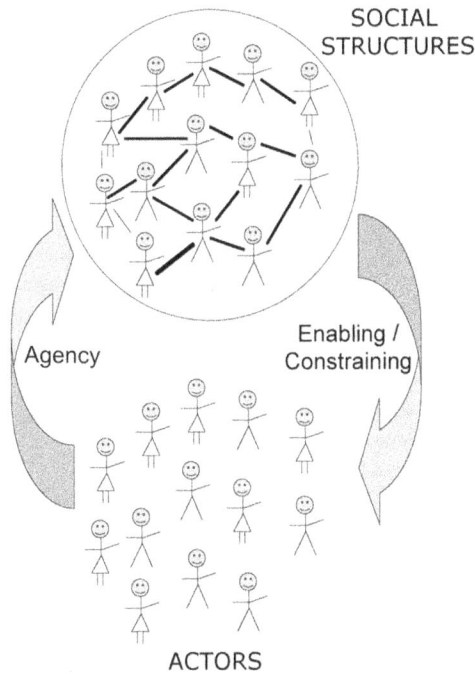

FIGURE 7.2   The dialectic of structure and agency in society (source: Fuchs 2008, 52)

belong to the economic systems; states, parliaments, political parties, and protest movements to the political system; universities, religions, libraries, museums, the mass media, hospitals, leisure clubs, and families to the cultural system. The economic, the political and the cultural system are society's subsystems. Each of these three systems consists of the networks of interaction between all humans and between all social systems that orient their communication and their social dialectic primarily on the (re) production of specific social structures. Table 7.1 and Figure 7.3 provide an overview of this distinction.

Society's subsystems are distinct, but not autonomous. They interact with each other. Politics and culture have in modern society their own economies: There are particular workers, who as their profession and in order to economically survive engage in the production of political and cultural structures. They are, however, not the only actors. There is also a multitude of voluntary activities. The political and cultural system are grounded in work that produces specific political and cultural use-values, but they at the same time go beyond these systems because political

TABLE 7.1 Structures in society

Dimension	Social structures	Definition	Social structures in modern society
Nature	Natural structures: Natural resources	Physical matter that is extracted in labour processes from nature and that is changed by human activities	Natural resources as the physical body of commodities
Society: Economy	Economic structures: Property	Use-values are created by human work, distributed and consumed in order to satisfy humans needs	Commodities and capital that objectify specific average amounts of human labour and take on the exchange-value form when being traded as commodities on markets
Society: Political system	Political structures: Decision-power	Collective decisions that define basic rules of behaviour in society	Laws and policies that regulate social conflicts in specific ways
Society: Cultural system	Cultural structures: Definitions, meanings	Collective definitions of reality that give meaning to social systems and provide identities to human actors	Knowledge, worldviews and ideologies that provide meaning to modern society's antagonisms and provide status and reputation to humans

decisions and cultural meanings take effect all over society. A basic premise of a cultural materialist approach in social theory is therefore that the economic and the non-economic are identical and non-identical at the same time (Fuchs 2016c, chapters 2 and 3).

Table 7.1 provides not only an overview of natural and social structures in general but also shows the forms they take on in modern society. Modern society is a societal formation that is based on the accumulation of economic, political, and cultural capital. In modernity, society's basic structures take on the form of capital that is accumulated. Modern society is in a general sense a capitalist society that is based on the logic of accumulation. In modern society, natural resources are the physical body of commodities, economic property is organised as commodities and capital, collective decisions take on the form of laws and policies, collective definitions and meanings are worldviews, knowledge and ideologies that provide status and reputation. The accumulation of various forms of capitalism shows that modern society is based on the logic of instrumental reason.

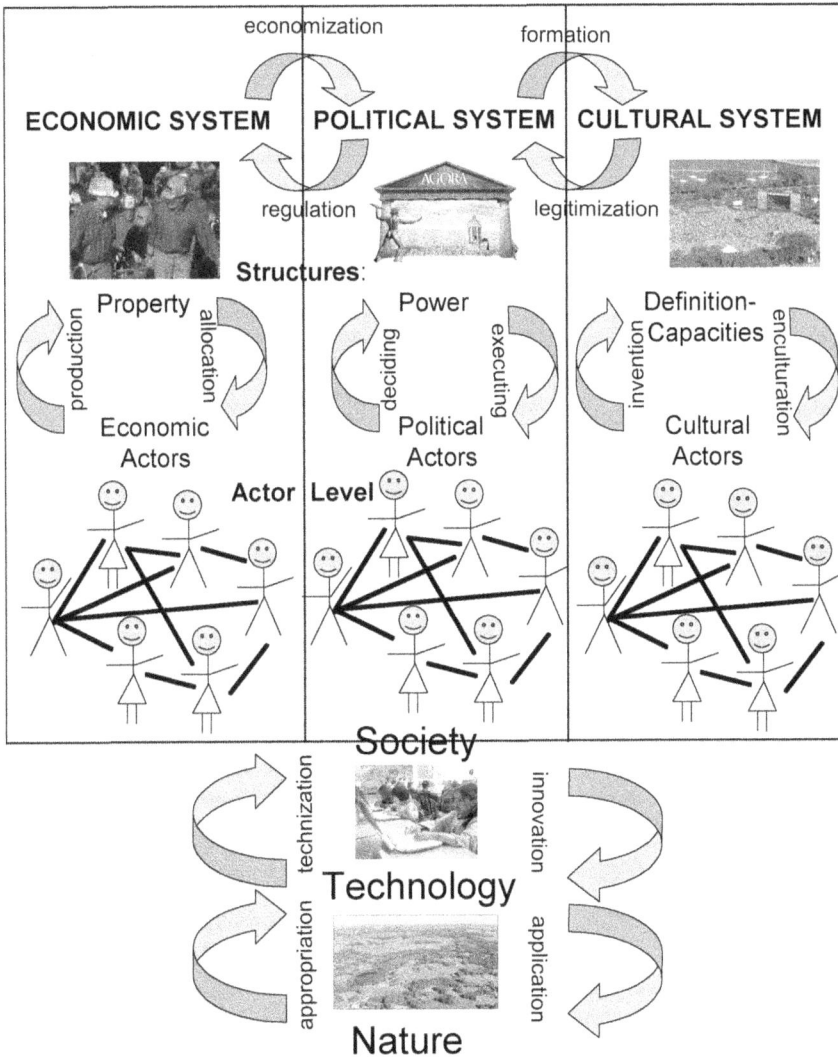

FIGURE 7.3 Society as a dialectic of dynamically reproducing subsystems (source: Fuchs 2008, 52)

7.7 Conclusion

I have in this article argued that critical social theory foundations of the sustainability concept are largely missing because critical sociology tends to see sustainability as ideology that neglects issues of capitalism and class. The approach that I suggest is not to abandon the notion of sustainability, but to sublate it based on a critical theory of society.

Sustainability is an inherently ethical concept (Ziegler and Ott 2015, 56) that poses the question: What is a good society? Sustainability asks the long-term question about how present and future generations can lead a good life in society. Table 7.2 provides an overview of the dimensions of sustainability and a check-list of questions that can be asked when determining the sustainable or unsustainable character of social systems.

This typology of un/sustainability is grounded in social theory. It suggests not just three dimensions of sustainability (environmental, economic, social), but distinguishes between environmental, economic, political, and cultural un/sustainability. The latter three constitute the societal dimension of un/sustainability of the communication between humans. The first aspect is the natural dimension in the interaction between society and nature. Sustainability has to do with the good life for all and the satisfaction of human needs for all.

Human needs are not fixed over time, but change historically with the development of society. Human needs today are different than 500 years ago. So for example today the Internet, a global communication system, exists as a still relatively novel form for the organisation of communication. It poses both opportunities and risks for society's organisation of the environment, the economy, politics, and culture (Fuchs 2008). Discussions about sustainability cannot ignore that Internet communication has become just like electricity supply, water supply, sewage systems, health care, and education systems a basic utility. Communications as utility form a basic human need today. The information society has developed both the communication and cultural capacities in society. It is therefore disturbing that discussions, policy agendas, and declarations have thus far not adequately taken communications and culture into account (see Parodi 2015).

The definition of cultural sustainability in Table 7.2 is based on an understanding of culture as the system of the reproduction of the human mind and body. The human mind can only develop if humans' identities and personalities are recognised in society and by others; if there are institutions that nourish human skills; if their ideas are taken serious, acknowledged and recognised; and if there are no large status and reputational inequalities. That the human body can reproduce itself means that there should be adequate amounts of leisure available to all that allows recreation and that health system protects humans from illnesses and helps them in the case of sickness. Cultural sustainability therefore has to do with the role of education, science, health care, personal and family life, arts and culture, leisure, entertainment, sports, the mass media, morality, and belief systems in society.

TABLE 7.2 Dimensions of un/sustainability

Dimension	Dimension of sustainability	Question	Dimension of unsustainability	Question
Nature	Environmental sustainability: Biodiversity	To which degree are natural resources protected and preserved so that the survival of nature and society is guaranteed? To which degree is there an equitable distribution of environmental harms and benefits to certain groups and places?	Environmental unsustainability: Environmental pollution, degradation and depletion	To which degree are natural resources depleted and polluted so that the survival of nature and society is threatened? To which degree is there an unequal and inequitable distribution of environmental harms and benefits to certain groups and places?
Society: Economy	Economic sustainability: Wealth for all	To which degree are economic relations organised in a way that allows the production of wealth for all and a fair distribution of wealth?	Economic unsustainability: Poverty, inequality, economic crisis	To which degree are economic relations organised in a manner that does not guarantee satisfaction of the needs of all humans (poverty), that results in unfair distribution of need satisfaction (inequality) or the irreproducibility of the economy (economic crisis)?
Society: Political system	Political sustainability: Participation and peace	To which degree does the political system enable humans to participate in collective decision-making? To which degree does the political system guarantee the peaceful existence and interaction of and within societies and the guarantee of basic rights?	Political unsustainability: Dictatorship and war	To which degree is the political system ruled by an elite that excludes the population from participation in collective decision-making? To which degree does the political system foster violence and the violation of basic rights and warfare?
Society: Cultural system	Cultural sustainability: Recognition	To which degree does culture enable the development of the human mind, the recognition of identities in society, and the reproduction of the human body?	Cultural unsustainability: Disrespect, ideology, and malrecognition	To which degree does culture limit the development of the human mind, the recognition of identities and the reproduction of the human body?

Conclusion

One should note that the typology of sustainability in Table 7.2 does not define economic sustainability in terms of GDP growth and monetary profitability of companies. It takes a critical perspective on economic sustainability that considers that it is labour and not capital that produces human wealth. The structures of modern society are class structures in that specific groups tend to accumulate economic, political and cultural capital and to exclude others from wealth, participation and recognition. Unsustainability arises in modern society to the extent that the class interests of elites become the governing principles of social systems and society's subsystems. Whereas we can speak of class relations in economic, political and cultural systems, it is not feasible to speak of a class relation between nature and society. Class is a specific social structure of human interaction.

James O'Connor argues that besides the social contradictions of modern society, there is a "second contradiction of capitalism" (O'Connor 1998, 158–177), "the contradiction between capitalist production relations (and productive forces) and the conditions of capitalist production, or 'capitalist relations and forces of social reproduction'" (O'Connor 1998, 160). Capitalism is based on social antagonisms in society, i.e. economic, political, and cultural antagonisms. What O'Connor terms the second contradiction is a contradiction between society's mode of production and natural forces. Productive forces turn into destructive forces in the metabolism of nature and society to the degree that they deplete and destroy natural resources. There are complex relations between class structures in society and environmental unsustainability. We have for example discussed that the poor tend to be most affected by environmental degradation that poses a threat to their lives.

The task for a critical theory of sustainability is to turn sustainability into a concept suited for the critique of capitalism, class, and power inequalities.

Note

1 Somalia, the country most at risk of climate change's impacts, was not included in the UN Human Development Report 2015.

References

Adorno, Theodor W., Hans Albert, Ralf Dahrendorf, Jürgen Habermas, Harald Pilot and Karl R. Popper. 1976. *The Positivist Dispute in German Sociology.* London: Heinemann.

Barro, Robert J. and Jong Wha Lee. 2013. A New Data Set of Educational Attainment in the World, 1950-2010. *Journal of Development Economics* 104: 184–198.

Beck, Ulrich. 1992. *Risk Society: Towards a New Modernity.* London: Sage.

Bell, Daniel. 1974. *The Coming of Post-Industrial Society.* London: Heinemann.

Bourdieu, Pierre. 1986. *Distinction: A Social Critique of the Judgement of Taste.* New York: Routledge.

Bukodi, Erzsébet and John H. Goldthorpe. 2013. Decomposing 'Social Origin': The Effects of Parents' Class, Status, and Education on the Educational Attainment of their Children. *European Sociological Review* 29 (5): 1024–1039.

Credit Suisse Research Institute (CSRI). 2015. *Global Wealth Databook 2015.* Zürich: Credit Suisse.

Credit Suisse Research Institute (CSRI). 2014. *Global Wealth Report 2014.* Zürich: Credit Suisse.

Deutz, Pauline. 2014. A Class-Based Analysis of Sustainable Development: Developing a Radical Perspective on Environmental Justice. *Sustainable Development* 22 (4): 243–252.

Enders, Judith C. and Moritz Remig. 2015. Theories of Sustainable Development: An Introduction. In *Theories of Sustainable Development*, ed. Judith C. Enders and Moritz Remig, 1–5. London: Routledge.

Foster, John Bellamy. 2002. *Ecology Against Capitalism.* New York. Monthly Review Press.

Fuchs, Christian. 2016a. Critical Theory. In *International Encyclopedia of Political Communication*, ed. Gianpietro Mazzoleni, Kevin Barnhurst, Ken'ichi Ikeda, Rouisley Mai and Hartmut Wessler. Hoboken, NJ: Wiley-Blackwell.

Fuchs, Christian. 2016b. *Critical Theory of Communication: New Readings of Lukács, Adorno, Marcuse, Honneth and Habermas in the Age of the Internet.* London: University of Westminster Press.

Fuchs, Christian. 2016c. *Reading Marx in the Information Age. A Media and Communication Studies Perspective on "Capital Volume I".* New York: Routledge.

Fuchs, Christian. 2014. The Dialectic: Not Just the Absolute Recoil, but the World's Living Fire That Extinguishes and Kindles Itself. Reflections on Slavoj Žižek's Version of Dialectical Philosophy in "Absolute Recoil: Towards a New Foundation of Dialectical Materialism". *tripleC: Communication, Capitalism & Critique* 12 (2): 848–875.

Fuchs, Christian. 2011. *Foundations of Critical Media and Information Studies.* New York: Routledge.

Fuchs, Christian. 2008. *Internet and Society: Social Theory in the Information Age.* New York: Routledge.

Fuchs, Christian. 2006. The Dialectic of the Nature-Society-System. *tripleC: Communication, Capitalism & Critique* 4 (1): 1–39.

Fuchs, Christian. 2003a. Some Implications of Pierre Bourdieu's Works for a Theory of Social Self-Organization. *European Journal of Social Theory* 6 (4): 387–408.

Fuchs, Christian. 2003b. Structuration Theory and Self-Organization. *Systemic Practice and Action Research* 16 (4): 133–167.

Giddens, Anthony. 1984. *The Constitution of Society. Outline of the Theory of Structuration.* Cambridge: Polity Press.

Giddings, Bob, Bill Hopwood and Geoff O'Brien. 2002. Environment, Economy and Society: Fitting Them Together into Sustainable Development. *Sustainable Development* 10 (4): 187–196.

Habermas, Jürgen. 1987. *Theory of Communicative Action. Vol. 2: Lifeworld and System.* Boston, MA: Beacon Press.

Harlow, John, Aaron Golub and Allenby Braden. 2011. A Review of Utopian Themes in Sustainable Development Discourse. *Sustainable Development* 21 (4): 270–280.

Heinrich Böll Foundation. 2002. *The Jo'burg Memo. Fairness in a Fragile World.* Berlin: Heinrich Böll Foundation.

Hopwood, Bill, Mary Mellor and Geoff O'Brien. 2005. Sustainable Development: Mapping Different Approaches. *Sustainable Development* 13 (1): 38–52.

International Labour Organization (ILO). 2015. *World Employment Social Outlook.* Geneva: International Labour Office.

Karabarbounis, Loukas and Brent Neiman. 2014. The Global Decline of the Labor Share. *The Quarterly Journal of Economics* 129 (1): 61–103.

Khan, M. Adil. 2015. Putting "Good Society" Ahead of Growth and/or "Development": Overcoming Neoliberalism's Growth Trap and its Costly Consequences. *Sustainable Development* 23 (2): 65–73.

Lukács, Georg. 1971. *History and Class Consciousness.* London: Merlin.

Luke, Timothy. 2005. Neither Sustainable nor Development: Reconsidering Sustainability in Development. *Sustainable Development* 13 (4): 228–238.

Magdoff, Fred and John Bellamy Foster. 2011. *What Every Environmentalist Needs to Know About Capitalism.* New York: Monthly Review Press.

Marx, Karl. 1988 [1844]. *Economic and Philosophic Manuscripts of 1844 and the Communist Manifesto.* Amherst, NY: Prometheus Books.

Marx, Karl. 1894. *Capital. Volume 3.* London: Penguin.

Marx, Karl. 1867. *Capital. Volume 1.* London: Penguin.

Marx, Karl. 1857/1858. *Grundrisse.* London: Penguin.

O'Connor, James. 1998. *Natural Causes. Essays in Ecological Marxism.* New York/London. Guilford Press.

O'Connor, James. 1994. Is Sustainable Capitalism Possible? In *Is Capitalism Sustainable?* ed. Martin O'Connor, 152–175. New York: Guilford Publications.

O'Mahony, Patrick and Tracey Skillington. 1996. Sustainable Development as an Organizing Principle for Discursive Democracy? *Sustainable Development* 4 (1): 42–51.

Parodi, Oliver. 2015. The Missing Aspect of Culture in Sustainability Concepts. In *Theories of Sustainable Development*, ed. Judith C. Enders and Moritz Remig, 169–187. London: Routledge.

Quental, Nuno, Júlia M. Lourenço and Fernando Nunes da Silva. 2011. Sustainable Development Policy: Goals, Targets and Political Cycles. *Sustainable Development* 19 (1): 15–29.

Redclift, Michael and Graham Woodgate. 2013. Sustainable Development and Nature: The Social and the Material. *Sustainable Development* 21 (2):92–100.

Redclift, Michael. 2005. Sustainable Development (1987-2005): An Oxymoron Comes of Age. *Sustainable Development* 13 (4): 212–227.

Serageldin, Ismail. 1995. The Human Face of the Urban Environment. In *Proceedings of the Second Annual World Bank Conference on Environmentally Sustainable Development: The Human Face of the Urban Environment*, ed. Ismail Serageldin et al., 16–20. September 19–21, 1994. Washington, D.C. World Bank.

Stiglitz, Joseph E., Amartya Sen and Jean-Paul Fitoussi. 2010. *Report by the Commission on the Measurement of Economic Performance and Social Progress.* Paris: Commission on the Measurement of Economic Performance and Social Progress.

Triventi, Moris. 2013. Stratification in Higher Education and its Relationship with Social Inequality: A Comparative Study of 11 European Countries. *European Sociological Review* 29 (3): 489–502.

United Nations. 2015. *Transforming Our World: The 2030 Agenda for Sustainable Development.* http://www.un.org/ga/search/view_doc.asp?symbol=A/RES/70/1&Lang=E

United Nations Conference on Environment & Development (UNCED). 1992. *Rio Declaration on Environment and Development. Adopted at the United Nations Conference on Environment & Development, Rio de Janeiro, Brazil, 3–14 June 1992.* http://www.un.org/documents/ga/conf151/aconf15126-1annex1.htm

United Nations Conference on Sustainable Development (UNCSD). 2012. *The Future We Want.* http://www.un.org/disabilities/documents/rio20_outcome_document_complete.pdf

United Nations Human Development Report 2015 (*UNHDR* 2015). New York: United Nations Development Programme.

United Nations University (UNU). 2014. *The Global E-Waste Monitor 2014. Quantities, Flows and Resources.* Tokyo: UNU-IAS.

World Commission on Environment and Development (WCED). 1987. *Our Common Future.* http://www.un-documents.net/our-common-future.pdf

World Summit on Sustainable Development (WSSD). 2002. *Johannesburg Declaration on Sustainable Development.* http://www.am.lt/VI/en/VI/files/0.038700001106642945.pdf

Ziegler, Rafael and Konrad Ott. 2015. The Quality of Sustainability Science: A Philosophical Perspective. In *Theories of Sustainable Development*, ed. Judith C. Enders and Moritz Remig, 43–64. London: Routledge.

Chapter Eight

The Relevance of C.L.R. James's Dialectical, Marxist-Humanist Philosophy in the Age of Donald Trump, Black Lives Matter, and Digital Capitalism

8.1 Introduction

Cyril Lionel Robert James (1901–1989) was a socialist theorist, activist, novelist, and journalist. He contributed to the development of Hegelian-Marxist Humanism. James was born and grew up in Trinidad. In 1932, he went to the UK to become a writer. He came in touch with the works of Marx, Lenin, and Trotsky and joined the Trotskyist movement. From 1938 until 1953, he lived in the USA. Together with Raya Dunayevskaya, he formed the Johnson-Forest Tendency. As socialist activist, James was engaged in anti-racist and anti-imperialist struggles. Among his best-known works are *The Black Jacobins: Toussaint L'Ouverture and the San Domingo Revolution*, *Beyond A Boundary*, *American Civilization*, *Mariners, Renegades and Castaways: The Story of Herman Melville and the World We Live In*, *Notes on Dialectics*, *A History of Pan-African Revolt*, *State Capitalism and World Revolution*; and *World Revolution, 1917–1936: The Rise and Fall of the Communist International*.

Selma James stresses that C.L.R. James's radical humanism led him to put an emphasis on the self-activity of the working class as key moment of socialist transformation: his "study of Marx and Lenin and of Hegel had led to uncovering a reading of Marx where the revolution was dependent on the self-activity of the working class, not on the leadership of a vanguard party. This was a Marx free of Stalinist influence. [...] the immediate question that CLR in his boldness began to address is: what kind of an

DOI: 10.4324/9781003199182-8

organization do you build which encourages rather than discourages self-activity?" (James 2012, 288). Stuart Hall (1998, 22) points out the importance of James's works for the critical understanding of the connection between racism and capitalism: James elevated "slavery to the world historical stage. That is the difference. And that has to do with the combination of Hegel and Marx, and his Caribbean background". Edward Said (1989, 128) characterises James as "a revolutionary champion of black struggle" and "a prodigiously gifted writer and political philosopher" (Said 1989, 128). In his biography of James, Buhle (2017, 169) writes: "He made Marxism coherent as a theory of mass revolt, and Leninism humane as an organized insight into the central role that Third World masses would play" (Buhle 2017, 169).

This chapter analyses James's interpretation of Hegel's dialectic. It focuses on the question: How relevant is C.L.R. James's dialectical philosophy today? Methodologically, the chapter discusses key aspects of James's philosophy and relates them to moments of contemporary society such as Donald Trump, fascism and racism today, digital capitalism, digital ideology, and Black Lives Matter. We give particular focus to James's (1980) book *Notes on Dialectics: Hegel, Marx, Lenin* (*NoD*) and his essay "Dialectical Materialism and the Fate of Humanity" (James 1989, 153–181).

Section 8.2 discusses James's concept of the dialectic and its focus on mediation and mediated communication. Section 8.3 analyses negative dialectics in the age of Donald Trump. Section 8.4 discusses ideology in the age of digital capitalism. Section 8.5's focus is on racism in the age of Black Lives Matter. Section 8.6 presents some conclusions.

8.2 Dialectical Mediation and Mediated Communication

8.2.1 Principles of the Dialectic

For James, the dialectic is a philosophy that studies change: "Dialectical logic is the science of tracing by what laws, in what way, notions, our concepts of things, change, to know that they change, to know how they change, constantly to examine these changes" (*NoD*, 55). Change takes place through contradictions that constitute negativity and the negation of this negativity into new contradictions:

> we are dealing with the spontaneous development of processes in real life, obvious also that any stage of these processes is a unity, consisting of opposites which are mutually exclusive but though unified are yet historically observable.

The next stage in the development (evolution) consists in the gathering strength of one of the opposites so that it overcomes the other, embraces it, and itself becomes the basis of a new stage in the Substance, in which the Subject, equally developing, is able to distinguish the new unity of further opposites.

(*NoD*, 8–9)

If we are analysing society we will note certain mass impulses, instinctive actions, spontaneous movements, the emergence of personalities, the incalculable activities which constitute a society. At a certain stage these apparently indeterminate activities coalesce into a hard knot [...] That knot constitutes the basis of new Substance. When the elements harden into a knot, Mind, Subject, can enter. Mind will observe, said Hegel, that the knot consists of two antagonistic elements locked together in unity. But it cannot remain as such. In a new historical period there are further impulses, instinctive actions, spontaneous movements, the emergence of personalities, calculable activities whereupon another knot is formed giving the basis to Subject, Mind, opportunity for further analysis.

(*NoD*, 9)

The question whether or not the dialectic exists only in society or also in nature has been hotly debated and contested in Marxist theory. Thinkers such as Lukács and Sartre stressed that the concept of dialectic of nature is prone to abuse by an undifferentiated application to society that results in mechanistic and deterministic concepts of society. They therefore argued that the dialectic only exists in the realm of humans. James shares with Lukács and Sartre the interest in Marxist Humanism, but does not deny that there is a dialectic of nature. He stresses that it is important to differentiate between how the dialectic works in the case of e.g. houses and mountains and in the realm of humans (*NoD*, 28). "Each object has its own particular dialectic, which is part of the general dialectic" (*NoD*, 28).

8.2.2 Mediation

In recent years, the concept of mediatisation has been used a lot in communication theory (see Fuchs 2020a, 69–73). "Mediatization therefore deals with the process in which these diverse types of media communication are established in varying contextual fields and the degree to which these fields are saturated with such types" (Hepp 2013, 68) "Mediatization, as defined here, means not only that the media play a role of their own determination, but that they at one and the same time have attained

Dialectical Mediation and Mediated Communication

the status of a semi-independent institution and provide the means by which other social institutions and players communicate" (Hjarvard 2013, 21). Krotz (2017, 108–109) sees mediatisation as "the transformation of everyday life, culture and society in the context of the transformation of the media". Mediatisation is the process where means of communication support the communication of human beings and play a role in society. It is a relational and processual concept. Based on Hegel, James uses the dialectical notion of mediation (*Vermittlung*) that goes beyond mediated communication and mediatisation in society. Mediation is the dialectical process of the reflection of contradictory moments that negate each other into each other. Moment A stands in a contradiction to moment B. A reaches into B. B reaches into A. Mediation is an aspect of society (including thought and communication) and nature.

> Mediated. A lovely word. Hug it to your bosom. I say, we say, that people's consciousness is one thing, immediacy, an entity that we can say has 'quality'. But as marxists we know that consciousness is in essence the reflection of economic and political, i.e. social environment. The social background, therefore, is mediated through consciousness. In the doctrine of Being, quality was, if you like, mediated into quantity. In the Doctrine of Essence quality is, or rather would be a Show of something which is reflecting itself through quality.
>
> (*NoD*, 80)

In the *Science of Logic*, Hegel introduces mediation as an aspect of the Doctrine of Essence. Mediation means "the concept as a system of *reflected determinations*, that is, of being as it passes over into the in-itselfness of the concept – a concept which is in this way not yet posited for itself *as such* but is also fettered by an immediate being still external to it" (Hegel 2010b, 40). "For mediation means to make a beginning and then to have proceeded to a second item, such that this second item is the way it is only insofar as one has arrived at it by starting with something that is an other over against it" (Hegel 2010a, 40, §12). Mediation grasps the relational and processual character of the dialectic in nature and society. A moment has an identity that exists in-itself. But nothing exists alone and in isolation. Something can only exist in relation to something else. Something is mediated with an Other:

> We have here, accordingly, two things: first, something immediate, a being *[Seiendes]*, and then, second, the same being as something mediated or posited. But now this is precisely the case when we reflect on an object or (as one would also say) *think it over [nachdenken]*. For what matters here is

not the object in its immediacy; we want instead to know *[wissen]* it as mediated. Indeed, according to the common construal of the task or purpose of philosophy, it is supposed to come to know the essence of things and that simply means that things are not supposed to be left in their immediacy but instead demonstrated to be mediated or justified by something else.

(Hegel 2010a, 174, addition to §112)

Raymond Williams (1983, 204–207) warns of the danger that one conceives of mediation in a dualistic manner as relation between separated moments. Adorno (1977, 374) points out that Hegel's notion of mediation operates in the object and not outside of it. Mediation is the process of how two dialectical moments negate each other, reach into each other, and sublate (*aufheben*) each other. "Hegel wants to say that the mediation is in the thing itself and not between several things" (Adorno 1993, 114).

Communication can only be found in humans and society as it presupposes consciousness and conscious production. Mediation and media can be found in all dialectical processes, i.e. in nature and society. Media and mediation are more general concepts than communication and mediatisation. Media are structures that enable and condition the relation between two dialectical moments so that One is reflected into an Other and the Other is reflected into the One. Mediation is the process of this reflection and interaction. In society, there is a dialectic of communication and media. Wolfgang Hofkirchner (2013) and Klaus Fuchs-Kittowski (1999, 2021) argue that information can be found in natural and social system. Hofkirchner (2013) points out that there is "mediation via a sign structure" (164) in physical, biological, and social systems. In physical systems, information as mediating structure takes on the form of patterns. In biological systems, it takes on the form of codes. And in human-social system, it takes on the form of sense/meaning (Hofkirchner 2013, 173–184). For Fuchs-Kittowski (1999, 342; 2021, figure 1), information is a triadic relation of form, content, and effect that exists on the levels of macromolecules, the nervous system, conscious individuals, and society. Hofkirchner and Fuchs-Kittowski conceive of information as dialectical and processual, which corresponds to Hegel's notion of mediation. Based on Hegel's and James's notion of mediation, Table 8.1 present the approach of the present author. It provides an overview of the role of media and mediation in nature and society. It identifies actors, media, and mediation processes at various levels of the organisation of matter.

Let us return to the question of mediatisation, or, as we say in Marxist theory, the role of the means of communication in society. James was very interested in the analysis of media, communication, and culture.

Dialectical Mediation and Mediated Communication

TABLE 8.1 Media and mediation in nature and society

Realm of Being	Medium	Mediation process	Actors
Inanimate matter	energy	movement of physical things	physical things
living beings	organism, environment	self-reproduction of cells and cell structures	cells
animal world	environment, nervous system, brain, organism	signal interpretation from the environment and responses to signals	animal
humanity	brain, body	thought, consciousness, self-consciousness	human individual
humanity	environment, nervous system, brain, sense organs (skin, tongue, nose, eyes, ears)	signal interpretation from the environment and active, conscious responses to signals	human individual
humanity	peripheral nerves, neurotransmitters, hormones, blood	inter-organic communication	human individual
humanity	cell adhesion molecules, gap junctions, extracellular matrix, neurotransmitters, growth factors, cytokines, hormones	intercellular communication	human individual
humanity	enzymes, helicase, gyrase, proteins, primase, DNA polymerase, nucleotide triphosphate, DNA ligase, mRNA, tRNA	intracellular communication	human individual
society	social structures	communication, social production	human individuals and groups
society: economy	resources, means of production	production of use-values	workers
society: politics	rules	production of collective decisions	citizens
society: culture	identities, ways of life, norms, moral, values	production of meanings	humans
society: media system	public sphere, information, and communication technologies	production of public information	media producers, audiences, users

8.2.3 The Means of Communication

Popular culture and communication was one of the topics that James continuously wrote about, including cricket, literature, visual art, and film. He wrote short stories and novels and worked as sports journalist and commentator. Whereas the mediatisation concept focuses on the media system, mediation is a more general dialectical notion. In society, we find a media system where mediation takes on the form of communication between conscious human beings that is mediated by means of communication. The media system is the totality of the means of communication and their uses in society. We can distinguish between five types of the means of communication depending on whether or not the production, distribution, and reception of information is mediated by media technology or not (see Fuchs 2020a, 159, table 6.2). For example, in Internet communication, digital machines and digital networks mediate the production, distribution, and consumption of information and consumers of information can act as prosumers (producing consumers) who generate digital content (Fuchs 2021).

There are three important moments in James's analysis of the means of communication. *First*, he stresses that in class societies, there are means of communication that disseminate ideologies:

> These concrete realities are reinforced by the literature and art of the system. The worker does not create these. He does not ask for anti-Negro literature. As workers do in every country, he reads the books, newspapers, and goes to the shows. From every one of these organs of communication and education his daily impressions about Negroes are reinforced. Movies reflect the society in which they are produced. The white worker constantly sees the Negro on the screen in situations which merely confirm his knowledge of the realities he himself has experienced. In books and magazines, all grace, strength, beauty, nobility, courage are automatically attributed to members of the white race. It isn't that the books are openly or even subtly anti-Negro. It is that in the mental and emotional stimulation which they provide, good or bad, the Negro is usually excluded. If he is included, he is placed in his usual menial position, made the butt of jokes or at the very best is portrayed as a good and loyal servant.
>
> (James 1996, 47)

James (1993, chapter 5) observes that during the Great Depression, US entertainment strongly focused on violence, sadism, and cruelty on the one hand and stars on the other hand as ways of how audiences release aggression, fears, and hopes. James (1993) points out that such entertainment offers are ways of how audiences release aggression (122) and flee from alienation (147).

Second, James writes that bourgeois culture keeps art ("high culture", "serious culture") and popular culture ("low culture", "entertainment culture") separate. He argues for their integration, "the coalescence of the cultural tradition with the popular audience" (James 1992, 253). James (1993, 36) argues that in the 20th century, popular film, popular music, and literature as "form of art and media of social communication"

Dialectical Mediation and Mediated Communication

resulted in artistic creations that "have hitherto been unknown in the history of civilization". James was an autodidact. What impressed him about the rise of the mass media is that he saw them as potential opportunities of learning that were cheaply accessible to a vast number of individuals (James 1989, 272).

James suggests that public service broadcasters should integrate different forms of programmes on one channel. "A great government corporation, like the British Broadcasting Corporation, frankly divides its cultural programme into two parts, the Third programme for the cultivated and popularisation for the mass" (James 1992, 253). The implication is that one should not create specialised content ghettos limited to specific channels, where similar content appeals to one group, but embrace diversity within one channel. Today, the commercialisation of the media system has resulted in an extreme fragmentation of the public sphere. As a consequence, human groups with different and opposing interests lack opportunities for common information and debate, which has created filter bubbles, where like-minded individuals meet in communicative ghettos that are isolated from each other. The alternative are lager public spheres where diverse humans engage with culture, encounter each other, debate, quarrel, agree, disagree, etc.

Third, James was interested in non-capitalist means of communication. For James (1992, 174), socialism means the end of society's mediation by capital, class relations, and the state. Socialism establishes an immediate unit of object and subject, the idea and the real, the concrete and the abstract (ibid.). The alternative to capitalist ownership is for James workers's self-management. He argues that self-management is also important in the context of the means of communication:

> The proletariat in England has some property, though not much. It has education, in some respects, social respects, the most advanced experience in the country. It has a press. It has a network of strategic positions – ask the bourgeoisie. It has a hierarchy of institutions. And what it hasn't got it could take over in 24 hours. *The Times? The Guardian?* The proletariat could take over that material and run it within two hours. In fact they run them now. As a matter of fact in Arab countries and in the rest of the underdeveloped countries, they know enough politics to know that when they make a revolution the first thing to do is to rush for the radio station. When they get hold of it they know what to say.
>
> (James 1999, 58)

Today, in the context of digital capitalism there are discussions about the creation of platform co-operatives (Scholz and Schneider 2016). A platform co-operative is a self-managed Internet platform that is owned and governed by digital workers. An example is the music streaming platform Resonate, an alternative to Spotify. Capitalist music streaming platforms have been criticised for undermining and reducing royalty payments to artists and contributing to precarious living conditions of musicians. Resonate pays artists a fair price for every streamed song. Let us have a look at how Resonate describes itself:

> STREAMING services wield too much power over discovery, and 'big pool' methods of splitting royalties are unfair. [...] INEFFICIENCIES plague the music industry and often lead to slow, inaccurate royalty payouts. [...] THE CO-OPERATIVE model fundamentally differentiates Resonate from other services. A one-member, one-share, one-vote system brings democracy to the platform, and gives all members a voice.[1]

In October 2020, there were 1,900 artists and 13,000 tracks on Resonate.[2] At the same time, there were more than 60 million tracks on Spotify.[3] Platform co-operatives and alternative projects have problems challenging and competing with capitalist monopoly corporations. Precarious resources and precarious labour are often the consequence of alternative, non-capitalist projects in a capitalist society. Is small always beautiful? Or is it rather precarious? Public service Internet platforms provided by public service media are viable, large scale non-capitalist alternatives to capitalist platforms such as YouTube (Fuchs 2021, chapter 15).

Having focused on the foundations of James's dialectical philosophy, we will next discuss negative dialectics in the age of Donald Trump. There are inherent potentials of capitalism to create catastrophes and barbarism. For critically analysing these potentials, James focuses on negative dialectics.

8.3 Negative Dialectics in the Age of Donald Trump

8.3.1 Negative Dialectics

James (1992, 155) argues that the contradiction is the fundamental law of dialectics. Capitalism is an antagonistic system. It creates on the one hand potentials for a society where all benefit and lead a good life and at the same time undermines the realisation of these potentials.

> Capitalism, being the greatest wealth-producing system so far known, has carried its contradictions to a pitch never known before. Thus it is that the moment when the world system of capitalism has demonstrated the greatest productive powers

in history is exactly the period when barbarism threatens to engulf the whole of society. The anti-dialecticians stand absolutely dumbfounded before the spectacle of the mastery of nature for human advancement and the degradation of human nature by this very mastery. The greater the means of transport, the less men are allowed to travel. The greater the means of communication, the less men freely interchange ideas. The greater the possibilities of living, the more men live in terror of mass annihilation.

(James 1992, 155)

James outlines a negative dialectic of capitalism that resembles Horkheimer and Adorno's (2002) dialectic of the Enlightenment. Horkheimer and Adorno (2002/1947, xvi) write that capitalism is based on the logic of the "self-destruction of enlightenment" (2002/1947, xvi) that advances "the reversion of enlightened civilization to barbarism" (xix). Capitalism's negative dialectic negates liberalism's own values such as the human rights. Its structures of exploitation and domination call forth inhumanity and barbarous catastrophes such as Auschwitz. Horkheimer (2004/1947, v) points out that in capitalism, Enlightenment tends to nullify itself and transform into its opposite, namely dehumanisation: "Advance in technical facilities for enlightenment is accompanied by a process of dehumanization. Thus progress threatens to nullify the very goal it is supposed to realize – the idea of man" (Horkheimer 2004/1947, v).

Dialectic of the Enlightenment was first published in 1944 and in its final version in 1947. James's essay "Dialectical Materialism and the Fate of Humanity", from which the longer quote just cited is taken, appeared in 1947. During and after the Second World War, Marxist thinkers wanted to make sense of how catastrophes such as Auschwitz or the transatlantic slave trade were possible. James, Horkheimer, and Adorno arrived at very similar conclusions. James added aspects of slavery to the negative dialectic of the Enlightenment.

8.3.2 Authoritarian Capitalism: Neoliberalism's Negative Dialectic

In the 1980s, Ronald Reagan and Margaret Thatcher were pioneers of neoliberal governance that dismantles welfare states and focuses on privatisation, deregulation of labour markets, the smashing of trade unions, the commodification of everything, and the advancement of the interests of transnational corporations. Reagonomics and Thatcherism influenced governments all over the world so that neoliberalism became a dominant global mode of capitalist regulation (see Harvey 2005).

Neoliberalism has advanced inequalities between the rich and the poor, labour and capital, urban and rural areas, global metropolises and deindustrialised regions, etc. The Gini coefficient is a measure of wealth and income inequality. It ranges between 0% and 100%. A Gini coefficient of 0% means that everyone controls the same amount of wealth, whereas a Gini coefficient of 100% means that one person owns everything and others own nothing. In the USA, Gini inequality increased from 34.5% in 1979 to 41.1% in 2016. In the UK, it increased from 28.4% in 1979 to 34.8% in 2016.[4]

Neoliberalism resulted in a negative dialectic of liberalism: the liberalisation of markets and increasing inequalities backfired against the basic freedom and moral values that liberalism propagates. New authoritarian forces emerged and gained power that constitute foundations of a new model of capitalism – authoritarian capitalism. Authoritarian capitalism advances top-down leadership, nationalism, the friend/enemy scheme (racism; xenophobia; hatred of socialists, liberals, intellectuals, experts, academics, liberal media, etc.), and militant patriarchy (law & order politics, militarism, warfare as means for managing conflicts, sexist politics) (Fuchs 2018). Together, these elements together distract attention from actual class inequality and structures of exploitation.

The biggest danger of authoritarian capitalism is the abolishment of democracy, the establishment of fascist regimes that practice and institutionalise terror, and the explosion of nationalism into a world war. James warned of fascism as consequence of capitalism's negative dialectic. For James, fascism and Stalinism were the complete negation of socialism that he conceived of as the essence of socialism. "The Stalinist state, the Nazi state, and in their varying degrees all states today, based upon property and privilege, are the negation of the complete democracy of the people. It is this state which is to be destroyed, that is to say, it is this state which is to be negated by the proletarian revolution" (James 1992, 161). For James, fascism is a form of Bonapartism that is capitalist, elevates the party above the state, suppresses socialist revolution and its forces, mobilises nationalism, and organises a war-waging one-party state (*NoD*, 177–178) – "the monster state" (*NoD*, 177). "There is no solution to the problems of society except every cook and every worker to a man administers the state and the economy. […] Without *that* you get fascism, imperialist war, barbarism of all kinds" (*NoD*, 203).

Forty years after the start of the Reagan- and Thatcher-eras, Donald Trump governs the USA and Boris Johnson the UK. In a comment in *The Telegraph*, Johnson (2018) wrote: "I would go further and say that it is absolutely ridiculous that people should choose to go

Negative Dialectics in the Age of Donald Trump

around looking like letter boxes" and "looking like a bank robber" (Johnson 2018). In another *Telegraph* comment, Johnson referred to Africans as "crowds of flag-waving piccaninnies" and "tribal warriors" who "break out in watermelon smiles" (Johnson 2002). Johnson compares black people and Muslims to things (letter boxes), criminals, and fruits. He denies these groups' humanity and ridicules them in order to construct scapegoats.

Also Trumps constructs scapegoats. Let us have a look at the tweet in Figure 8.1.

In this tweet, Trump constructs Latin American as traffickers, drug dealers, and criminals. He argues for law and order politics in the form of "STRONG Border Security" and building a border wall. He claims that Latin Americans mean "no Security". By using capitalisation ("STRONG", "KEEP OUT!") he presents himself as strongman who takes tough measures to keep immigrants out. Racism, top-down leadership, the friend/enemy-scheme, and law and order politics are key elements of authoritarianism.

How would C.L.R. James assess Trump and Johnson? He'd argue that authoritarian politics are the result of capitalism's exclusion of workers from the administration of the state and the economy and argue for a socialist politics that advances self-management through concrete measures so that economic and political alienation is reduced. "Marx said that capitalism would inevitably come to the stage where the workers would take over. If they don't or can't, he added, society would relapse into barbarism. Look at the world we live in and judge" (James 2013, 146)

James was interested in the Hegelian notions of essence and truth and in ideology critique. The next section will focus on James's analysis of ideology.

With Caravans marching through Mexico and toward our Country, Republicans must be prepared to do whatever is necessary for STRONG Border Security. Dems do nothing. If there is no Wall, there is no Security. Human Trafficking, Drugs and Criminals of all dimensions – KEEP OUT!

11:03 PM · Feb 3, 2019 · Twitter for iPhone

29K Retweets   **3.7K** Quote Tweets   **126.2K** Likes

FIGURE 8.1   Tweet by Donald Trump, https://twitter.com/realDonaldTrump/status/1092181733825490945

8.4 Ideology in the Age of Digital Capitalism

8.4.1 Socialism as Essence and Truth

In the *Science of Logic*'s section on the Doctrine of Essence, Hegel introduces the notion of Essence:

> The immediate being of things is represented here, as it were, as a crust or as a curtain behind which the essence is hidden. – The further claim that 'all things have an essence' is a way of declaring that they are not truly what they immediately show themselves to be. It then is also not enough merely to traipse from one quality to another and merely proceed from the qualitative to the quantitative and vice versa; instead, there is something enduring in things and this primarily is the essence.
>
> (Hegel 2010a, 174, addition to §112)

A thing's essence is its true and fundamental character. The essence is not always and not automatically visible. It can be hidden behind appearances. "The essence is the fact that something continually becomes something else and negates it because it isn't what the thing that is becoming wants to be" (*NoD*, 76).

Based on Marx's philosophical writings, James argues that the human being's essence is that humans are social beings who work and thereby produce and reproduce society:

> Marx's philosophy was a philosophy of the activity of man, of man as active in the labour process. The free individual was he whose labour by its very nature ensured his freedom. If he was not free in his labour he could not be free in any sense. [...] Family, education, relations between the sexes, religion, all would lose their destructive alienated quality in a new mode of production in which the universality of the individual would be the starting point and source of all progress, beginning with economic progress.
>
> (James 1984, 67, 69)

A socialist society, where political and economic alienation are overcome and humans collectively self-manage the economy and politics beyond class and the state is for James the essence of humans and society. "The need and desire for socialism, for complete democracy, for complete freedom, that is the 'real' nature of man" (James 1992, 162). James (2013, 119) sees freedom as self-realisation and creativity of all, "creative universality".

While Hegel's Doctrine of Being focuses on the world's contradictions and dialectical development and the Doctrine of Essence deals with the essences, grounds, and truths that are hidden behind appearances, the Doctrine of the Notion/Concept is the world of consciousness, ideas, and human thought, where humans interpret being and essence. The Concept/Notion/Idea is the subject-object, the subject's interpretation of the object. "the absolutely concrete, and indeed is so insofar as it contains in itself being and essence, and accordingly contains the entire richness of these two spheres in an ideal *[ideeller]* unity" (Hegel 2010a, addition to §160, 233). The Doctrine of the Notion culminates in the Absolute Idea, which is "the absolute truth" (Hegel 2010a, §162, 235). "The idea is the *adequate concept*, the objectively *true*, or the *true as such*" (Hegel 2010b, 670).

James outlines that for Hegel truth means the correspondence of essence and existence of a phenomenon (*NoD*, 43–47).

> In the philosophical sense, by contrast, truth means in general the agreement of a content with itself, to put it abstractly [...] Coincidentally, the deeper (i.e. philosophical) meaning of truth can already be found to some extent in the ordinary use of language. Thus, for instance, we speak of a *true* friend and mean by that someone whose way of acting conforms to the concept of friendship. Similarly, we speak of a *true* work of art. Untrue then means as much as bad, something in itself inadequate. In this sense, a bad state is an untrue state, and what is bad and untrue generally consists in the contradiction that obtains between the determination or the concept and the concrete existence of the object.
>
> (Hegel 2010a, 62, addition 1 to §24)

For Hegel, truth lies in totality. "The true is the whole. However, the whole is only the essence completing itself through its own development. This much must be said of the absolute: It is essentially a *result*, and only at the *end* is it what it is in truth" (Hegel 2018, 13). And this focus on the truth of the whole brings Hegel in his *Logic* to the notion of the Absolute Idea. "The idea as the unity of the subjective and the objective idea is the concept of the idea, for which the idea as such is the object *[Gegenstand]*, for which it is the object *[Objekt]* – an object *[Objekt]* into which all determinations have gone together. This unity is accordingly the *absolute and entire truth*, the idea thinking itself, and here, indeed, *as* thinking, as the *logical* idea" (Hegel 2010a, 299, §236).

For Hegel, "God alone is the true agreement of the concept with reality" (Hegel 2010a, 62, addition 1 to §24), the absolute and entire truth if the world. James interprets truth at the level of society as totality and argues that socialism is a true society: "The Absolute Idea has another truth, the inner truth of the Idea itself, a truly democratic non-bourgeois socialist international" (*NoD*, 43). James here seems to have the socialist international as political movement and "the abolition of the distinction between party and mass" (*NoD*, 180) in working-class self-activity in mind. But of the socialist movement's goal is (international) socialism, as James points out: "When the masses, not the philosophers, grasp the dialectic, the logic, the unity of theoretical, practical, methodological, we have reached the Absolute Idea of society, i.e., social man. There begins the development of human power for its own sake" (James 1949, 1626). Raya Dunayevskaya (1958) argues that working class struggles for Humanist Socialism are an "acting out of Hegel's Absolute Idea" (Dunayevskaya 1958, 37) and the Absolute Idea is "the new society gestating in the old" (Dunayevskaya 2002, 24). Dunayevskaya (1958, 125) particularly has Marx's (1867, 928) formulation in mind that the capitalist antagonism of productive forces and relations of production creates "new forces and new passions" that "spring up in the bosom of society". Socialism is society's Absolute Idea, the unity of the social Essence and Existence of humanity and society. James and Dunayevskaysa remind us that socialism is both subject and object, social movement and society, praxis and totality. The Absolute Idea operates at both levels. It is the subject-object of socialism. Hegel (2010a) argues that the Absolute Idea means "*reason*" (§214, 284), the "*truth* of the good" (§235, 299), "*the absolute and entire truth*" (§236, 299). By combining Hegel and Marx, James and Dunayevskaysa show that socialism is reason in society, society's truth that means a good life of all.

For James (1992, 153), socialism is "the complete expression of democracy", the Absolute Idea of society. Socialism abolishes exploitation and domination, it is the negation of the negation of alienation. It means humans' democratic control of the conditions that shape their working life, politics, and culture. James's dialectic contributes to "the conception of a participatory democratic ethos, and not, or at least not directly, to any figuration of the ideal structures and institutions of a democratic state" (Douglas 2008, 438)

In socialist society, the human being becomes truly human "by the release of his human function – creative action in labour" (*NoD*, 175) under the conditions of the abolition of the division of labour, a high development of the productive forces, the abolition of classes, etc., which includes the abolition of the division between "manual and intellectual labour" and between "being and knowing" (*NoD*, 175). For James, this means the disappearance of the party and the state and the organisation of the economy and politics under direct workers' control (*NoD*, 176). James argues that every cook should learn to govern, and every worker should become an administrator of the economy and the state so that "the party as knowing could not be in opposition to the proletariat as being" and would wither away (*NoD*, 176).

8.4.2 Alienation and Ideology

Actuality means the correspondence of Essence and Existence. Not everything that exists, i.e. real being, is actual. Hegel writes that "*what is reasonable is actual, and what is actual is reasonable*" (Hegel 1970, §6, 47, translation from German). Hegel thereby does not mean that everything that exists is reasonable. In contrast, Hegel opposes positivism. The Actual is reasonable because it is existence that has been made reasonable through social struggles. The Actual is a manifestation or anticipation of the good society. In his discussion of Hegel's *Philosophy of Right* (where Hegel first used the formulation that actuality is reasonable and reason is actual), Marx (1843, 266) writes: "That the rational is actual is proved precisely in the *contradiction* of *irrational actuality*, which everywhere is the contrary of what it asserts, and asserts the contrary of what it is". The Actual is the sublation of unreasonable conditions such as exploitation, domination, and ideology. In his reading of Hegel's *Science of Logic*, Herbert Marcuse (1941/1955, 149) argues: "The essence can 'achieve' its existence when the potentialities of things have ripened in and through the conditions of reality. Hegel describes this process as the transition into actuality".

For Marx (1844), alienation means that humans do not control their conditions of existence. Alienation means that a product is "*alien, hostile,* powerful object independent of" humans (278), "a *power independent* of the producer" (272). Alienation means that humans and society cannot realise their potentials and Essence. Class society alienates humans from their and society's Essence. It reduces humans to the status of animals, things, and machines by turning them into instruments that are dominated and exploited. For Hegel, "without thought there is no man, not a damned thing but another animal. Man thinks or he is nothing – another animal. Marx (from this point of view) will say the same thing: 'The proletariat is revolutionary or it is nothing'. The proletariat is revolutionary or it is just another animal" (*NoD*, 163–164).

For James, Stalinist Russia was the alienation of socialism from its Essence so that it turned into socialism's opposite, a specific form of capitalism. James argues that both Bernsteinism, i.e. revisionist social democracy, and Stalinism meant that organisation "had become an end in itself" (*NoD*, 116) in the form of top-down, bureaucratic control of the working class. Organisation became an Actuality that was alienated from the

Essence of socialism (*NoD,* 117). The solution would be to introduce spontaneity – "the free creative activity of the proletariat" (*NoD,* 117). Bernsteinism and Stalinism are an alienation of Existence from Essence. The Soviet system was an alienated society and as ideology alienated consciousness. James argues that Stalinism and Bernsteinism meat that the petty bourgeoisie as administrative caste controlled the working class (*NoD,* 200–201, 219–220).

At the level of consciousness, ideology is the attempt to create alienated consciousness, consciousness that cannot see the essence of the world. " *'ideological' is a social reality whose very existence implies the non-knowledge of its participants as to its essence*" (Žižek 1989/2008, 21). More than this, we can add that fetishism and ideology aim at reducing the working class' critical capacities so that workers are influenced by bourgeois thought and forget their own interest. Ideology reifies consciousness: it tries to reduce humans to the status of things and animals that do not think freely and creatively. For Marx, the human being is not just, as for Hegel, a conscious and thinking being, but a working and producing and social being.

The dialectic of proletarian consciousness means that the proletarian class' consciousness is situated, can shift and develop on a continuum between two extremes: in the most radical case, it turns into its opposite, namely bourgeois consciousness, it then becomes "permeated through and through with a capitalist content"; on the opposite end of the spectrum, it is socialist consciousness that realises "truer, more rich, more clear, i.e. more concrete, categories of its own truly proletarian nature, its unending fight against capital" (*NoD,* 58). False consciousness of the proletariat means a "contradiction between *its* consciousness and its being" (*NoD,* 59). The "contradiction between the proletariat and its consciousness" is a part and form of "the contradiction between capital and labour" (*NoD,* 59).

James (1992, 155) outlines that bourgeois ideology postulates "the inevitability of bourgeois society, natural division of labour, more particularly of men into capitalists and workers, constantly expanding technical progress, constantly expanding production, constantly expanding democracy, constantly rising culture". Dialectical logic is anti-ideological. It challenges the logic of inevitability and domination without alternatives. It stresses that the antagonisms of capitalism and class societies create social problems and inequalities.

Let us next discuss ideology in digital capitalism.

Ideology in the Age of Digital Capitalism

8.4.3 Digital Capitalism's Ideology

In 2020, Facebook was the world's 39th largest transnational corporation.[5] In 2019, it made profits of US$21 billion. It is one of the largest digital corporations operating in digital capitalism.

For attracting users, Facebook presents itself as social medium that empowers communities and brings humans together. Facebook's mission statement therefore reads: "Mission: Give people the power to build community and bring the world closer together".[6] Facebook furthermore claims: "Our products empower more than 3 billion people around the world to share ideas, offer support and make a difference. [...] Our services help people connect, and when they're at their best, they bring people closer together".[7] "At the Facebook company, we are constantly iterating, solving problems and working together to connect people all over the world through our apps and technologies".[8]

Facebook's self-promotion sounds like it advances an unalienated, socialist society where humans live together in solidarity. It appeals to the social experiences that users make at the level of the interface, i.e. the level of users' existence. But as Hegel and James tell us, there are essences behind appearances that often remain hidden. When Facebook speaks to its users, it employs a positivistic, ideological language that claims there are trillions of advantages that the company advances. It operates purely at the level of use-value. Users do not directly experience their online activities' and data's commodification that generates Facebook's profits. Exchange-value and commodity exchange remain hidden from the users. Facebook hides its exploitation of users' activities, their digital labour that creates data and content and online attention that Facebook uses for selling targeted ads and making massive profits (Fuchs 2021).

Let us have a look at some excerpts from pages where Facebook talks to another type of actor, namely its customers, those who are interested to buy ads on Facebook:

> Millions of businesses, big and small, connect with people on Facebook.
>
> Make connections that matter. 2.5 billion people use Facebook every month to connect with friends and family and to discover things that matter. Find new customers and build lasting relationships with them.[9]
>
> You also choose who you want to see your ad. You can use demographics, such as age, gender and current cities, to connect with people, or things such as interests, devices or past actions.[10]

> If you have ads on a Facebook platform, you have Facebook measurement.
>
> Anyone can get started with Facebook measurement. If you have ads running on Facebook, Instagram, Messenger or Audience Network, visit Ads Manager, where you can monitor your campaign performance, view reach and demographics breakdowns and review the cost of your ads over any period of time.[...] With Facebook, you can learn more about your audience.[11]

Facebook here argues with the mass of users on its platforms in order to attract advertising customers. It points out that it has big data of users that allows targeting ads and that in addition big data allows audience measurement and access of advertising to audience measurement data.

Whereas Facebook's language focuses on the qualities of community, the social, empowerment, connection when it addresses users, it focuses on quantitative categories such as measurement, large user numbers, big data, campaign performance, campaign reach, demographic breakdowns, ad costs, etc. when speaking to advertisers. This linguistic gap reveals that Facebook uses an engaging/connecting/sharing-ideology (Fuchs 2021, chapter 10) that stresses the social in order to hide its logic of operation that drives its capital accumulation model, namely the collection of big data, audience measurement, and the sale of more and more ads that are targeted at users. Facebook's idealisation of the social tries to hide its exploitation of its users' activities and that users perform digital labour. While Facebook's Essence is the exploitation of digital labours, the Appearance it wants to create to users is that it is purely focused on the use-values of sociality and community. We know from James that ideology means attempts to hide domination and exploitation from the dominated and exploited. By spreading the engaging/connecting/sharing-ideology, Facebook tries to create a contradiction between the digital proletariats' "consciousness and its being" (*NoD*, 59). James would say that the existence of digital ideology shows that there is a contradiction between digital capital and digital labour.

"In fact Hegel says there are three broad divisions of cognition. 1. Simple, everyday, common sense, vulgar empiricism, ordinary perception. 2. Understanding. 3. Dialectic" (*NoD*, 18). The first one is intuition. Also the dialectic requires empiricism and understanding that fixes the world in categories (*NoD*, 20). But only as its starting point. "Understanding is dialectic to the extent that it negates" (*NoD*, 20). Understanding creates differences, it differentiates and separates. Ideologies, such as Facebook's digital ideology of engaging/connecting/sharing, operate at the level of common sense and empiricism.

In the Doctrine of the Notion, Hegel (2010b, 689–734) distinguishes between different forms of cognition: analytical cognition (e.g. arithmetic and analysis in mathematics; the analysis of identity and immediacy), synthetic cognition (the analysis of mediation, difference, contradictions; the analysis of the universal, the particular and the individual), the Absolute Idea ("Dialectic Cognition", "the Cognition of Creative Cognition", James 1980, 157). "the absolute idea alone is *being*, imperishable *life*, *self-knowing truth*, and is *all truth*. It is the sole subject matter and content of philosophy" (Hegel 2010b, 735). Dialectical logic is the mode of thought, the method, of the Absolute Idea. James in his discussion of the Hegelian forms of cognition outlines that analytical cognition "is concerned only with what simply *is*", synthetic cognition grasps differences that "divide the object" and sees their unity (James 1980, 158). The Absolute Idea is dialectical thought that grasps the world's identity, differences, contradictions, unity of contradictions, nodal points of change where quantity turns into new qualities, negations of negations, sublations. It is based on and sublates analytical and synthetic thought. In it, dialectical moments are sublated, eliminated, preserved, and constituted at a higher level. These are dialectical moments such as "*subject-object, [...] the unity of the ideal and the real, of the finite and the infinite, of the soul and the body, as the possibility that can only be conceived as existing*, and so forth" (Hegel 2010a, §214, 284–285).

Digital ideology operates at the level of analytical cognition. It tries to convince users that their immediate experience of sociality is society's truth. Critical reason operates at the level of dialectical cognition. It analyses Facebook and sees the promises it makes to its users. It identifies the underlying capitalist interest of Facebook as essence and moment that contradicts the users' interest. Three of the major criticisms of Facebook are that a) the corporation's big data practices violate users' privacy, b) commodify users' online behaviour, and c) have enabled the emergence of online fake news that, as the Cambridge Analytica scandal showed, threatens democracy (Fuchs 2021, chapter 6). The dialectic stresses the potentials of sublation (*Aufhebung*) and the negation of the negation. Analysing Facebook, James would call users to engage in digital class struggles and create self-managed alternatives to Facebook, digital capital, and digital capitalism. James would today be an advocate of digital socialism (Fuchs 2020b).

The analysis of racism was an important aspect of James's work. We will next focus on this dimension.

8.5 Racism in the Age of Black Lives Matter

8.5.1 Racism and Capitalism

James pinpoints the inherent connection of racism and capitalism in the following manner: "They have been lynching me and my people, giving us the dirtiest jobs, at the lowest pay, Jim Crowing us, taking the taxes we pay to teach white children, treating us worth than they treat their dogs" (James 1996, 19–20).

Racism is an ideology that propagates and practices the inferiority of certain groups that are identified as "races" or cultures or nations or ethnicities. It is also a mode of governance, a politics that discriminates against racialised groups. And it is a mode of production in which racialised groups face high levels of exploitation. Racism is not an economy or a politics or an ideology. It is all of that. Racism is a system of power.

James stresses that the origins and development of capitalism were based on the exploitation of slaves: "the wealth which went toward the building up of the bourgeoisie so that they could challenge the ancient regime came from the slave trade and slavery" (James 1984, 193). In a comparable manner, Marx wrote: "The slave-owner buys his worker in the same way as he buys his horse. If he loses his slave, he loses a piece of capital, which he must replace by fresh expenditure on the slave-market. [...] For slave trade, read labour-market, for Kentucky and Virginia, Ireland and the agricultural districts of England, Scotland and Wales, for Africa, Germany" (Marx 1867, 377, 378)

James points out that there is an inherent connection of imperialism and racism. Capitalism's origins were based on the imperialist conquer of Africa that resulted in slave trade:

> Imperialism vaunts its exploitation of the wealth of Africa for the benefit of civilisation. In reality, from the very nature of its system of production for profit it strangles the real wealth of the continent-the creative capacity of the African people.
>
> (James 1989, 377)

European contact with Africa began with the rise of European imperialism. A new continent, America, was discovered and Africa, which had always lain within easy reach of European ships, was penetrated. Commercial capitalism developed the mercantile system, which needed labor in the American tropical plantation. When the Indians proved unsatisfactory, slaves were brought from Africa. On the basis of the wealth created by the slave trade and the colonial trade directly dependent upon it, the commercial capitalists of Europe and

America built up from their ranks a new section of the capitalist class, the industrial capitalists. These, whose chief function was the application of large-scale organization and science to industry, came inevitably into conflict with the planters: slave labor was too expensive, too backward for the new methods. This economic conflict was the basis for political conflict. The commercial bourgeoisie and the feudal aristocracy still had the political power their former economic predominance had given them, and for the new rising class of industrial bourgeoisie, to wrest it from them meant a struggle.

(James 1996, 96–97)

W.E.B. Du Bois (1935/1998) analyses slavery in the United States. He writes that slavery is "the ultimate degradation of" humans (Du Bois 1935/1998, 9). Slaves are treated like chattel and things (10), which makes slaves "the ultimate exploited" (15). Slavery is based on "direct barter in human flesh" (11). "Here is the real modern labor problem. Here is the kernel of the problem of Religion and Democracy, of Humanity. Words and futile gestures avail nothing. Out of the exploitation of the dark proletariat comes the Surplus Value filched from human beasts which, in cultured lands, the Machine and harnessed Power veil and conceal. The emancipation of man is the emancipation of labor and the emancipation of labor is the freeing of that basic majority of workers who are yellow, brown and black" (16).

The American Civil War was result of the conflict between two factions of US capital, agricultural capital and industrial capital. Its results were the abolition of slavery, the integration of Afro-Americans into the system of wage-labour, and the creation of new forms of discrimination and exploitation. Du Bois (1935/1998) describes how after the American Civil War, US capital utilised racism in order to split black and white workers and stabilise and deepen capitalist exploitation of the working class. He shows that racist ideology has played an important role in the stabilization and legitimation of capitalist rule.

The race element was emphasized in order that property-holders could get the support of the majority of white laborers and make it more possible to exploit Negro labor. But the race philosophy came as a new and terrible thing to make labor unity or labor class-consciousness impossible. So long as the Southern white laborers could be induced to prefer poverty to equality with the Negro, just so long was a labor movement in the South made impossible. [...] There was but one way to break up this threatened coalition, and that was to unite poor and rich whites by the shibboleth of race, and despite divergent economic interests. The work of secret orders in 1868–1872 [such as the Ku Klux Klan] frustrated any mass movement toward union of white and black labor.

(Du Bois 1935/1998, 680)

According to James (1992, 13), tyrannies such as Nazism operate by creating "an illusion of universality". For example, Hitler argued the Nazi movement and he as its leader stood for the universality of the "Aryan race" organised as folk community (*Volksgemeinschaft*). But this universality is in reality a particularistic ideology that crates an outside (Jews, people of colour, socialists, liberals, etc.) who are presented as enemies and whom the regime aims to annihilate. Racism has an ideological dimension. "To deaden the consciousness of exploitation among the white workers it [the American capitalist class] taught them to despise Negroes" (James 1996, 40)

James (1984, 34–35) argues that black and white workers should "fight together on the basis of economic struggle". For James, anti-racist struggles are "a constituent part of the struggle for socialism" and can "exercise a powerful influence on the revolutionary proletariat" (James 1992, 183). James (1996, 8) argues that black separatism, as for example advanced by Marcus Garvey, is "an inverted segregation" and "economically reactionary". He worked for the organisation of a black movement that fights against racism and over time through everyday political work explicitly adopts socialism as its political perspective (James 1996, 3–16).

If James were alive today, he'd be interested in and supporting Black Lives Matter.

8.5.2 Black Lives Matter

In February 2012, George Zimmermann, who was part of a neighbourhood watch group in Sanford, Florida, shot the 17-year-old African-American high school student Trayvon Martin, who died from the gunshot wounds. Zimmermann's acquittal sparked off the creation of the Twitter hashtag #BlackLivesMatter and the creation of the Black Lives Matter (BLM) movement. Following the police killings of Afro-Americans Michael Brown in Ferguson, Missouri, and Eric Garner in New York City in summer 2014, large protests against police violence and racism emerged. In May 2020, police in Minneapolis, Minnesota, killed the black man George Floyd. White police officer Derek Chauvin kneed on Floyd's neck for almost eight minutes. Chauvin did not release Floyd who repeatedly screamed "I can't breathe!". George Floyd's killing triggered mass protests of millions of people in many cities in and beyond the USA.

BLM characterises itself in the following way:

> #BlackLivesMatter was founded in 2013 in response to the acquittal of Trayvon Martin's murderer. Black Lives Matter Global Network Foundation, Inc. is a global organization in the US, UK, and Canada, whose mission is to eradicate white supremacy and build local power to intervene in violence inflicted on Black communities by the state and vigilantes. By combating and countering acts of violence, creating space for Black imagination and innovation, and centering Black joy, we are winning immediate improvements in our lives. [...] We are working for a world where Black lives are no longer systematically targeted for demise. We affirm our humanity, our contributions to this society, and our resilience in the face of deadly oppression. The call for Black lives to matter is a rallying cry for ALL Black lives striving for liberation.[12]

BLM is a humanist movement that opposes and protests against the dehumanisation of black people by racist violence and discrimination. It demands the treatment of blacks as full human beings. If C.L.R. James witnessed BLM, he would not just participate in the movement, but would also argue that it is a necessary response to the racist forms of alienation that deny black people their humanity. He would point out that racism is a form of dehumanisation that treats humans like and reduces them to the status of things. James (1993, 202) argues that the situation of black people in the USA is an economic and a political question and "primarily a question of human relations".

James would today say that it is important to point out in the context of BLM the relationship of class, capitalism, and racism. James analysed the connection of capitalism and racist violence. He writes about the lynching of black people in the USA: "lynching is rooted in the economic system and even the very forms it takes are conditioned by the specific class relations of the two races" (James 1996, 35). Capitalism is "the root source of lynching" (James 1996, 36). The white supremacist who exerts terror against black people, the police that shoots black people and the politician who legitimates violence against blacks act "in accordance with the three hundred-year-old policy of American capitalism – nor could it be otherwise. The state, says Marx, is the executive committee of the ruling class. The American capitalist class has gained untold riches by its specially brutal exploitation of Negroes" (James 1996, 40).

Slave-owners were allowed to kill slaves they owned. The Ku Klux Klan (KKK) was founded in 1866. Lynching black people became part of the KKK's practices of killing, frightening, and controlling black people. Racist police killings of black people show that racist violence is not confined to fascist civil society groups such as the KKK but is also part of the practices of repressive state apparatuses. From 1 January until 19 October 2020, 874 people were shot dead by the US police. 179 (20.5%) of these 874 people were black, although blacks account for only 13% of the US population.[13] From 2013–2020, 98.3% of deadly police shootings did not result in criminal charges against officers.[14]

In the context of BLM, C.L.R. James would today argue that racist police killings of blacks are a continuation of and institutionalisation of racist lynching. And he would add that the police, the military and the prison systems are inherently and systematically racist institutions that reflect the connection of racism, capitalism, and violence.

There can also be a capitalist state where socialists and anti-racists are part of the government, which implies that not all institutions of capitalist society are necessarily racist. But repressive state apparatuses uphold the ruling order by a state monopoly of violence. The police and the military are necessarily organisations built on the logic of violence. Capitalism exploits and excludes people of colour and drives them into precarity and poverty. Part of the police's tasks is to control the population in order to prevent uprisings of the poor and precarious. Capitalism needs to control potential rebellions of the poor and the exploited in order to reproduce itself and capital accumulation. The police and the military to a certain degree attract authoritarian personalities, who have a sadomasochistic personality, believe in top-down leadership and the friend/enemy-scheme, and enjoy exerting violence. Such individuals are prone to exert racist violence. In the USA, the police are often ordered to control segregated neighbourhoods and inner-city ghettos where lots of black people live. Given the strong presence of police in such areas and institutionalised racism, police actions such as stop and search and arrests to a disproportionate degree affect black people, which reinforces a spiral of the police targeting of blacks and the state's perception of blacks as criminals who need to be policed.

It is a logical consequence that BLM demands defunding of the police. Opal Tometi, a founding member of BLM, explains:

> The police forces' "budgets are overly bloated. And we can see this in many ways, but I think the most symbolic ways – and not even symbolic, it's material – are that we see they are militarized and we see all the equipment

they have been able to lay out overnight or in hours. So we know they have a vast amount of resources. This overpolicing of largely poor communities, which are largely people of color because poverty is racialized in this country, means that we are the ones interacting with law enforcement more. And with all this racial bias, of course, we see this brutality and these murders. [....] And what we concluded is that we need social workers. We need these resources to go to our social workers and educators. We need it to go to our schools. We would love to have mental-health professionals when we have certain crises in our communities. [....] And so I say all this to say that, yes, a defunding of police looks like an investment in the community.

(Chotiner 2020)

If C.L.R. James were alive today, he would argue that BLM's anti-racist practices are important in themselves and should be actively organised as "a constituent part of the struggle for socialism" (James 1992, 183). He would argue for seeing the interconnection of capitalism and racism in the form of black unemployment and the high exploitation and discrimination of black workers. Black people are over-represented in precarious, low-paid service jobs such as waiters, cleaners, fast food workers, and clerks. Racialised groups often face higher unemployment and higher underemployment, are concentrated in undesirable economic sectors and occupations, are more likely to be precariously self-employed, face high levels of discrimination at work, and are more likely to lose their jobs in crises (Bhattacharyya 2018, 107–108). Capitalism is racialised capitalism. James would argue for joint struggles of BLM and the working-class movement, including trade unions, on labour questions.

Right-wingers have presented BLM as a Marxist movement in order to utilise anti-Marxist sentiments and argue that BLM is a danger to America. They often refer to a 2015 video in which BLM co-founders Patrise Cullors describes herself and other BLM co-founders as "trained Marxists" (Kertscher 2020). There is no Marxist movement. Marx said of himself that "I myself am not a Marxist" (Engels 1882, 356). Marx opposed personalisation. Socialism is a movement for a fair and just, commons-based society that abolishes the private property of the means of production, not a movement defined by specific persons. Personalisation implies the degeneration of socialism. It makes sense to ask if BLM is a socialist movement.

Patrisse Cullors points out the ideological purpose of calling her a Marxist and says that "everybody called Dr. Martin Luther King a communist. That was the terrible word he was called forever up until he was assassinated". She argues as a political or-ganiser she learned about Marx in order to understand "the system we were criticising – capitalism" and that she believes that "we can get to a place where there is a socio-economic system that does not oppress some groups of people and only uplifts a few" (Cullors 2020).

There are scholars who point out the importance of situating anti-racism in the context of class and capitalism. One of them is the socialist political scientist Adolph Reed Jr., who warns of an identity politics that that ignores class politics. Reed and his col-leagues argue that identity politics focuses simply on "equal access to hierarchically distributed social goods" instead of questioning asymmetric distribution, exploitation, and domination as such (Warren, Reed, Johnson, Reed, Smith and Legette 2016). Reed warns of a liberal anti-racism that propagates that society is "just if one percent of the population controlled 90 percent of the resources so long as 12 percent of the one percent were black, half were female, and so on" (Reed 2016, 33). Reed argues that all social movements should be aware of the importance of anti-class politics.

Reed writes that police violence is "the product of an approach to policing that emerges from an imperative to contain and suppress the pockets of economically marginal and sub-employed working class populations produced by revanchist capitalism"; the "deeper roots of the pattern of police violence" lie "in enforcement of the neoliberal regime of sharply regressive upward redistribution and its social entailments" (Reed 2020). Reed points out that it would not be sufficient if persons of colour were proportionally re-presented among the victims of police violence because police violence would then still persist. He argues against separating police violence from political economy.

Reed is critical of critiques of Bernie Sanders from within BLM, especially the two occasions when BLM activists stormed the stage of Sanders rallies on 16 July 2015 in Phoenix and on 8 August 2015 in Seattle to demand attention for the demands of BLM. Reed comments that the "most telling moments of the 2016 Democratic presidential nomination campaign included when the random, self-selected Black Lives Matter activists attacked Sanders for supposedly not declaring his opposition to racism in a way that suited their tastes" (2018, 113). He points out that "every nearly item on the Sanders campaign's policy agenda – from the Robin Hood tax on billionaires to free public higher education to the $15/h minimum wage, a single-payer health care system, etc. (Sanders for President) – would disproportionately benefit black and Hispanic populations that are disproportionately working class" (Reed 2018, 110). To be fair, one should stress that there has been support of the Bernie Sanders campaigns by important BLM activists. BLM co-founder Patrisse Cullors, who was among those who disrupted the event in Phoenix, supported Sanders and Warren in the 2020 Democratic primaries.

The bottom line of the critique advanced by Reed and his colleagues is that anti-racist movements should have an explicitly anti-capitalist character and situate the critique of racism in relation to the critique of class in order to avoid the trap of an equal-opportunity liberalism.[15] Reed and his colleagues argue for a broad coalition of progressive forces for socialism, what Touré F. Reed (2020, 160) describes as "interracial political coalitions centered on the shared material concerns of poor and working-class people (groups in which blacks are overrepresented)" and a politics that is built on the insight that "the fate of poor and working-class African Americans – who are unquestionably overrepresented among neoliberalism's vic-tims – is linked to that of other poor and working-class Americans" (172). C.L.R. James stressed the connection of racism and capitalism and would therefore today point out the importance of criticising racism in the context of capitalism. BLM is not automatically a socialist movement, but contains socialist strands and ele-ments. Thinking Reed's critique to the end does not imply that BLM does not have socialist potentials but that the movement's socialist potentials and elements should become the dominant strand.

In 2016, the Movement for Black Lives (2016), a coalition that includes BLM, issued *A Vision for Black Lives: Policy Demands for Black Power, Freedom and Justice*. The section on economic justice demands economic justice for all, federal and state job programmes that provide a living wage, the progressive restructuring of tax codes to organise the redistribution of wealth, the strengthening of the right of workers to organise especially in the on-demand economy, the break-up of large banks, the ad-vancement of co-operatives, and the protection of workers in unregulated sectors. There are certainly important parallels of these demands to the Bernie Sanders campaign, which means that it contains socialist elements. *A Vision for Black Lives* says that the policy platform that formulated the vision stands "against the ravages of global capitalism and anti-Black racism, human-made climate change, war, and ex-ploitation". BLM Portland defines itself as organisation "against colonialism, capit-alism, imperialism, and all intersections of oppression therein. We organize so that our people can be free" (Black Lives Matter 2017, 26). There are socialist elements in BLM. C.L.R. James would just like Adolph Reed point out that racism, war, imperialism, environmental problems, etc. do not exist side by side but exist as part of the capitalist totality and class society.

If C.L.R. James had been alive in 2020, he would have been a supporter of and activist in BLM. He would stress that BLM's anti-racist struggle should be seen in the context of capitalism, be organised as part of the struggle for socialism, and work together with socialist movements such as the Bernie Sanders campaign.

8.6 Conclusion

This chapter asked: How relevant is C.L.R. James's dialectical philosophy today? The overall finding is that C.L.R. James's dialectical, Marxist-Humanist philosophy remains highly topical today for understanding phenomena such as authoritarian capitalism, Donald Trump, fascism and racial capitalism today, digital capitalism, digital ideology, and Black Lives Matter.

Of particular relevance for critical analysis today are James's concepts of the dialectic as mediation, his negative dialectics of capitalism and barbarism, his focus on truth and ideology critique, and his analysis of the dialectic of capitalism and racism.

Let us summarise the main findings:

- Dialectical mediation: James stresses that nature and society are dialectical. In a dialectic, contradictory moments are mediated with each other, which has the potential for a negation of the negation that results in development in the form of the constitution of new contradictions.
- Means of communication: There are three key aspects of James's analysis of the means of communication. He stresses that a) there are means of communication that disseminate ideologies in class societies, b) art and popular culture should be integrated, and c) self-managed media are a viable and democratic alternative to capitalist media. These moments are relevant today in the context of filter bubbles, fragmented public spheres, digital capitalism, platform co-operatives, and public service Internet platforms.
- Negative dialectics of capitalism and barbarism: Comparable to Horkheimer's and Adorno's *Dialectic of the Enlightenment*, James argues that capitalism has a negative dialectic so that it reaches points where there is the danger of society descending into fascist barbarism. Today, the rise of new authoritarianisms is an expression of neoliberal capitalism's negative dialectic. James would argue that such developments are the consequence of economic and political alienation and that measures are needed that reduce alienation and advance self-management and socialism.

- Essence, truth, and ideology critique: James was interested in the Hegelian notions of essence and truth and in ideology critique. He stresses that humans are in essence social and working being and that socialism is the society that corresponds to human Essence. With Marx, he sees capitalism, fascism, and Stalinism as alienated forms of society. For James, ideology means attempts to hide the world's essence from dominated and exploited classes, a contradiction between *their* consciousness and their being. In digital capitalism, we encounter new forms of ideology such as the engaging/connecting/sharing-ideology that tries to hide digital corporations' profit logic and the exploitation of digital labour by idealising the immediate social experiences of digital platform users. If James analysed Facebook and similar companies, he would call users to engage in digital class struggles and create self-managed alternatives to Facebook, digital capital, and digital capitalism. He would advocate for the digital proletariat's self-activity and praxis and the struggle for digital socialism.

- Racial capitalism: James stressed the connection of capitalism and racism. He points out that the origins and development of capitalism and imperialism were based on the enslavement of Africans. Black Lives Matter (BLM) is a humanist movement that opposes and protests against the dehumanisation of black people by racist violence and discrimination. If James were alive today, he would stress that BLM is a reaction to the inherent connection of racism and the police in capitalist society. If C.L.R. James had been alive in 2020, he would have been a supporter of and activist in BLM. He would stress that BLM's anti-racist struggle should be seen in the context of capitalism, be organised as part of the struggle for socialism, and work together with socialist movements such as the Bernie Sanders campaign.

James (1992, 164) argues that progressive social struggles are struggles for making "the abstract universal concrete", struggles that aim "to negate what impedes his movement towards freedom and happiness". For Marx and Engels, the proletariat is the universal class because its objective interest is not the establishment of another class rule but the creation of a classless society (see James 1992, 164–174). James points out the important "role of the proletariat in the preservation of society from barbarism" (James 1992, 328, 329). In the age of racial, authoritarian, digital capitalism, C.L.R. James's dialectical, Marxist-Humanist philosophy remains an important inspiration for the critical analysis of capitalism and for struggles against barbarism and for socialism.

Notes

1 https://resonate.is/about/, accessed on 27 October 2020.
2 https://resonate.is/about/, accessed on 27 October 2020.
3 https://newsroom.spotify.com/company-info/, accessed on 29 October 2020.
4 Data source: World Bank Data, https://data.worldbank.org, accessed on 29 October 2020.
5 https://www.forbes.com/global2000, accessed on 27 October 2020.
6 https://www.facebook.com/pg/facebook/about/, accessed on 28 October 2020.
7 https://about.fb.com/company-info/, accessed on 28 October 2020.
8 https://www.facebook.com/pg/facebook/about/, accessed on 28 October 2020.
9 https://www.facebook.com/business/marketing/facebook, accessed on 28 October 2020.
10 https://www.facebook.com/business/ads/pricing, accessed on 28 October 2020.
11 https://www.facebook.com/business/measurement, accessed on 28 October 2020.
12 https://blacklivesmatter.com/about/, accessed on 28 October 2020.
13 Data source: https://mappingpoliceviolence.org/, accessed on 28 October 2020.
14 Data source: https://mappingpoliceviolence.org/, accessed on 28 October 2020.
15 In summer 2020, a talk by Reed at the Democratic Socialists of America's New York chapter was cancelled because groups such as the Afrosocialists and Socialists of Color Caucus argued that letting him talk was "reactionary, class reductionist and at best, tone deaf" (Powell 2020). Cornel West commented: "God have mercy, Adolph is the greatest democratic theorist of his generation, [...] He has taken some very unpopular stands on identity politics, but he has a track record of a half-century. If you give up discussion, your movement moves toward narrowness" (Powell 2020).

References

Adorno, Theodor W. 1993. *Hegel. Three Studies.* Cambridge, MA: The MIT Press.
Adorno, Theodor W. 1977. *Kulturkritik und Gesellchaft I: Prismen. Ohne Leitbild.* Frankfurt am Main: Suhrkamp.
Bhattacharyya, Gargi. 2018. *Rethinking Racial Capitalism. Questions of Reproduction and Survival.* London: Rowman & Littlefield.
Black Lives Matter. 2017. *Celebrating Four Years of Organizing to Protect Black Lives.* https://drive.google.com/file/d/0B0pJEXffvS0uOHdJREJnZ2JJYTA/view
Buhle, Paul. 2017. *C.L.R. James: The Artist as Revolutionary.* London: Verso.
Chotiner, Isaac. A Black Lives Matter Co-Founder Explains Why This Time is Different. *The New Yorker*, 3 June 2020, https://www.newyorker.com/news/q-and-a/a-black-lives-matter-co-founder-explains-why-this-time-is-different
Cullors, Patrisse. 2020. Am I A Marxist? https://www.youtube.com/watch?v=rEp1kxg58kE

References

Douglas, Andrew J. 2008. Democratizing Dialectics with C.L.R. James. *The Review of Politics* 70 (3): 420–441.

Du Bois, W. E. B. 1935/1998. *Black Reconstruction: An Essay Toward a History of the Part which Black Folk Played in the Attempt to Reconstruct Democracy in America, 1860–1880.* New York: The Free Press.

Dunayevskaya, Raya. 2002. *The Power of Negativity. Selected Writings on the Dialectic in Marx and Hegel.* Lanham, MD: Lexington.

Dunayevskaya, Raya. 1958. *Marxism and Freedom ... From 1776 Until Today.* New York: Bookman Associates.

Engels, Friedrich. 1882. Engels to Bernstein. 2-3 November 1882. In *Marx & Engels Collected Works (MECW)Volume 46*, 353–358. London: Lawrence & Wishart.

Fuchs, Christian. 2021. *Social Media: A Critical Introduction.* London: Sage. Third edition.

Fuchs, Christian. 2020a. *Communication and Capitalism: A Critical Theory.* London: University of Westminster Press. https://doi.org/10.16997/book45

Fuchs, Christian, ed. 2020b. Communicative Socialism/Digital Socialism. *tripleC: Communication Capitalism & Critique* 18 (1): 1–285.

Fuchs, Christian. 2018. *Digital Demagogue. Authoritarian Capitalism in the Age of Trump and Twitter.* London: Pluto.

Fuchs-Kittowski, Klaus. 2021. On the Categories of Possibility, Limiting Conditions and the Qualitative Development Stages of Matter in the Thought of Friedrich Engels. *tripleC: Communication, Capitalism & Critique* 19 (1): 125–139.

Fuchs-Kittowski, Klaus. 1999. Information – Neither Matter nor Mind – On the Essence and on the Evolutionary Stage Conception of Information. In *The Quest for a Unified Theory of Information*, ed. Wolfgang Hofkirchner, 331–350. Abingdon: Routledge.

Hall, Stuart. 1998. Breaking Bread with History: C. L. R. James and *The Black Jacobins*. Stuart Hall Interviewed by Bill Schwarz. *History Workshop Journal* 46: 17–32.

Harvey, David. 2005. *A Brief History of Neoliberalism.* Oxford: Oxford University Press.

Hegel, Georg Wilhelm Friedrich. 2018. *The Phenomenology of Spirit.* Cambridge: Cambridge University Press.

Hegel, Georg Wilhelm Friedrich. 2010a. *Encyclopedia of the Philosophical Sciences in Basic Outline. Part I: Science of Logic.* Cambridge: Cambridge University Press.

Hegel, Georg Wilhelm Friedrich. 2010b. *The Science of Logic.* Cambridge: Cambridge University Press.

Hegel, Georg Wilhelm Friedrich. 2007. *Philosophy of Mind. Hegel's Encyclopaedia of the Philosophical Sciences Volume 3.* Oxford: Oxford University Press.

Hegel, Georg Wilhelm Friedrich. 1970. *Enzklopädie der philosophischen Wissenschaften im Grundrisse. 1830. Erster Teil: Die Wissenschaft der Logik. Mit den mündlchen Zusätzen.* Frankfurt am Main: Suhrkamp.

Hepp, Andreas. 2013. *Cultures of Mediatization.* Cambridge: Polity.

Hjarvard, Stig. 2013. *The Mediatization of Culture and Society.* Abingdon: Routledge.

Hofkirchner, Wolfgang. 2013. *Emergent Information. A Unified Theory of Information Framework.* Singapore: World Scientific.

Horkheimer, Max. 2004/1947. *Eclipse of Reason.* London: Continuum.

Horkheimer, Max and Theodor W. Adorno. 2002/1947. *Dialectic of Enlightenment: Philosophical Fragments.* Stanford, CA: Stanford University Press.

James, C.L.R. 2017. *World Revolution 1917-1936. The Rise and Fall of the Communist International.* Durham, NC: Duke University Press.

James, C.L.R. 2013. *Modern Politics.* Oakland, CA: PM Press.

James, C.L.R. 1999. *Marxism for Our Times: C.L.R. James on Revolutionary Organization,* ed. Martin Glaberman. Jackson, MS: University Press of Mississippi.

James, C.L.R. 1996. *C.L.R. James on the "Negro Question",* ed. Scott McLemee. Jackson, MS: University Press of Mississippi.

James, C.L.R. 1993. *American Civilization.* Cambridge, MA: Blackwell.

James, C.L.R. 1992. *The C.L.R. James Reader,* ed. Anna Grimshaw. Oxford: Blackwell.

James, C.L.R. 1989. *The Black Jacobins: Toussaint L'Ouverture and the San Domingo Revolution.* New York: Vintage Books. Second edition.

James, C.L.R. 1984. *At the Rendezvous of Victory. Selected Writings.* London: Allison & Busby.

James, C.L.R. 1980. *Notes on Dialectics: Hegel, Marx, Lenin.* Westport, CT: Lawrence Hill & Co.

James, C.L.R. 1949. Letter to Raya Dunayevskaya, 13 June 1949. In *The Raya Dunayevskaya Collection: List of 35 Letters in Philosophical Correspondence 1949-50,* 1626–1629. http://rayadunayevskaya.org/ArchivePDFs/1595.pdf

James, Selma. 2012. *Sex, Race, and Class – The Perspective of Winning: A Selection of Writings, 1952–2011.* Oakland, CA: PM Press.

Johnson, Boris. 2018. Denmark Has Got it Wrong. Yes, the Burka is Oppressive and Ridiculous – but That's Still no Reason to Ban it. *The Telegraph,* 5 August 2018.

Johnson, Boris. 2002. If Blair's so Good at Running the Congo, Let Him Stay There. *The Telegraph,* 10 January 2002.

Kertscher, Tom. 2020. Is Black Lives Matter a Marxist Movement? *PolitiFact,* 70 2020. https://www.politifact.com/article/2020/jul/21/black-lives-matter-marxist-movement/

Krotz, Friedrich. 2017. Explaining the Mediatisation Approach. *Javnost – The Public* 24 (2): 103–118.

Marcuse, Herbert. 1941/1955. *Reason and Revolution. Hegel and the Rise of Social Theory.* London: Routledge & Kegan Paul. Second edition.

Marx, Karl. 1867. *Capital Volume I.* London: Penguin.

Marx, Karl. 1844. Economic and Philosophic Manuscripts of 1844. In *Marx & Engels Collected Works (MECW) Volume 3,* 229–346. London: Lawrence & Wishart.

Marx, Karl. 1843. Contribution to the Critique of Hegel's Philosophy of Law. In *Marx & Engels Collected Works (MECW) Volume 3,* 3–129. London: Lawrence & Wishart.

References

Movement for Black Lives. 2016. *A Vision for Black Lives: Policy Demands for Black Power, Freedom and Justice*. https://web.archive.org/web/20160828130258/https://policy.m4bl.org/platform/

Powell, Michael. 2020. A Black Marxist Scholar Wanted to Talk About Race. It Ignited a Fury. *New York Times*, 14 August 2020. https://www.nytimes.com/2020/08/14/us/adolph-reed-controversy.html

Reed, Adolph Jr. 2020. How Racial Disparity Does Not Help Make Sense of Patterns of Police Violence. *NonSite* 33, 9 June 2020. https://nonsite.org/how-racial-disparity-does-not-help-make-sense-of-patterns-of-police-violence-2/

Reed, Adolph Jr. 2018. Antiracism: A Neoliberal Alternative to a Left. *Dialectical Anthropology* 42 (2): 105–115.

Reed, Adolph Jr. 2016. The Black-Labor-Left-Alliance in the Neoliberal Age. *New Labor Forum* 25 (2): 28–34.

Reed, Touré F. 2020. *Toward Freedom: The Case Against Race Reductionism*. London: Verso.

Said, Edward. 1989. C.L.R. James: The Artist as Revolutionary. *New Left Review* 175: 126–128.

Scholz, Trebor and Nathan Schneider, eds. 2016. *Ours to Hack and to Own: The Rise of Platform Cooperativism, a New Vision for the Future of Work and a Fairer Internet*. New York: OR Books.

Warren, Kenneth, Adolph Reed Jr., Cedric Johnson, Touré F. Reed, Preston Smith II and Willie Legette. 2016. On the End(s) of Black Politics. *NonSite*, 16 September 2016. https://nonsite.org/on-the-ends-of-black-politics/

Williams, Raymond. 1983. *Keywords*. New York: Oxford University Press.

Žižek, Slavoj. 1989/2008. *The Sublime Object of Ideology*, new ed. London: Verso.

Chapter Nine
Cornel West and Marxist Humanism

9.1 Introduction: Foundations of Marxist Humanism

This chapter asks and tries to answer the following questions: How can Cornel West's works inform a contemporary Marxist-Humanist theory of society? Taking West's works as a starting point, what are key elements of a Marxist-Humanist theory of society?

The approach this chapter takes is theoretical in nature. It develops theory and contributes to sociological theory and critical theories of society. It does not involve empirical, data-focused research. It engages with key works of West, sets them into the context of Marxist Humanism, and takes West's writings as a starting point for an update of Marxist-Humanist theory. The discussion of West's theory and the update of Marxist Humanism inspired by West focus on key aspects of Marxist-Humanist theory, namely alienation, organic intellectuality, praxis, culture, and the critique of ideology.

Two key concepts that underlie the present chapter are humanism and Marxist Humanism. We therefore have to first ask: What is humanism? What is Marxist Humanism?

Humanism is a particular philosophical tradition and worldview that focuses on the human being as central moment of society. "'humanism' established itself in the late 19th century as an umbrella term for any disposition of thought stressing the centrality of 'Man' or the human" (Soper 1991, 187). Humanism "places human beings, as opposed to God, at the center of the universe. [...] [It is based on the] conviction that human destiny is entirely in human hands" (Kraye 2005, 477). "At its broadest, 'humanism' means little more than a system of thought in which human values, interests, and dignity are considered particularly important. [...] Humanism's focus is on the 'big

DOI: 10.4324/9781003199182-9

questions', for example of what ultimately is real; of what ultimately makes life worth living; of what is morally right or wrong, and why; and of how best to order our society" (Law 2011, 1, 6)

Synthesising these understandings, we can define humanism as a philosophical tradition and worldview that considers the human being as the central aspect of society, takes the human being as starting point for theory, ethics, and politics, asks and deals with big questions about the human being's role in society such as what the good life of humans in society is and how it can be achieved.

Luik (1998) identifies four philosophical forms of modern humanism: Marxist Humanism, pragmatist humanism, existentialist humanism, and Heideggerian humanism. Marxist Humanism is a form of humanism. It is a particular type and approach of critical social theory that is informed by Karl Marx's works. Its representatives include, for example, Raya Dunayevskaya, Paulo Freire, Erich Fromm, C.L.R. James, Henri Lefebvre, Georg Lukács, Herbert Marcuse, M.N. Roy, E.P. Thompson, and Raymond Williams (see the contributions in Fromm (1965) and Alderson and Spencer (2017) for an introduction). Key features of Marxist-Humanist theory are a strong influence by Hegel's dialectical philosophy and Marx's philosophical writings such as the *Economic and Philosophic Manuscripts of 1844*; the stress of the importance of practices, praxis and class struggles in class societies; the use and further development of Marx's notion of alienation; and the development of a theory and philosophy of praxis where theorists act as organic intellectuals who inform struggles for Democratic Socialism and Socialist Democracy (Fuchs 2021, 2020a, 2020b).

Kate Soper (1991, 188) provides the following characterisation of Marxist Humanism:

> Marxist and socialist humanists have wanted to respect the 'dialectic' between human agency and the circumstances in which it is exercised, but there has been a certain polarization in their argument: the existentialist approach has placed an emphasis on consciousness which is difficult to reconcile with the idea of 'unwilled' social forces whilst the Hegelian-Lukácsian school has emphasized the loss of humanity inflicted by generalized processes of reification and alienation, though perhaps at the cost of making them appear inescapable. In contrast to both these positions, structuralist and 'post-structuralist' anti-humanists either insist on the subordination of individuals to economic structures, codes and regulating forces (modes of production, kinship systems, the Unconscious, etc.) or

attempt to 'deconstruct' the very idea of a 'human meaning' prior to the discourse and cultural systems whose qualities it is supposed to explain.

Anti-humanists can on the one hand be found in the structuralist-Marxist theory tradition. Its representatives include, for example, Edward Bernstein, Karl Kautsky, Henryk Grossmann, Louis Althusser, Étienne Balibar, Nicos Poulantzas, Ralph Miliband, Galvano della Volpe, Lucio Colletti, Alain Badiou, and Jacques Rancière. On the other hand, postmodern and post-structuralist thought is anti-humanist. Examples are the approaches of Roland Barthes, Jean Baudrillard, Judith Butler, Gilles Deleuze, Jacques Derrida, Michel Foucault, Félix Guattari, Julia Kristeva, Ernesto Laclau, Jean-François Lyotard, Chantal Mouffe, and Bernard Stiegler. The common feature of anti-humanism is the structuralist assumption that not human beings and their practices are central in society, but structures that act on and constrain humans who are mere bearers and executors of structures.

Returning to the above-mentioned definition of humanism, we can define Marxist Humanism as a philosophical tradition and worldview inspired by Marx that considers the human being as the central aspect of society, takes the human being as starting point for the theoretical and practical analysis and critique of alienation, capitalism and class society, puts an emphasis on human practices and class struggles, and sees democratic socialism as the good society that enables a good life for all humans. For example, Marx gave a humanist analysis of class struggle when he said that humans "make their own history, but they do not make it just as they please; they do not make it under circumstances chosen by themselves, but under circumstances directly encountered, given and transmitted from the past" (Marx 1852, 103). The point here is that structures condition class struggles but that significant social change in class societies can only be achieved when the exploited unite and collectively organise and struggle.

Humanity has experienced an explosion of anti-humanism (Fuchs 2021, 2020a, 2020b) in three forms:

a) In many countries, there has been the rise of authoritarian governments, leaders, parties, and movements that threaten democracy and appeal to citizens who feel disenfranchised by capitalism by nationalism, racism, and demagoguery;

b) Postmodern culture has put so much stress on and fetishized difference that we have experienced the rise of filter bubbles that disable humans to see, put a stress on and talk about commonalities;

c) Global problems such as global inequalities, the global environmental crisis, the coronavirus crisis, and violent global conflicts threaten the survival of humanity.

Taken together, these factors have contributed to a crisis of the human being and society. The imminent danger is that violence and global problems escalate and that humanity is destroyed. The renewal of humanism is a proper political answer to this danger. Marxist Humanism stresses that Democratic Socialism is the proper alternative to the social formation that created global problems that threaten the survival of humanity.

Cornel West is one of the leading critical intellectuals today. He is an organic intellectual who has been highly visible in the public sphere through public interventions such as the support of the Bernie Sanders campaign, Black Lives Matter, and the Occupy movement. His work has been influenced by, has fused and has contributed to the development of anti-racist theory, Black Liberation Theology, Marxist theory, pragmatism, and existentialism.

West describes his basic theoretical and political motivation in the following way: "I have tried to be a man of letters in love with ideas in order to be a wiser and more loving person, hoping to leave the world just a little better than I found it" (West 1999, 19). Stuart Hall (1996/2019, 83) characterises West's work as "brilliantly concise and insightful". At a 2009 public event in New York, the German philosopher Jürgen Habermas was so impressed by Cornel West's communication and argumentation skills, that he said that given West's "prophetic speech" and "moving rhetoric", "the only possible response would be to stand up and to change one's life" (Butler et al. 2011, 114). Philosopher George Yancy (2001, 1–2) characterises West as "radical democrat, humanist, race-transcending prophet, spiritual gadfly, social and cultural critical, advocate on the side of 'the least of these', political activist (combining elements of *theoria* and *praxis*), astute critic of our postmodern moment". bell hooks writes that Cornel West is one of the "few intellectuals in the United States able to speak in an informed way about so many subjects, whose influence reaches far beyond the academy" (hooks and West 1991/2017, 23–24).

This range of comments is an indication of the extraordinary power of Cornel West's thought and praxis. Anyone interested in the question of how we can save humanity from its destruction today, shouldn't ignore and should engage with the works of Cornel West. This chapter asks the question of how Cornel West's theory can inform the renewal of Marxist Humanism. Section 9.2 provides an analysis of Cornel West's Marxist-Christian humanism. Section 9.3 analyses his concept of culture. Section 9.4 presents conclusions.

9.2 Marxist-Christian Humanism: Black Liberation Theology & Marxist Humanism

In his book *Prophesy Deliverance! An Afro-American Revolutionary Christianity*, Cornel West (1982/2002) outlines foundations of a combination of Black Liberation Theology and Marxist theory. He advances a Marxist-Christian version of humanism. There are three distinctive features of West's Marxist-Christian humanism:

a. the focus on alienation;
b. the critique of exploitation and domination;
c. organic critical intellectuals.

9.2.1 Alienation

Humanism is for Cornel West a commonality of Black Liberation Theology and the version of Marxist theory he subscribes to. It is expressed in the insight that "every individual regardless of class, country, caste, race, or sex should have the opportunity to fulfil his or her potentials" (1982/2002, 16). This insight is based on Hegel's philosophical dialectic of essence and existence, to which West explicitly refers (1982/2002, 16 & 150, footnote 5). Progressive Marxism and Christian Liberation Theology are both committed to the negation of domination and exploitation and the advancement of democracy and individuality (101). They are critiques of capitalist civilisation (101).

Hegel (1956) argues that Spirit is "alien to itself" and that the truth of history is that essence and existence of Spirit can be reconciled (319), which means the realisation of freedom (17). While Hegel was confident that history automatically results in the "progress of the consciousness of Freedom" (19), Marx substituted Hegel's principle of Spirit in history by the principle of class struggle: in class societies, the exploited are alienated from the good life and the realisation of the full potentials of all humans and society. Class struggle is the way of realising these potentials. It makes history open and uncertain. West (1991) interprets Marx as a radical historicist. He argues that for Marx, "the real ground or basis of history" are "the dynamic social practices and the constellation of institutions erected thereon by human beings" (90). In *The Manifesto of the Communist Party*, Marx and Engels (1848, 482) expressed the dynamic and practical character of human history by saying: "The history of all hitherto existing society is the history of class struggles". In Christianity, egalitarianism is derived from the assumption that humanity was created by God, which endows all humans "with a certain dignity and respect which warrants a particular treatment, including a chance to fulfil their capacities and potentialities" (West 1988, 130).

West (1991) stresses that Marx sees common life and sociality as key features of human beings and that alienation is a form of dehumanisation:

> Marx seems to appeal to human nature and social freedom as ideals which contrast sharply with alienation and de-humanization. But it is important to note that he understands human nature as the true common life of social persons created and produced by those persons. Alienation is an impediment for this true common life of people, a humanization of this social intercourse and interaction of people. In this sense, Marx conceives human nature *as* social freedom and alienation *as* dehumanization, with the former morally desirable and the latter morally undesirable. Social freedom consists of the mutual ownership of products by producers; alienation consists of the private ownership of products by nonproducers.
>
> (West 1991, 47–48)

West advances a Hegelian-Marxist concept of alienation as disempowerment and de-humanisation. He argues that forms of domination such as capitalism, racism, and patriarchy disempower and dehumanise individuals, which means that they do not allow them to realise their capacities and full potentials. He therefore also stresses the critique of exploitation and domination.

9.2.2 The Critique of Exploitation and Domination

McGary (2001) argues that humanists see human experiences and humans needs as basis for morality, believe in the positive capacities of human reason, and are concerned with the good life and social justice. He points out that Cornel West is a humanist because he "questions any form of human oppression" (289), stresses the need for humans' "common struggle for human dignity" (283), and that "democratic control over the major institutions that regulate" society is the major step needed towards conditions where "every human is valued and respected" (291).

West argues that there are four major forms of oppression today: "imperialist oppression, class exploitation, racial oppression, and sexual oppression" (West 1982/2002, 123). This means that he focuses on the critique of (global) capitalism, racism, and patriarchy and their interactions. West doesn't assume that all of these factors are equally influencing the living conditions of humans in contemporary societies. He argues that "class position contributes more than racial status to the basic form of powerlessness in America" (West 1982/2002, 115). He understands class in a Marxian sense as "the population's relation to the mode of production [...] in terms of their role or lack thereof in decision-making processes for effective control over investment choices" (West 1988, 52). He writes that overstating

> region, sex, age, ethnicity, and race" and ignoring class results in a "petit bourgeois viewpoint that clamors for a bigger piece of the ever-growing American pie, rarely asking fundamental questions such as why it never gets recut more equally or how it gets baked in the first place.
>
> (West 1982/2002, 116)

> For sophisticated Marxists, this does not mean that class explains every major event in the past or present, or that economic struggles supersede all others. It simply suggests that in capitalist societies, the dynamic processes of capital accumulation and the commodification of labor condition social and cultural practices in an inescapable manner.
>
> (West 1991, xxiii)

That West is a humanist means he stresses the commonalities of black and white workers. The interaction of racism and capitalism causes "powerlessness among black people", which includes unemployment, low wages, bad housing, health care and educational conditions, and so on (West 1982/2002, 114). Afro-Americans face exacerbated powerlessness (115), and many American workers have "no substantive control over their lives, little participation in the decision-making process of the major institutions that regulate their lives" (114–115).

West argues that racism and sexism are "integral to the class exploitative capitalist system of production as well as its repressive imperialist tentacles abroad" and that individuals face "the crucial existential issue of death, disease, despair, dread, and disappointment [...] within the context of these present circumstances" (West 1982/2002, 106; see also hooks and West 1991/2017, 33). There is a substantial influence of existentialist philosophy, such as Kierkegaard's approach, on West's thinking. Racism buttresses "the current mode of production, concealing the unequal distribution of wealth, and portraying the lethargy of the political system" (West 1982/2002, 114). For West (1999, xvi), humanism means the insight that "to be human, at the most profound level, is to encounter honestly the inescapable circumstances that constrain us, yet

Marxist-Christian Humanism: Black Liberation Theology & Marxist Humanism

muster the courage to struggle compassionately, for our own unique individualities and for more democratic and free societies".

Based on Ernest Mandel's work, West (1988, 74) distinguishes three phases of capitalist development:

1. industrial capitalism;
2. monopoly capitalism;
3. multinational corporate capitalism.

He discusses the role of racism in each of the three stages, which means that he sees racism as integral feature of capitalism:

1. Industrial capitalism was based on slavery and the military conquest of indigenous peoples and places of the world where people of colour live (West 1988, 104);
2. Monopoly capitalism in the USA and other countries installed racist laws that discriminated based on skin colour and secured high levels of exploitation of people of colour (104–105);
3. In multinational corporate capitalism, equality was formally established. On the one hand, there is an "expanding middle class of people of colour", on the other hand "the underclass of black and brown working and poor people at the margins of society has grown", people of colour face educational inequality, and are especially affected by neoliberal cuts to public services and the establishment of a low wage service sector (106).

West (1982/2002, chapter 3) defines humanism as one of four responses to US racial capitalism. The other responses are the propagation of Afro-American exceptionalism, assimilation into white American capitalism, and individualistic rebellions against marginalisation. West characterises these responses as petty-bourgeois. The Afro-American humanist tradition that West subscribes to and propagates "affirms Afro-American membership in the human race, not above or below it" (71).

West provides important heuristic principles of how critical theories of society can thinking of the relationship of exploitation and domination. But he has not outlined a systematic theorisation of this relationship. Building on West's insight, we can further develop his approach. What follows next is the present author's own theorisation of the relation of class and domination that has been inspired by reading West's works and takes these works as a starting point. It is in this context important to theorise the relationship of capitalism, racism, and patriarchy.

Society is a realm of social production. Human beings are producing and social beings who produce in social relations and (re)produce their sociality. Production is an economic principle that shapes all realms of society and all social relations. Georg Lukács (1984, 1986) characterises production as *teleological positing*: Humans produce teleologically, which means they produce in order to achieve certain goals that satisfy their needs, wants, and desires (see Fuchs 2020a, 2016 [chapter 2] for a more detailed discussion of teleological positing). Production is, however, not the same in every realm of society. Human practices have distinct, relatively autonomous qualities and results in the different realms and systems that make up society as totality.

Capitalist society is a society that is shaped by the logic of accumulation and instrumental reason. In the economy, accumulation means the accumulation of capital. In the political system, accumulation means the accumulation of decision-power. In the cultural system, accumulation means the accumulation of reputation and attention. Accumulation results in alienation that creates structures that cause injustices. Injustice means that humans are denied a good life, the realisation of their potentials, and control of the conditions that shape their lives. Accumulation and alienation are forms of inhumanity. Table 9.1 provides an overview of the three forms of injustice as alienation.

Instrumental reason is a logic that instrumentalises humans in order to realise the partial interests of the ruling class and dominant groups. Through exploitation, domination, and ideology, instrumental reason turns humans into instruments that advance partial

TABLE 9.1 Alienation as injustice

Sphere	General features	Structure	Process	Antagonism	Injustice
Economy	Production of use-values	Class relation between capital and labour	Capital accumulation	Capital vs. labour	Capitalist exploitation: capital's private ownership of the means of production, capital, and created products implies the working class' non-ownership and exploitation
Politics	Production of collective decisions	Nation-state	Accumulation of decision-power and influence	Bureaucracy vs. citizens	Domination: citizens' lack of influence on political decisions as consequence of the asymmetric distribution of decision-power and influence
Culture	Production of meanings	Ideologies	Accumulation of reputation, attention and respect	Ideologues and celebrities vs. everyday people	Invisibility, disrespect: lack of recognition as consequence of an asymmetric attention economy and ideological scapegoating

Marxist-Christian Humanism: Black Liberation Theology & Marxist Humanism

interests of classes and groups that dominate society. In capitalist society, instrumental reason takes on the form of accumulation and results in inequalities. Instrumental reason undermines human equality. Exploitation, domination, and ideology deny humans their humanity. They are forms of alienation. Alienation means anti-humanism.

Capitalism, racism, and patriarchy are three modes of power relations that each combine economic alienation, political alienation, and cultural alienation. Capitalism, racism, and patriarchy involve specific forms of exploitation, domination, and disrespect (see Table 9.2).

The three forms of alienation are interacting in particular forms of power relations. Capitalism, racism, and patriarchy/gender-related oppression are inherently connected and interacting. The economy plays a particular role in this interaction because these power relations are relations of production and accumulation of power. Table 9.3 provides an overview of the interactions of capitalism, racism, and patriarchy.

The capitalist economy creates forms of highly exploited, insecure, precarious labour – including racialised labour, unpaid labour, reproductive labour, and gender-defined labour – in order to maximise profits. Racism and patriarchy have economic, political, and ideological dimensions. In capitalism, these dimensions are united by the logic of accumulation. Class,

TABLE 9.2 The economic, political, and cultural-ideological dimensions of capitalism, racism, and patriarchy

	Capitalism	Racism	Patriarchy
Economic dimension	The exploitation of the working class	The exploitation and super-exploitation of racialised groups	The exploitation and super-exploitation of gender-defined groups, including houseworkers, female care workers, and female wage-workers
Political dimension	Bureaucratic discrimination of, surveillance of, state control of, and violence directed against dominated classes (such as wage-workers, slave-workers, particular types of workers, etc.)	Bureaucratic discrimination of, surveillance of, state control of, and violence directed against racialised groups	Bureaucratic discrimination of, surveillance of, state control of, and violence directed against gender-defined groups
Cultural-ideological dimension	Denial of voice, respect, recognition, attention and visibility of the working class, ideological scapegoating of the working class	Racist ideology: assumption that race exists as cultural and/or biological essence; denial of voice, respect, recognition, attention and visibility of racialised groups, ideological scapegoating of racialised groups,	Denial of voice, respect, recognition, attention and visibility of gender-defined groups, ideological scapegoating of gender-defined groups

TABLE 9.3 The interaction of class, racism, and gender-based oppression

	Class	Racism	Gender-based oppression, patriarchy
Class	Exploitation	Racist exploitation	Gender-structured exploitation
Racism	Racist exploitation	Racism	Discrimination of racialised individuals or groups of a particular gender
Gender-related oppression, patriarchy	Gender-structured exploitation	Discrimination of racialised individuals or groups of a particular gender	Gender-based discrimination

racism, and gender-based oppression/patriarchy are the three main forms of power relations that advance alienation, deny humans their humanity, and create damaged lives. Reed (2002, 272) argues that "racial and class hierarchies" have "their common foundation in the capitalist labor relation". We can extend this insight by saying that in capitalist society, class relations, racism, and gender relations have their common foundation in the capitalist labour relation, which means that wage labour, racialised labour, reproductive labour, and unpaid labour constitute the common foundation of class, racism, and patriarchy.

Humans produce society. Communication is the process of the production of sociality. Class, racism, and gender are social relations, which implies that communication is a process that helps producing and reproducing class, racism, and gender.

Table 9.4 gives an overview of how class, racism, and patriarchy play in role in the mediated production, distribution, and use of capitalism, racism, and patriarchy (see also Gandy 1998). The mediated communication process is in this context conceived of existing of processes of production, distribution, and consumption/use of content.

9.2.3 Organic Critical Intellectuals

Italian Marxist philosopher Antonio Gramsci argues that all humans "are intellectuals, one could therefore say; but not all men have in society the function of intellectuals" (Gramsci 2000, 304). For Gramsci, all humans have the capacity to contribute to the public analysis and debate of society. But in class societies, there is a division of labour between mental and manual labour and an asymmetric cultural power that results in the exclusionary character of educational institutions. The rise of the "knowledge society" has made access to higher education more open so that academic education has become a feature of a larger number and share of workers. But education continues to be asymmetrically distributed. Gramsci argues that progressive political change requires

TABLE 9.4 Aspects of class, racism, and patriarchy in the context of media production, circulation, and use

Aspect of the media	Dimension
Media production process	Exploitation, racist exploitation, gender-structured exploitation of media workers;
	Class-based, sexist, or racist division of labour in media production;
	Working class-hatred, sexism, or racism in laws that regulate media production and content;
	Alternative and public service media that commit to avoid working-class hatred, sexism, and racism in their code of conduct or public service remit
Content that is distributed	Public communication of content that supports the capitalist class, racism, or patriarchy;
	Algorithms and software that encode and advance working-class hatred, sexism, and racism.
	Exclusion of, misrepresentation of, ignorance of, or advancement of biases against, ideologies about and stereotypes about workers, racialised groups or gender-defined groups;
Media use and consumption	Class-based, racist, or sexist discrimination, segmentation, tracking, surveillance, and targeting of audiences and users for the purpose of accumulating capital and/or selling advertisements;
	Acceptance of, reproduction of, partial acceptance of, partial questioning of, questioning of, or resistance against ideologies that advance capitalism, racism, or patriarchy

organic intellectuals, who as "organic" part of the working-class movement provide inputs to the working-class' ideas (Gramsci 1971, 1–43; Gramsci 2000, 300–322). Organic intellectuals are the "organic category of every social group" (Gramsci 1996, 202). Gramsci distinguishes organic intellectuals from traditional intellectuals who operate intellectually without connection to social groups and "remain comfortably nested in the academy" (West 1989, 234). Also the bourgeoisie has organic intellectuals. That's why socialist politics is interested in a particular type of organic intellectuals, namely those that represent, defend, analyse, argue for and inform working-class interests – that is, the interest in the establishment of a socialist society.

Cornel West has been strongly influenced by Gramsci's works. He argues that it is important that intellectuals act as organic intellectuals that are "leaders and thinkers directly tied into a particular cultural group primarily by means of institutional af-filiations. Organic intellectuals combine theory and action, and relate popular culture and religion to structural social change" (West 1982/2002, 121). West thinks that the humanism immanent in the combination of Christian Liberation Theology, Marxism, and pragmatism compels the intellectual to be "entrenched in and affiliated with organi-zations, associations, and, possibly, movements of grass-roots folk" (West 1989, 234).

Johnson (2001) argues that West is a humanistic scholar because he acts as organic intellectual who puts "the life of the mind to praxis" (330) by public political engagement and activist in organisations such as the Congressional Black Caucus and the Democratic Socialists of America. West's Marxism is a humanist Marxism, his theology is a radical, humanist, socialist theology. He characterises this approach as Black Theology of Liberation and Critique of Capitalist Civilisation (West 1982/2002, 106). "Human struggle sits at the center" of West's approach (West 1989, 229). He considers it important "to keep alive the sense of alternative ways of life and of struggles based on the best of the past" (West 1989, 229). His focus on praxis is oriented on social struggles for a good society that fosters the common good for all humans. Through such struggles practice becomes a "material force" (West 1989, 232).

Politically, West's socialism is close to council communism, an approach developed by organic intellectuals such as Rosa Luxemburg, Anton Pannekoek, and Karl Korsch that supports prefigurative politics and favours "the self-organization and self-guidance of the working class movement" (West 1982/2002, 136). West's adherence to councilist ideas also explains why he stresses the importance of self-management in the economy and politics and argues for participatory democracy.

The Afro-American humanist tradition that West stands for argues for participatory democracy as condition for overcoming racism, i.e. "the democratic control over institutions in the productive and political processes" (West 1982/2002, 89). It stresses the powerlessness of Afro-Americans in politics and the capitalist economy (90) and the need for institutional transformations. According to West, creating a participatory democracy requires that "the black and white poor and working classes unite against corporate domination of the economy and government" (90). Participatory democracy enables all humans to fulfil their "potentialities and capacities" and advances self-management (91). "Human liberation occurs only when people participate substantively in the decision-making processes in the major institutions that regulate their lives" (112). This includes that companies should be self-managed by their workers (114). West argues that, for Marxism, empowerment and the democratic control of institutions is the indicator for the quality of life, whereas for Weberians it is high incomes (West 1988, 52).

West has a particular style of public speaking. He characterises it as a "passionate rhetoric" that is "involved, engaged, passionate", has been influenced by Afro-American styles of preaching, and that is a reflection of his philosophical, moral, and

Marxist-Christian Humanism: Black Liberation Theology & Marxist Humanism political engagement with the world and the concern for a better society that overflows with passion (West 1999, 21). West calls his approach prophetic because it "harks back to the Jewish and Christian tradition of prophets who brought urgent and compassionate critique to bear on the evils of their day" (West 1989, 233). For West (1993b, 3–6), prophetic thought is the combination of discernment, connection, tracking hypocrisy, and hope. It is a broad and deep analysis of power (discernment); considers the humanity of others as key principle (human connection); courageously challenges the gaps between rhetoric and reality (tracking hypocrisy); and wants to make a difference to galvanise, energise, inspire, and invigorate world-weary individuals and groups (hope).

West is a very active speaker who gives lots of talks and interviews and participates in a variety of events. He sees books as an important public intervention into intellectual life, culture, politics, and society. West's books such as *Race Matters* have been widely read and discussed. West is convinced that books as media of public intervention are not enough, which is why he has tried to utilise popular culture as political means of communication. Cornel West recorded three rap albums (Sketches of my Culture, 2001; Street Knowledge, 2005; Cornel West & BMWMB: Never Forget: A Journey of Revelations, 2008), which shows the importance he gives to popular culture in political activism and communication. West also has a highly visible presence on social media. In January 2021, his Twitter profile @CornelWest had more than a million followers, and his Facebook page https://www.facebook.com/drcornelwest/ had more than 800,000 followers. Together with sociologist Tricia Rose, Cornel West hosts the podcast The Tight Rope. Until January 2021, Rose and West had moderated 48 episodes that had reached around 350,000 downloads on the podcast hosting service Podbean. (https://spkerboxmedia.podbean.com/).

One criticism of Cornel West is that he is too much focused on socialist preaching than on being part of actual social struggles. Lester Spence (2015, 104, 129) writes in this context:

> Cornel West wouldn't spend so much of his time speaking to black audiences if he didn't believe speaking to them had an effect on their politics. But in relying primarily on rhetoric that emphasizes a certain type of political leadership he misses other important aspects of political action. [...] while we should in general be wary of using religious metaphors in talking and writing about political struggle, we should be particularly wary about the use

of prophetic language because it places more value on powerful speech (often articulated by charismatic male figures) than on labor, and hence, privileges individuals over communities, and privileges an aristocracy (based on speech) over democracy.

Cornel West's popularity, influence, and skills as a speaker do not make him a charismatic leader, but rather an organic intellectual who supports radical movements in several respects. Let us take Black Lives Matter (BLM) and The Movement for Black Lives (M4BL) as an example. As organic intellectual, West has supported these movements in several respects. First, he points out the importance of the movement in his interviews, talks, and popular writing, which helps the movement in countering prejudices. Via West, BLM and M4BL reach a mainstream audience that hears positive views and assessments of the movement. For example, in an interview in the *Guardian*, West said that Black Lives Matter is a "beautiful new moment in the struggle for black freedom" (Muir 2020). After the murder of George Floyd, West told CNN that Black Lives Matter is a "movement for love and justice"[1] and moved moderator Anderson Cooper to tears. Second, West has helped to not just raise awareness of the movement but to also organise financial support. For example, in August 2020 West participated in the Fundraiser for Black Lives that brought in US$10,000.[2] Third, West has supported the organisation of protests. For example, when The Movement for Black Lives (M4BL) organised protests under the name "Six Nineteen: Defend Black Lives" on Juneteenth 2020 (https://sixnineteen.com/), West appeared in a video, in which he called for participation (see https://www.facebook.com/watch/?v=250818662887419).

West in various ways also supported, for example, Bernie Sanders, the Occupy movement, the Democratic Socialists of America, or the Campaign for Peace and Democracy. He initiated the Stop Mass Incarceration Network (http://www.stoppoliceterror.org) and participated in the counter-demonstration to the Unite the Right Rally that took place in Charlottesville in August 2017. West is not simply an idealist socialist preacher but in a very materialist way an organic intellectual – in Gramsci's sense of the term – who is grounded in and supportive of left-wing movements. West has the skill to move humans not just to tears, but also onto the streets.

Adolph Reed Jr. (2000) criticises that Cornel West and other black public intellectuals speak to white audiences about black lives. He would thereby act as "Moral Voice for white elites" (86) and as "star [...] in the white left" (73); "white forums, particularly those associated with the left, have become the primary arenas for elaboration of black commentary and critical public discourse, an all-purpose message, equally suitable for corporate boards, rarefied academic conferences, White House dinners, and common folk. And, unsurprisingly, the white audience overwhelms and sets the terms for the black, repeating an ironic pattern begun with Washington" (83, 84). Reed's essay that formulated this criticism first appeared in *Village Voice*, a New York-based alternative weekly whose audience its promotion manager described as "young, hip, and affluent".[3] Reed spoke to the same "white elites" that West and others according to him spoke to. If a critical public intellectual were to speak to only one audience, then they would contribute to the fragmentation of the public sphere and the creation of small, powerless micro-publics. West speaks in different context to different audiences – blacks, whites, multicultural, working class, middle class, etc. – because he is a socialist universalist who believes in the need for forging alliances in social struggle against capital, racism, fascism, and patriarchy. Like West, Reed acts as socialist public intellectual who appears on popular YouTube channels such as Jacobin, The Michael Brooks Show, or Rolling Stone-magazine's Useful Idiots, where he passionately and effectively makes arguments for socialism and Marxist analysis.

At the bottom line, Reed's and West's politics have important commonalities, which has for example become evident in their support of Bernie Sanders. Let us compare what both said about Sanders. Adolph Reed Jr.:

> [Sanders] located a discourse frame and message that resonated broadly among the working-class population. (I define "working class" in line with Michael Zweig's simple criterion – those who take rather than give orders at work – which includes many who are routinely characterized as middle class by virtue, for example, of home ownership or white-collar employment.). Sanders showed in dramatic fashion what some on the Left have insisted for a long time, that very many Americans of all races, genders, and sexual orientations feel that their concerns, worries, and aspirations are ignored by both political parties and that they will respond affirmatively to voices that do attempt to connect with them.
>
> (Reed 2018, xiii)

In September 2015, West introduced Sanders at a Democratic primary rally in South Carolina:

> We are here in fact to highlight our dear brother Bernie Sanders. [...] he represents so much of the best and the latest in Martin Luther King Jr. and Rabbi

Abraham Joshua Herschel and Dorothy Day and Miriam McCloud Bethune and so many others who said what? We are concerned with unarmed truth and the condition of truth is to allow suffering to speak. And if you are concerned about truth in politics you have to push out the big money. If you're concerned about truth in politics you're going to have to keep track of the poor children. You have to keep track of the elderly and the orphans and the widows and the working people whose wages have stagnated. And you have got to keep track of the 1% who now own 42% of the wealth. And in the richest nation of the world, 22% of children, 42% of black children, brown children, red children still live in poverty. [...] Are you concerned about the decrepit schools? Are you discerned about the dilapidated housing? Are you concerned about the massive unemployment and underemployment that are not reflected in the statistics because they don't count those folks who are not looking for work or part time workers? [...] Bernie Sanders is calling for a political revolution predicated on a moral and spiritual awakening. [...] Come together across colour, across class, across sexual orientation, across region. That's what Bernie Sanders' campaign is all about.

(West 2015)

Both Reed and West stress that Sanders appeals to the working class that they both see as consisting of a broad range of workers who are dispossessed and disempowered by the capitalist class. Both argue that that a broad working-class alliance across colour, working class faction, sexual orientation, gender, etc. is needed. And they see the Sanders campaign as the platform that can make such united struggles possible. Both Reed[4] and West stress that humans have to come together and organise around their common interests in the struggle for socialism. They both put an emphasis on the importance of class struggle. Reed (2000, xiii-xiv) argues that structuralist Marxism forgets that "the course of history is dynamic and open-ended, that *people* actually do make history, even if not 'as they please, under circumstances chosen by themselves'". Like Reed, West in his interpretation of Marx stresses the role of praxis – that is, class struggle:

What separates Marx's own brand of emancipation from the others is that his communism rests upon the kind of human productive activity which promotes social freedom, that is, satisfies evolving human needs and permits the ex pression of human properties and faculties. [...] Marx's materialist conception of history is supported by his radical historicist viewpoint in that both focus on the dynamic social practices of people.

(West 1991, 59, 87)

For Marx (1844, 182), praxis is social struggle that aims at overthrowing "*all relations* in which man is a debased, enslaved, forsaken, despicable being" Praxis wants to establish an "absolute humanism" (Gramsci 1971, 330) – socialism. Cornel West has contributed as organic intellectual with a variety of praxis forms to the struggle for socialism.

West is an organic intellectual who is part of and informs progressive social movements that struggle for Democratic Socialism and participatory democracy and makes use of popular culture for passionate political interventions. Culture is naturally important for organic critical intellectuals such as West. Already Marxist-Humanists such as Gramsci and Lukács had a particular interest in culture and the relationship of culture and political economy. The engagement with culture is an important feature of many Marxist-Humanist approaches. We will therefore next look at Cornel West's analysis of culture.

9.3 Cornel West on Communication and Culture

There are four dimensions of West's engagement with culture:

a. the concept of culture;
b. humanist culture and the public sphere;
c. the critique of ideology; and
d. popular culture.

9.3.1 The Concept of Culture

West (1988, 100) gives the following definition of culture:

> Cultural practices are the medium through which selves are produced. We are who and what we are owing primarily to cultural practices. The complex process of people shaping and being shaped by cultural practices involves the use of language, psychological factors, sexual identities, and aesthetic conceptions that cannot be adequately grasped by a social theory primarily focused on modes of production at the macrostructural level.

For West (1993/2017, 12), culture is "rooted in institutions such as families, schools, churches, synagogues, mosques, and communication industries (television, radio, video, music)". Today we have to add the information, communication and collaboration capacities of the Internet and social media to the institutions that enable and shape human meaning-making. For West, cultural institutions have their economies and politics just like culture operates in the economy and politics because they "promote particular cultural ideals" (West 1993/2017, 12).

West defines culture as practices focused on the formation of identity, the self, and how humans make meaning of themselves, each other and society. The humanist character of his understanding is evident from West's focus on cultural practices.

West says about language and communication:

> Language cannot be a model for social systems, since it is inseparable from other forms of power relations, other forms of social practices. I recognize, as Gadamer does, the radical linguisticality of human existence; I recognize, as Derrida does, the ways which forms of textualization mediate all our claims about the world but the linguistic model itself must be questioned. The multilevel operations of power within social practices – of which language one is one – are more important.
>
> (Stephanson and West 1989, 270–271)

In his definitions of culture just cited, West limits the communication industries and the use of language to culture. West tends to relegate language and communication to the realm of culture. But humans also use language in the workplace and in political groups and organisations. Language and communication are fundamental aspects of human existence that play a role in all realms of society and all social systems. West also sees production as limited to the economic realm. But he says himself that there is the cultural production of selves, which shows that production processes extend beyond the economy into all realms of society. The economy as the realm of production operates in all realms of society, including political and cultural relations, groups, organisations, and institutions. There is a dialectic of communication and production (Fuchs 2020a): Humans produce communicatively; communication is the production of understanding and human sociality. Communication is a form of production. Production is also communication. The communication industry and communication workers such as journalists, academics, and artists show that communication is economic just like it is cultural.

An often discussed and controversial issue in Marxist theory is the base/superstructure-problem. It deals with the question of how the economic and the non-economic (politics, culture) are related. West is critical of structuralists such as Althusser who argue that the economic mode of production turns humans into bearers of structures whose actions are economically programmed. West stresses that there is "not a history without a subject propagated by the structuralist Louis Althusser, but rather a history made by the praxis of human subjects which often results in complex structures of discourses which have relative autonomy from (or is not fully accountable in terms of) the intentions, aims, needs, interests, and objectives of human subjects" (West 1982/2002, 49). There is "no direct correspondence between nondiscursive structures, such as a system of production (or, in Marxist terms, an economic base), and discursive structures, such as theoretical formations (or, in Marxist terms, an ideological superstructure)" (49). It is important to add that there is a common element between all realms of society and between all types of practices, namely social production. Production is part of all human activities. It is the unifying and common element of society. Raymond Williams stresses that culture is material (see Fuchs 2017 for a detailed discussion). He speaks of "the material character of the production of a cultural order" (Williams 1977, 93). Ideas do not stand outside of material activity, but are produced socially in society. For Williams, there is no immateriality.

West (1999, 257) follows Raymond Williams neo-Marxist conception of the relation between the economic and the non-economic, in which there is "the mutual setting of limits and exerting of pressures" (see Williams' essay "Base and Superstructure in Marxist Cultural Theory", Williams 2005, 31–49).[5] There is the "multi-leveled interplay between historically situated subjects who act and materially grounded structures that circumscribe, i.e. enable and constrain, such action" (West 1999, 257). For West, there is "privilege" of "the economic sphere without viewing the other spheres as mere expressions of the economic" (258). This means that West sees the economic as key sphere of society, but he stresses that the non-economic cannot be reduced to the economic although it is grounded in it. West does not advance a proper vocabulary for conceptualising this complex, dialectical relationship of the economic and the non-economic. But we can, inspired by and based on Cornel West, update the Marxist-Humanist understanding of the economic and the non-economic. So what follows next is the present author's own understanding that takes West's theoretical works as one of its starting points.

In his "Base and Superstructure" essay, Williams solved the base/superstructure problem in the form of an interactive dualism that sees the economic and the non-economic as interacting but leaves them separate. Starting with his book *Marxism and Literature* (Williams 1977), Williams advanced a fully developed cultural materialism, where the economic and the non-economic are identical and separate. Cultural materialism has an "emphasis on production" (Williams 1981, 12), which includes economic production, political production, and cultural production as material processes in society (see

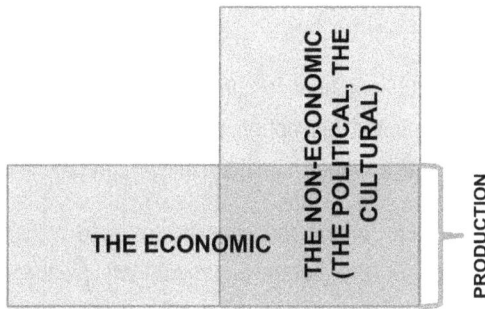

FIGURE 9.1   The relationship of the economic and the non-economic

Fuchs 2017). Based on cultural materialism, Figure 9.1 visualises the relationship of the economic and the non-economic. Economic production operates in all economic and non-economic relations in society but does not determine the content and form of the non-economic. The non-economic has emergent qualities that are non-reduceable to the economy, sublate the economic, and interact with the economic. The economic and the non-economic are identical, non-identical, intersecting, and interacting.

9.3.2 Humanist Culture and the Public Sphere

The public sphere is a realm of society that stands in-between, mediates, and inter-faces the economy, politics, and culture. In the public sphere, humans communicate about matters that are of public relevance – that is, concern the many. "[C]ritical public debate" (Habermas 1991, 52) is a key feature of the public sphere. The public sphere has a political-economic dimension in the form of organisations of the public sphere that have certain forms of ownership, resources, funding, and so forth, and a cultural dimension of meaning-making.

West argues for a humanist culture of the public sphere, where humans encounter each other as humans, brothers and sisters, and friends in dialogue, also when they disagree. He stresses the importance of dialogue as principle of the public sphere. "West is a deep believer in dialogue as a means of breaking down the walls that separate people" (Cone 2001, 111). For West (1999), dialogue is a "free encounter of the mind, soul and body that relates to others in order to be unsettled, unnerved and unhoused" (xvii-xviii), I is "the I-Thou relation with the uncontrolled other" (xviii). He argues that dialogue has the potential to "broaden the scope of empathy and imagination" (Butler et al. 2011, 95).

West's notion of the public sphere is comparable to the one of Jürgen Habermas. Habermas has complemented his notion of the public sphere (Habermas 1991) by discourse ethics, a practice where humans achieve agreement via rational discourse.

> [In] rational discourse, where the speaker seeks to convince his audience through the force of the better argument, we presuppose a dialogical situation that satisfies ideal conditions in a number of respects, including, as we have seen, freedom of access, equal rights to participate, truthfulness on the part of participants, absence of coercion in taking positions, and so forth.
>
> (Habermas 1994, 56)

Cornel West shows how racism undermines the democratic character of the public sphere. People of colour have frequently been banned from or marginalised from politics and therefore also from the public sphere and political communication in the public sphere. Culture is about meaning-making, recognition, voice, visibility, and attention. In class and heteronomous societies, cultural power is asymmetrically visible. In racist societies, racialised groups are not just highly exploited, killed at will, and denied political participation; their voices, minds, and bodies are also excluded from culture. They are culturally disrespected, ignored, kept voiceless, and made invisible. West (1999, 10) argues in this context:

> every major institution in American society — churches, universities, courts, academies of science, governments, economies, newspapers, magazines, television, film and others — attempted to exclude black people from the human family in the name of white-supremacist ideology. This unrelenting assault on black humanity produced the fundamental condition of black culture — that of *black invisibility and namelessness*.

Black invisibility and namelessness constitute a form of cultural disrespect and mal-recognition. Disrespect is also political when it extends to invisibility in the public sphere and exclusion from political decision-making. It is also economic to the degree that people of colour are excluded from the control of organisations and institutions such as the mass media that play a role in public meaning-making. West (1999, 115) argues based on W.E.B. Du Bois' (1903/2007) *The Souls of Black Folk* that racism has in the USA also meant "the relative lack of communication across the Veil of color" (West 1999, 115). Du Bois (1903/2007) speaks of the "Veil of Color" that forces blacks in America to live a double-life, "as a Negro and as an American" (136). Du Bois refers to the Veil also as "color-line" (e.g. 32, 68, 113, 124, 125) and Veil of Race (55, 57, 184). Racism deeply divides the economy, politics, culture, everyday life, private life, public life – society – along the lines of racialisation. It is an economic, political, cultural system of social classification that creates a society of two classes, where one is conceived of and treated as being fully human and the other one as subhuman, inhuman, not fully human. Racism that denies black people humanity and individuality creates a veil that "separates the black and white worlds. [...] This Veil not just precludes honest communication between blacks and whites; it also forces blacks to live in two worlds in order to survive" (West 1999, 104). "The unique combination of American terrorism – Jim Crow and lynching – as well as American barbarism – slave trade and slave labor – bears witness to the distinctive American assault on black humanity" (West 1993/2017, vii).

The US public sphere has marginalised black voices. The "public sphere is racialized" (West 1999, 487). In racial capitalism, the public sphere is "regulated by and for well-to-do, white males in the name of freedom and democracy" (West 1993a, 27). Corporate market institutions have greatly contributed to the "shattering of black civil society" and "the weakening of black cultural institutions" (West 1993/2017, 16). When racialised groups are denied voice, names, visibility, and attention in the public sphere, what Habermas terms the re-feudalisation of the public sphere takes on the form of disrespect and malrecogition as dehumanising racist culture.

Some observers have criticised West, and especially his book *Race Matters*, for focusing too much on the politics of cultural recognition instead of political economic redistribution (see e.g. Joseph 2001; Steinberg 1994). Such claims overlook that West argues for the combination and a dialectic of the politics of redistribution and recognition. "If the elimination of black poverty is a necessary condition of substantive black progress, then the affirmation of black humanity, especially among black people themselves, is a sufficient condition of such progress. [...] Any progressive discussion about the future of racial equality must speak to black poverty and black identity" (West 1993/2017, 65, 67). Together with Tavis Smiley, West wrote a book about poverty that ends with a manifesto that makes socialist demands for the eradication of poverty that resemble many of Bernie Sanders' demands (Smiley and West 2012).

Like Habermas (1991), West is critical of the reduction of the public sphere to entertainment, consumerism, and market culture (West 1999, 115). Habermas (1991) speaks in this context of the re-feudalisation of the public sphere. As a consequence, "public discourse has degenerated into petty name-calling and finger-pointing – with

Cornel West on Communication and Culture

little room for mutual respect and empathetic exchange" (West 1999, 115). Big Money's rule of culture has resulted in "market-driven celebrities who thrive to glitzy spectacles and seductive brands" (West 1993/2017, xvi). Status became an obsession and capitalist consumer culture advanced an individualism that has harmed communal relations and solidarity (West 1993/2017, 36–37). For West (1993/2017, 6), also contemporary politics is dominated by "images, not ideas", which contributes to the destruction of the public sphere. According to West (1993/2017, 14). The consequence of neoliberalism and the destruction of the public sphere is nihilism in society – meaninglessness, hopelessness, lovelessness.

West envisions a public sphere where everyone can be heard as a human being in-dependent of their colour, class, gender, and other classifications. This requires a new framework and new languages (West 1993/2017, 6) that focus on empathy and com-passion (8), the extension of public infrastructure and public services (6), large-scale public intervention to ensure access to basic social goods (7), an invigoration of "common life" and "the common good" (7), a love ethic (18–19), grassroots democratic organisations (19), race-transcending prophetic leaders (39–40, 46), race-transcending intellectuals (42–43), and cultural hybridity (101). For West, strengthening the public sphere has a political economy dimension – the elimination of poverty and socio-economic injustices; a political dimension – political participation; and a cultural side – cultural frameworks that make human voices visible and allow humans to come together and form communities that cut across dividing lines. West (1989) is critical of John Dewey's reduction of the public sphere to a cultural democracy – what Dewey calls "the great community" where de-mocracy is purely achieved by "pedagogical and dialogical means", which means Dewey "falls back on 'communication'" (106). West stresses the importance of economic and political self-management of organisations that operate in the public sphere.

9.3.3 The Critique of Ideology

For Marx, "to be dialectical is to unmask, unearth, to bring to light" (West 1982/2002, 110). The critique of ideology is an important aspect of Marx's works. Marx especially analysed the ideological concepts of society advanced by bourgeois economists. In addition, he analysed how politicians, newspapers, philosophers, religion, science, and the commodity form (the fetishism of the commodity) advance ideology.

Based on Marx, West (1982/2002, 119) understands ideology as "the set of formal ideas and beliefs promoted by the ruling class for the purpose of preserving its privileged position in society". West, based on Gramsci, stresses that ideology needs a hegemonic culture that

> subtly and effectively encourages people to identify themselves with the habits, sensibilities, and world views supportive of the status quo and the class interests that dominate it. It is a culture successful in persuading people to 'consent' to their oppression and exploitation.
>
> (West 1982/2002, 119)

Counter-hegemony means the practice of oppositional world views, sensibilities, and habits that challenge hegemonic culture (West 1982/2002, 120, 121). "Human struggle is always a possibility in any society and culture" (120). Culture and religion therefore have the capacity "to be instruments of freedom or domination, vehicles of liberation or pacification" (120).

For West, racism has a political-economic role that interacts with ideology. A political economy aspect of racism is that slaves were used as gratis labour forces and that many black workers in contemporary capitalism are highly exploited: "racism provided the chief ideological justification for the use of Africans as slaves in the Americas; and sexism was employed to defend the abuse of women both on the plantations in the Americas and within the mills in Britain" (West 1982/2002, 124). West (1982/2002) argues that the rise of racism had besides a political-economic dimension also a cultural-ideological dimension. Racism "is as much a product of the interaction of cultural ways of life as it is of modern capitalism" (West 1988, 100). Racism in the form of white supremacy is a form of anti-humanism that emerged in the period between the late 17th century and the late 19th century based on theories such as natural history's definition of races as well as phrenology and physiognomy in anthropology that defined racial differences and the superiority of whites over blacks (West 1982/2002, chapter 2). West stresses that the emergence of racism not just had to do with the "exploitative (oligopolistic) capitalist system of production but also" with "cultural attitudes and sensibilities, including alienating ideals of beauty" (West 1982/2002, 65).

9.3.4 Popular Culture

Referring to Gramsci and Raymond Williams, West (1982/2002, 118–121) argues that class struggle not just takes place in the work situation but also "takes the form of cultural and religious conflict over which attitudes, values, and beliefs will dominate the thought and behaviour of people" (119). He is interested in popular culture because he sees it as a potential realm of and a cultural dimension of class struggle.

West stresses that Black Liberation Theology takes seriously the role of culture and the reality of social, civic, physical, psychic, and spiritual death of Black people in contemporary societies (1982/2002, 6; 2001, 348). He is interested in progressive Christianity because it allows "suffering to speak" (Butler et al. 2011, 99). West (1988, 19) argues that the major contribution that religion can make to left strategy is to show that the *"culture of the oppressed"* matters for the formation of community and political action.

For Afro-Americans, Methodist and Baptist churches and music (black gospel, blues, jazz, rhythm and blues [R&B], soul, funk, rap) have been important aspects of everyday life under racist conditions and of coming together and forming communities. For slaves in the United States, composing and singing spirituals was an expression of their sorrows, joys, and hopes. Spirituals influenced the development of blues, jazz, gospel music, and rhythm and blues. "Among large numbers of black youth, it is black music which serves as the central influence for the shaping of their psyches" (West 1988, 69). Black music appeals to "alienated young people" (West 1988, 177). It is "a countercultural practice with deep roots in modes of religious transcendence and political opposition" (West 1988, 177). West is interested in popular culture, especially music, because it is one of the areas "where Black humanity is most powerfully expressed, where Black people have been able to articulate their sense of the world in a profound manner" (hooks and West 1991/2017, 37).

West argues that Afro-American music expresses "what it is like to be human under black skin in America" and is Afro-American humanism (1982/2002, 86). Afro-American folklore, spirituals, gospels, blues, and jazz convey a "profound message of personal and communal struggles – of persistent negation and transformation of prevailing realities" (88). Songs, singing, and concerts "serve as media of social communication which express the values for the joint communal existence of Afro-Americans" (88). Black culture is an expression of "the ontological wounds, psychic scars and existential bruises of black people" (West 1999, 102). For groups that have faced existential threats and experiences such as genocide, war, racist violence, exploitation, and so on popular culture is an important form of working through and expressing their experiences in artistic forms, an expression of rage about injustices (West 1999, 108–109), and also of keep on keepin' on (103). Popular culture is in this context the hope that things will be different. Popular cultural expressions of Afro-Americans' cries and moan go

> back to the indescribable cries of Africans on the slave ships during the cruel transatlantic voyages to America and the indecipherable moans of enslaved Afro-Americans on Wednesday nights or Sunday morning near godforsaken creeks or on wooden benches at prayer meetings in makeshift churches.
>
> (West 1999, 102)

West sees books and talks as possibilities for critical interventions into the public spheres. But he says that this is not enough because in capitalism, not everyone has the time and capacities to engage with books. He therefore stresses that music, television, film, and video are important means for critical public communication (hooks and West 1991/2017, 45). Today, we also have to add the Internet, social media, and podcasts. West stresses that Black voices are marginalised in the capitalist media, "the Black infrastructure for intellectual discourse and dialogue is nearly non-existent" (134). Inspired by the council communist idea of self-management, West therefore argues for the creation of self-managed cultural and media organisations so that "Black intellectuals [...] establish and sustain their own institutional mechanism of criticism and self-criticism, organized in such a way that people of whatever colour would be able to contribute to it" (134). "We must have Black cultural workers within television, film, and video who are presenting alternative perspectives [...] We also need more Black journalists who are writing in widely accessible newspapers and magazines" (45).

West argues that rap's speed and "linguistic versatility" resembles the style of preaching and "recovers and revises elements of black rhetorical styles" (West 1988, 186). Music and preaching are for West (Stephanson and West 1989, 280) *the* black means of cultural expression. He considers the two as inseparable (281). Influenced by the political spoken-word performances and soul and jazz poetry of Gil Scott-Heron, rap is partly directly political (political rap) and is a "cry of desperation and celebration of the black underclass and poor working class, a cry which openly acknowledges and confronts the wave of personal cold-heartedness, criminal cruelty, and existential hopelessness in the black ghettos of Afro-America" (West 1988, 186).

Rap gives particular stress to communication and language. A rap song contains a vast amount of poetry and words, spoken very quickly. Rap is a form of public political communication. Political rap and conscious rap are political at the content level; many forms of rap are political at the level of social form where they are complex reflections and expressions of life in racist capitalism. Rap, like all music, appeals not just to our reason, but also to our emotions, affects, and bodies. Dancing, singing, listening, performing music, and concerts are social acts where humans come together. Hip hop culture's appeal to white youth can create "a shared cultural space where some humane interaction" between black and white humans takes place (West 1993/2017, 84). West sees popular culture and music as an important form of community building that he likes to see as one possible means of socialist culture, praxis and consciousness-raising. Popular culture alone isn't politics, but it is an important way of how humans come together and can form bonds that can bind together communities and allows them to form and express their collective identity. Socialism therefore should appropriate popular culture as one of the means for attaining socialist ends.

Adolph Reed Jr. (2000) is critical of West's cultural politics. "West loads up on Continental theory to explain why the music he listened to in his undergraduate dorm is the apotheosis of black culture and why poor people need moral rearmament" (Reed 2000, 87). Reed speaks of cultural politics as a

> quietistic alternative to real political analysis. It boils down to nothing more than an insistence that authentic, meaningful political engagement for black Americans is expressed not in relation to the institutions of public authority – the state – or the workplace – but in the clandestine significance assigned to apparently apolitical rituals. Black people, according to this logic, don't mobilize through overt collective action. They do it surreptitiously when they look like they're just dancing, or as a colleague of mine ironically described it, 'dressing for resistance.
>
> (88–89)

West and others who take culture serious do not suggest that popular culture can or should replace trade unions, political parties, or street protests. West is active in political groups just like he attends street protests and appears in movies, podcasts, and hip hop songs. In the age of communicative and digital capitalism, leaving the realm of popular culture aside as one of the spaces of struggle means to render socialist politics less effective because popular culture and the Internet are important meeting places for large groups of people. If entertainment replaces politics, as Horkheimer and Adorno (2002) feared, then popular culture indeed acts as ideology. But West and others politicise popular culture. They want to create a left-wing cultural politics that contributes to political mobilisation. Every social movement has a particular culture that it practices in the form of songs, images, chants, jokes, symbols, dances, aesthetics, and so on. A rebellion not just needs political ideas, demands, strategies, and tactics but also music, dancing, means of internal and public communication and so forth.

West isn't affirmative of popular culture. He argues that the capitalist profit-motive has introduced a dumbing down of music "for pecuniary gain", "eliminated most soulful group performers for big-name celebrities-to-be, and unleashed vicious stereotypes of women, men, LGBTQ people, and others" (West 1993/2017, xxii). In a way, West here to a certain degree reflects Horkheimer's and Adorno's (2002) concept of the culture industry. West is critical of anti-Semitism, sexism, the glorification of capitalism and so forth in black culture. He blames the capitalist focus on "spectacle, image, money, status" for such tendencies that he characterises as "neoliberal spiritual warfare" and "a market-driven attack on the very souls of Black folk" (West 1993/2017, xxii). He also characterises the commodification and brutalisation of culture as "[p]ostmodern culture" (5).

West's analysis of popular culture differs from the one we find in mainstream Cultural Studies. For West, counter-hegemony is no automatism, but a possibility. He stresses that popular culture has a potential to be a means of creating community and helping progressive political groups to form, come together, and express their identity and demands, but it isn't always progressive. Popular culture is a necessary but not a sufficient dimension of socialist movements. Such movements also require political organisation, programmes, resources and so on.

In American Cultural Studies, John Fiske has advanced deterministic concepts of counter-hegemony and popular culture. He sees popular culture as necessarily political and resistant: "Popular culture [...] always bears traces of the constant struggle between domination and subordination, between power and various forms of resistance to it or evasions of it, between military strategy guerrilla tactics" (Fiske 1989, 19). For Fiske (1989, 168), the consumption of popular culture means "always relationships of domination and subordination, always ones of top-down power and of bottom-up power resisting or evading it" (Fiske 1989, 168). "Discursive struggles are an *inevitable* part of life in societies whose power and resources are inequitably distributed" (Fiske 1996, 5).

In British Cultural Studies, Stuart Hall presented popular culture as a constant battlefield where resistance is inevitable: "In the study of popular culture, we should always start here: with the double-stake in popular culture, the double movement of containment and resistance, which is always inevitably inside it" (Hall 1981/2019, 348).

> There are points of resistance; there are also moments of supersession. This is the dialectic of cultural struggle. In our times, it goes on continuously, in the complex lines of resistance and acceptance, refusal and capitulation, which make the field of culture a sort of constant battlefield.
>
> (Hall 1981/2019, 354)

Hall's use of the terms "inevitability", "continuity", and "constancy" here implies a determinism of resistance, political resistance as necessary element of popular culture. These formulations exclude the alternative of resistance and counter-hegemonies as possibilities that are forestalled.

Cornel West shares with Hall the insight that popular culture "is one of the places where socialism might be constituted. That is why 'popular culture' matters. Otherwise, to tell you the truth, I don't give a damn about it" (Hall 1981/2019, 361). But West rejects a deterministic concept of class struggle, counter-hegemony, and resistant as necessary and inevitable. For Cornel West, popular culture is a potential means of social and class struggles for socialism. He sees socialist counter-hegemony and class struggles as conditioned potentials shaped by society's dialectic of chance and necessity. West's humanism is different from the Althusserian structuralism that has influenced thinkers such as Stuart Hall, in whose works we can hardly find human beings that act, but rather structures that act (Fuchs 2019, 4–6; Fuchs 2017, 759–760).

9.4 Conclusion

This chapter dealt with the following two questions: How can Cornel West's works inform a contemporary Marxist-Humanist theory of society? Taking West's works as a starting point, what are key elements of a Marxist-Humanist theory of society?

Cornel West is a role model of a critical public intellectual who has contributed to the fusion of socialist theory and praxis. His works and praxis can inform the reinvigoration of Marxist Humanism in the age of authoritarian capitalism as a socialist response. His thought can and should inform the analysis of alienation, exploitation, domination, culture, the public sphere, the critique of ideology, and popular culture.

West is a representative of a Marxist-Christian Humanism that combines Black Liberation Theology and Marxist Humanism. His Marxist-Christian Humanism has three core features: a) the focus on alienation; b) the critique of exploitation and domination; c) organic critical intellectuals.

With respect to *alienation*, West advances a Hegelian-Marxist concept of alienation as disempowerment and de-humanisation. He argues that forms of domination such as capitalism, racism, and patriarchy disempower and dehumanise individuals, which means that they do not allow them to realise their capacities and full potentials.

With respect to the *critique of exploitation and domination*, West is both critical of economic reductionism that purely focuses on class and identity politics-reductionism that focuses on malrecognition and disregards class and capitalism. He focuses on the critique of capitalism, racism, and patriarchy and their interactions. West gives a particular attention to the economy by stressing that class underpins all forms of oppression, including racism and patriarchy. West argues that capitalism, racism, and patriarchy and their interactions deny humans their humanity.

West provides important heuristic principles of how critical theories of society can think of the relationship between exploitation and domination. But he has not outlined a systematic theorisation of this relationship. Building on West's insight, we can further develop his approach. In this chapter, such an attempt was presented that identified economic, political, and cultural-ideological dimensions of capitalism, racism, and patriarchy and analysed how capitalism, racism, and patriarchy interact.

With respect to *organic critical intellectuality*, West understands himself as an organic intellectual in Gramsci's sense of the term. Influenced by council communism, West argues for self-managed organisations and participatory democracy as the realisation of a humanist society. West is a passionate speaker who understands how to move his listeners emotionally and politically. He uses books, public talks, interviews in the popular press, rap music, social media, and podcasts as political means of communication in the public sphere. West is an organic critical intellectual who is part of and informs progressive social movements that struggle for Democratic Socialism and participatory democracy. He makes use of popular culture for passionate political interventions.

There are four dimensions of West's engagement with culture:

a. the concept of culture;
b. humanist culture and the public sphere;
c. the critique of ideology; and
d. popular culture.

West argues for a *concept of culture* that solves the base/superstructure-model in a dialectical manner so that the non-economic spheres of society such as culture are based on but cannot be reduced to the economy. Cultural materialism has established a more concrete theoretical language and models for the dialectic of the economic and the non-economic.

West argues for a *humanist culture of the public sphere*, where humans encounter each other as humans, brothers and sisters, and friends in dialogue, also when they disagree. West's notion of the public sphere is comparable to the one of Jürgen Habermas. He shows how racism undermines the democratic character of the public sphere. When racialised groups are denied voice, names, visibility, and attention in the public sphere, what Habermas terms the re-feudalisation of the public sphere takes on the form of disrespect and malrecogition as dehumanising racist culture.

Marx and Gramsci influenced West's concept of *ideology*. West stresses the inter-action of ideology and hegemony and that there is always the *possibility* for counter-hegemonic struggles. For West, racist ideology is the cultural dimension of racism that interacts with the latter' political economy.

West is interested in *popular culture* such as black music as potential means of and cultural dimension of class struggle. Popular culture, including religion and music, has been an important aspect of black people's experience of and reaction to racism in the United States. Cornel West is himself popular culture. His passionate way of talking in the public sphere is influenced by the culture of blues, jazz, and rap. Cornel West is critical theory's and academia's Gil Scott-Heron. West doesn't see all popular culture as progressive and resistant. He argues that the profit motive of capitalist consumer culture dumbs down, depoliticises, and alienates popular culture. West rejects de-terministic understandings of class struggle, counter-hegemony and resistance as necessary and inevitable. For Cornel West, popular culture is a potential means of social and class struggles for socialism.

Donald Trump is the prototype of the contemporary authoritarian personality. But there is not just one Trump. There are one, two, many Donald Trumps. Donald Trump is just a symbol and manifestation of authoritarian capitalism. Renewing Socialist Humanism is an urgent political task as counter-hegemonic antidote to the Donald Trumps of this world and their systems. West (2017) argues that Donald Trump is "a product of American civilization, the vicious legacies of white supremacy still operating" (27) and means "neo-liberal economy on steroids" and the betrayal of the working class (28).

Given the age of de-humanisation we live in, Socialist Humanism is the truly viable alternative to and necessary form of struggle against authoritarian capitalism.

We live in a world where multiple crises intersect: the economic crisis-proneness of capitalism, a crisis of social inequalities, the COVID-19 pandemic-health crisis, the climate crisis, the crisis of democracy posed by new nationalism and right-wing authoritarianism, and so on. The world's divisionists stress human being's differences and that they should be separated along the lines of friends and enemies. To overcome the world's multiple, intersecting crises, we need international solidarity and class struggles that overcome division and unite the working class by what it has in common and what it can struggle for in common. The 21st century poses the political alternative between socialism and barbarism in new forms. It is uncertain how society will look like in 10, 20, 30, and 50 years from now. Democratic Socialism is the humanist alternative to the divisionist pathways of war, fascism, and destruction. Cornel West's humanism reminds us that class and social struggles in the moment we are now in have to focus on the struggle for the realisation of everyone's human dignity, which means the struggle for Democratic Socialism in the light of the dawning of barbarism. West shows that humanism means both the dedication to Democratic Socialism and the insight that only human praxis – that is, struggle – can realise democratic socialism as the full development of humanity.

Notes

1 https://edition.cnn.com/videos/us/2020/06/10/cornel-west-george-floyd-cooper-ac360-vpx.cnn, accessed on 22 November 2020.
2 http://bostonreview.net/race/boston-review-where-do-we-go-here-fundraiser, accessed on 8 May 2021.
3 https://www.encyclopedia.com/marketing/encyclopedias-almanacs-transcripts-and-maps/village-voice-llc, accessed on 21 June 2021.
4 Reed argues that identity politics' attacks on what its representatives call "class reductionism" results in a form of neoliberalism so that "identity politics is not an alternative to class politics; it *is* a class politics" (Reed 2020, 39) that constitutes the left-wing of neoliberalism. He argues that the alternative is the focus on anti-capitalist politics. Reed advances the Marxist-Humanist agenda of focusing on the common by arguing that labour is the common feature of the oppressed and exploited.
5 West (1989, 172) characterises Williams as socialist intellectual who highlights, "in relatively cold moments in human societies", that "class conflict is mediated through social, cultural or educational changes that insure the muting of class struggle".

References

Alderson, David and Robert Spencer, eds. 2017. *For Humanism. Explorations in Theory and Politics.* London: Pluto.

Butler, Judith, Jürgen Habermas, Charles Taylor and Cornel West. 2011. *The Power of Religion in the Public Sphere.* New York: Columbia University Press.

Cone, James H. 2001. "Let Suffering Speak": The Vocation of a Black Intellectual. In *Cornel West: A Critical Reader*, ed. George Yancy, 105–114. Malden, MA: Blackwell.

Du Bois, W.E.B. 1903/2007. *The Souls of Black Folk.* Oxford: Oxford University Press.

Fiske, John. 1996. *Media Matters. Everyday Culture and Political Change.* Minneapolis: University of Minnesota Press.

Fiske, John. 1989. *Understanding the Popular.* New York: Routledge.

Fromm, Erich, ed. 1965. *Socialist Humanism. An International Symposium.* Garden City, NY: Doubleday.

Fuchs, Christian. 2021. *Marxist Humanism & Communication Theory Communication & Society Volume 1.* New York: Routledge.

Fuchs, Christian. 2020a. *Communication and Capitalism: A Critical Theory.* London: University of Westminster Press. https://doi.org/10.16997/book45

Fuchs, Christian. 2020b. Towards a Critical Theory of Communication as Renewal and Update of Marxist Humanism in the Age of Digital Capitalism. *Journal for the Theory of Social Behaviour* 50 (3): 335–356. https://doi.org/10.1111/jtsb.12247

Fuchs, Christian. 2019. Revisiting the Althusser/E. P. Thompson-Controversy: Towards a Marxist Theory of Communication. *Communication and the Public* 4 (1): 3–20.

Fuchs, Christian. 2017. Raymond Williams' Communicative Materialism. *European Journal of Cultural Studies* 20 (6): 744–762.

Fuchs, Christian. 2016. *Critical Theory of Communication: New Readings of Lukács, Adorno, Marcuse, Honneth and Habermas in the Age of the Internet.* London: University of Westminster Press. https://doi.org/10.16997/book1

Gandy, Oscar H. 1998. *Communication and Race. A Structural Perspective.* London: Arnold.

Gramsci, Antonio. 2000. *The Gramsci Reader*, ed. David Forgacs. New York: New York University Press.

Gramsci, Antonio. 1996. *Prison Notebooks Volume II.* New York: Columbia University Press.

Gramsci, Antonio. 1971. *Selections from the Prison Notebooks.* New York: International Publishers.

Habermas, Jürgen. 1994. *Justification and Application. Remarks on Discourse Ethics.* Cambridge, MA: The MIT Press.

Habermas, Jürgen. 1991. *The Structural Transformation of the Public Sphere. An Inquiry into a Category of Bourgeois Society.* Cambridge, MA: MIT Press.

Hall, Stuart. 1996/2019. What Is This "Black" in Black Popular Culture. In *Essential Essays Volume 2: Identity and Diaspora*, ed. David Morley, 83–94. Durham, NC: Duke University Press.

Hall, Stuart. 1981/2019. Notes on Deconstructing "the Popular". In *Essential Essays Volume 1: Foundations of Cultural Studies*, ed. David Morley, 347–361. Durham, NC: Duke University Press.

Hegel, Georg Wilhelm Friedrich. 1956. *The Philosophy of History*. New York: Dover.

hooks, bell and Cornel West. 1991/2017. *Breaking Bread: Insurgent Black Intellectual Life*. New York: Routledge.

Horkheimer, Max and Theodor W. Adorno. 2002. *Dialectic of Enlightenment*. Stanford, CA: Stanford University Press.

Johnson, Clarence Shole. 2001. Reading Cornel West as a Humanistic Scholar: Rhetoric and Practice. In *Cornel West: A Critical Reader*, ed. George Yancy, 312–334. Malden, MA: Blackwell.

Joseph, Peniel E. 2001. "Its Dark and Hell is Hot:" Cornel West, the Crisis of African-American Intellectuals and the Cultural Politics of Race. In *Cornel West: A Critical Reader*, ed. George Yancy, 295–311. Malden, MA: Blackwell.

Kraye, Jill. 2005. Humanism. In *Encyclopedia of Philosophy*, ed. Donald M. Borchert, 477–481. Farmington Hills, MI: Thomson Gale. Second edition.

Law, Stephen. 2011. *Humanism: A Very Short Introduction*. Oxford: Oxford University.

Luik, John C. 1998. Humanism. In *Routledge Encyclopedia of Philosophy*, ed. Edward Craig. http://doi.org/10.4324/9780415249126-N025-1

Lukács, Georg. 1986. *Zur Ontologie des gesellschaftlichen Seins. Zweiter Halbband. Georg Lukács Werke, Band 14*. Darmstadt: Luchterhand.

Lukács, Georg. 1984. *Zur Ontologie des gesellschaftlichen Seins. Erster Halbband. Georg Lukács Werke, Band 13*. Darmstadt: Luchterhand.

Marx, Karl. 1852. The Eighteenth Brumaire of Louis Bonaparte. In *Marx & Engels Collected Works (MECW) Volume 1*, 99–197. London: Lawrence & Wishart.

Marx, Karl. 1844. Contribution to the Critique of Hegel's Philosophy of Law. Introduction. In *Marx & Engels Collected Works (MECW) Volume 3*, 175–187. London: Lawrence & Wishart.

Marx, Karl and Friedrich Engels. 1848. The Manifesto of the Communist Party. In *Marx & Engels Collected Works (MECW) Volume 6*, 477–519. London: Lawrence & Wishart.

McGary, Howard Jr. 2001. The Political Philosophy and Humanism of Cornel West. In *Cornel West: A Critical Reader*, ed. George Yancy, 280–292. Malden, MA: Blackwell.

Muir, Hugh. 2020. Cornel West: "George Floyd's Public Lynching Pulled the Cover Off Who We Really Are". *The Guardian*, 19 October 2020. https://www.theguardian.com/us-news/2020/oct/19/cornel-west-george-floyds-public-lynching-pulled-the-cover-off-who-we-really-are

Reed, Adolph Jr. 2020. Socialism and the Argument Against Race Reductionism. *New Labor Forum* 29 (2): 36–43.

Reed, Adolph Jr. 2018. Foreword. In *Crashing the Party*, ed. Heather Gautney, ix–xxiii. London: Verso.

Reed, Adolph Jr. 2002. Unraveling the Relation of Race and Class in American Politics. *Political Power and Social Theory* 15: 265–274.

Reed, Adolph Jr. 2000. *Class Notes: Posing as Politics and Other Thoughts on the American Scene.* New York: New Press.

Smiley, Tavis and Cornel West. 2012. *The Rich and the Rest of Us. A Poverty Manifesto.* New York: Smiley Books.

Soper, Kate. 1991. Humanism. In *The Concise Encyclopedia of Western Philosophy and Philosophers*, ed. J. O. Urmson and Jonathan Rée, 187–188. London: Routledge.

Spence, Lester K. 2015. *Knocking the Hustle. Against the Neoliberal Turn in Black Politics.* Brooklyn, NY: Punctum.

Steinberg, Stephen. 1994. The Liberal Retreat from Race. *New Politics* 4 (1): 30–51.

Stephanson, Andrew and Cornel West. 1989. Interview with Cornel West. *Social Text* 21: 269–286.

West, Cornel. 2017. The Trump Era: Hope in a Time of Escalating Despair. *Transition* 122: 22–41.

West, Cornel. 2015. Cornel West Introduces Bernie Sanders in South Carolina. Florence, South Carolina. 15 September, 2015. https://www.youtube.com/watch?v=W8cex4VTrwg

West, Cornel. 1999. *The Cornel West Reader.* New York: Basic Civitas Books.

West, Cornel. 1993/2017. *Race Matters. 25th Anniversary Edition.* Boston, MA: Beacon Press.

West, Cornel. 1993a. *Keeping Faith. Philosophy and Race in America.* New York: Routledge.

West, Cornel. 1993b. *Prophetic Thought in Postmodern Times.* Monroe, ME: Common Courage Press.

West, Cornel. 1991. *The Ethical Dimensions of Marxist Thought.* New York: Monthly Review Press.

West, Cornel. 1989. *The American Evasion of Philosophy. A Genealogy of Pragmatism.* Madison, WI: The University of Wisconsin Press.

West, Cornel. 1988. *Prophetic Fragments. Illuminations of the Crisis in American Religion & Culture.* Grand Rapids, MI: Wm. B. Eerdmans.

West, Cornel. 1982/2002. *Prophesy Deliverance! An Afro-American Revolutionary Christianity.* Louisville, KT: Westminster John Knox Press.

Williams, Raymond. 2005. *Culture and Materialism. Selected Essays.* London: Verso.

Williams, Raymond. 1981. Introduction. In *Contact: Human Communication and Its History*, 7–20. London: Thames and Hudson.

Williams, Raymond. 1977. *Marxism and Literature.* Oxford: Oxford University Press

Yancy, George. 2001. Cornel West: The Vanguard of Existential and Democratic Hope. In *Cornel West: A Critical Reader*, ed. George Yancy, 1–16. Malden, MA: Blackwell.

Chapter Ten

Rosa Luxemburg and Karl Marx

10.1 Introduction

10.2 Karl Marx, by Rosa Luxemburg

10.3 Karl Marx & Rosa Luxemburg, by Christian Fuchs

References

> "The philosophers have only *interpreted* the world in various ways; the point is to *change* it"
>
> Marx's 11th thesis on Feuerbach (1845, 5)

10.1 Introduction

Marx died on 14 March 1883. Exactly 20 years later, on 14 March 1903, Rosa Luxemburg's reflections on Karl Marx were published in German in *Vorwärts*, the newspaper of the Social Democratic Party of Germany. We here publish an English translation of Luxemburg's essay. Christian Fuchs reflects on the question of how we can make sense of Rosa Luxemburg's reading today. Source of the German original: Luxemburg, Rosa. 1903. Karl Marx. *Vorwärts* 62: 1–2.

10.2 Karl Marx, by Rosa Luxemburg

Twenty years ago, Marx laid his towering head to rest. And although we only experienced a couple of years ago what in the language of German professors is called "the crisis of Marxism", it suffices to throw a glance at the masses that today follow socialism alone in Germany and at socialism's importance in all so-called civilised countries, in order to grasp the immensity of the work of Marx's thoughts.

If it mattered to express in few words what Marx did for the contemporary working class, then one could say: Marx has uncovered the modern working class as historical category, that is, as a class with particular historical conditions of existence and laws of motion. A mass of wage-workers, who were led to solidarity by the similarity of their social existence in bourgeois society and looked for a way out of their condition and partly for a bridge to the promised land of socialism, arguably existed in capitalist

DOI: 10.4324/9781003199182-10

countries before Marx. Marx was the first who elevated workers to the working *class* by linking them through the specific historical task of conquering political power in the socialist revolution.

Class struggle for conquering political power was the bridge that Marx built between socialism and the proletarian movement that elementarily rises up from the ground of contemporary society.

The bourgeoisie has always shown sure instinct when it followed the proletariat's *political* aspirations with hatred and fear. Already in November 1831, when reporting on the working class' initial impulses on the continent to the French Chamber of Deputies, Casimir Périer[1] said: "Gentlemen, we can be relieved! *Nothing* politically has emerged from Lyon's labour movement". The dominant classes namely considered every political impulse of the proletariat as an early sign of the coming emancipation of the workers from the bourgeoisie's paternalism.

It was only Marx who succeeded in putting working class-politics on the foundation of conscious class struggle and to thereby forge it into a deadly weapon directed against existing society's order. The *materialist conception of history* in general and the Marxian *theory of capitalist development* in particular form the foundation of contemporary social democratic labour politics. Only someone to whom the essence of social democratic politics and the essence of Marxism are equally a mystery can think of class conscious labour politics outside of Marxian theory.

In his *Feuerbach*, Engels (1886) formulated the essence of philosophy as the eternal question about the relationship between thought and being, the question of human consciousness in the objective, material world. If we transfer the concepts of *being* and *thought* from the abstract world of nature and individual speculation, whereto professional philosophers stick with iron determination, to the realm of societal life, then the same can in a particular sense be said about *socialism*. Socialism has always been the feeling for and the search for means and ways to bring being into accord with thought, namely to bring the historical forms of existence into accord with societal consciousness.

It was left to Marx and his friend Engels to find the solution to a centuries-old painstaking task. Marx has revealed history's most important driving force by discovering that the history of all hitherto-existing societies is *in the last instance* the history of its relations of production and exchange, whose development manifests itself under the rule of private property in the political and social institutions as class struggle. Thereby we gained an explanation of the necessary disparity between con-sciousness and being in all hitherto-existing forms of society, between human will and social action, and between intentions and results.

Humanity first uncovered the secret behind its own societal process thanks to Marxian ideas. Furthermore, the discovery of the laws of capitalist development also expounded the way that society took from its natural, unconscious stage, during which history was made in the manner that bees construct their honeycombs, to the stage of conscious, deliberate, true *human* history, wherein for the first time society's will and action come into accord with each other so that the social human will for the first time in millennia do *that* what (s)he *wants* to do.

To speak with Engels (1886/87, 270), this final "leap from the kingdom of necessity to the kingdom of freedom" that only the socialist revolution will realise for society as a whole, already takes place *within the existing order* – in *social-democratic politics.*[2] With the Ariadne thread of Marx's theory in its hand, the workers' party is today the only party that *knows* from the historical point of view *what it does* and therefore does *what it desires.* This is the whole secret of social democracy's power.

The bourgeois world has long been puzzled by social democracy's astonishing resi-lience and steady progress. From time to time there are single senile silly-billies who, blinded by special moral successes of our politics, advise the bourgeoisie to learn a lesson from "our example" and from social democracy's secret wisdom and idealism. They do not understand that what is a source of life and fountain of youth and energy for the aspiring working class-politics is deadly poison for the bourgeois parties.

Because what is it that in fact gives us the inner moral strength to endure and shake off the biggest repression, such as a dozen years of the law against socialists,[3] with such laughing courage? Is it for instance the disinherited's keenness to pursue small im-provements of their condition? The modern proletariat is unlike the philistine and the petty bourgeois not willing to become a hero for the sake of everyday comforts. The plain, sober bigotry of the world of English trade unions shows how little the pure prospect of small material gains for the working class is capable of creating a moral flight of fancy.

Is it the ascetic stoicism of a sect that as among the original Christians flickers up all the more brightly the more persecution there is? The modern proletarian is, as heir and pupil of bourgeois society, far too much a born materialist and a healthy sensual human of flesh and blood to alone draw love and strength for his ideas from torture in accordance with slave morality.

Is it, finally, the "justice" of our cause that makes us so impregnable? The causes of the Chartists, the followers of Weitling,[4] and the utopian socialist schools were no less "just" than our cause, but nonetheless they all soon succumbed to modern society's resilience.

If the contemporary labour movement victoriously shakes the manes, defying all the acts of violence of the enemy world, then this is especially due to its calm understanding of the lawfulness of the objective historical development, the understanding of the fact that "capitalist production" begets "with the inexorability of a natural process [...] its own negation" (Marx 1867, 929) – namely the expropriation of the expropriators, the socialist revolution. It is this insight, from which the labour movement draws the firm guarantee of its final victory, not just impetuosity, but also the patience, the power to action and the courage to endure.

The first condition of successful politics of struggle is understanding the movements of the opponent. But what is the key to understanding bourgeois politics down to its smallest ramifications and the labyrinths of daily politics so that we are equally protected from surprises and illusions? The key is nothing more than the insight that one must explain all forms of societal consciousness in their inner turmoil from the interests of classes and groups, from the antagonisms of material life and in the last instance from "the conflict existing between the social forces of production and the relations of production" (Marx 1859, 263).

And what gives us the capability to adapt our politics to new appearances of political life, such as for example world politics, and especially to assess it, also without special talent and profundity, with the depth of judgement that gets to the core of the appearance itself, while the most talented bourgeois critics only scratch on its surface or get caught up in hopeless antagonisms at every glance into the depth? Again, nothing else than the overview of historical development based on the law that the "mode of production of material life conditions the general process of social, political and intellectual life" (Marx 1859, 263).

What is it that provides us above all with a measure for avoiding in the selection of struggles' ways and means aimless experiments and utopian escapades that are a waste of energy? Once the direction of the economic and political process of contemporary society has been understood, this understanding can act as a measure not just of the overall direction of our campaign plan, but also of every detail of our political efforts. Thanks to this guideline the working class has managed for the first time to transform the idea of socialism as the ultimate aim into daily politics' divisional coins and to elevate the everyday political detail work to the big idea's executive tool. There was bourgeois politics led by workers and there was revolutionary socialism before Marx. But only since Marx and through Marx has a *socialist working class-politics* existed that is at the same time and in the fullest meaning of both words *revolutionary Realpolitik.*

If we understand by Realpolitik a politics that only sets itself achievable goals that it pursues to obtain by the most effective means in the shortest time, then the difference between proletarian class-politics that stands in the Marxian spirit and bourgeois politics is that bourgeois politics is real from the standpoint of *material daily politics*, whereas socialist politics is real from the standpoint of the historical *tendency of development*. Exactly the same difference can be found between a vulgar economic theory of value that conceives of value as a thing in appearance from the standpoint of the market stall and Marxian theory that conceives of value as a societal relation in a particular historical epoch.

But proletarian Realpolitik is also revolutionary in that it goes in all the parts of its endeavours beyond the bounds of the existing order in which it operates, by consciously regarding itself only as the preliminary stage of the act that turns proletarian Realpolitik into the politics of the ruling, revolutionary proletariat.

In this manner, Marx's theory penetrates and enlightens everything – the moral power, by which we overcome perils; our tactics of struggle, even its last details; our critique of opponents; our everyday agitation, by which we win the masses; our entire work down to the tips of the fingers. And if we here and there indulge in the illusion that our politics is today with all its inner power independent from Marx's theory, then this only shows that our praxis speaks in Marx's terms although we do not know it, just like Molière's bourgeois spoke in prose.

It suffices that we visualise Marx's achievements in order to understand that bourgeois society made him its deadly enemy because of his concept of the working class's socialist revolution. It became evident to the dominant classes that overcoming the modern labour movement meant overcoming Marx. In the 20 years since Marx's death, we have seen a constant series of attempts to destroy Marx's spirit in the labour movement's theory and praxis.

The labour movement has from the start of its history navigated between the two poles of revolutionary-socialist utopianism and bourgeois Realpolitik. Wholly absolutist or semi-absolutist pre-bourgeois society formed the historical soil of the first. The revolutionary-utopian stage of socialism in Western Europe is by and large concluded by the development of bourgeois class rule, although we can observe single relapses into it until today. The other danger – getting lost in bourgeois Realpolitik's patchwork – has only emerged in the course of the labour movement's strengthening on the floor of parliamentarism.

The idea was that bourgeois parliamentarism would provide weapons for *practically* overcoming the proletariat's revolutionary politics and that the democratic union of the classes and social peace brought about by reforms should replace class struggle.

And what has been achieved? The illusion may have here and there lasted for a while, but the unsuitability of Realpolitik's bourgeois methods for the working class became immediately evident. The fiasco of ministerialism in France,[5] the betrayal by liberalism in Belgium,[6] the breakdown of parliamentarism in Germany[7] – the short dream of "quiet development" strike by strike broke to pieces. The Marxian law of the tendency of the sharpening of social contrasts as foundation of class struggle asserted itself. And every day brings new signs and wonders. In the Netherlands, 24 hours of the railway strike like an earthquake overnight opened up a yawning gap in the middle of society, from which class struggle blazed out. Holland is on fire.[8]

So in the light of the "march of the worker battalions", the base of bourgeois democracy and bourgeois legislation breaks down like a thin ice sheet and again and again makes the working class aware that its final goal can *not* be achieved on this base. All of this is the result of the many attempts to "practically" overcome Marx.

Hundreds of industrious apologists have made the *theoretical* overcoming of Marxism their life-task and the springboard of their careers. What have they achieved? They have managed to create in the circles of the faithful intelligentsia the conviction that Marx's works are "one-sided" and "exaggerated". But even those of the bourgeois ideologues, who can be taken serious, such as Stammler,[9] have understood that nothing can be achieved with "'a bit more or a bit less' half-truths" against "such a deep and profound theory". But what can bourgeois academia oppose to Marxian theory *at a whole*?

Since Marx has emphasised the historical standpoint of the working class in the fields of philosophy, history, and economics, bourgeois research in these fields has lost the thread. The classical philosophy of nature has come to an end. The bourgeois philosophy of history has come to an end. Scientific political economy has come to an end.

In historical research, as far as there is not the dominance of an unconscious and inconsequent materialism, an eclecticism shimmering in all colours has taken the place of any unified theory. So there is the relinquishment of the unified explanation of the process of history, i.e. of the philosophy of history as such. Economics oscillates between two schools, the "historical" one and the "subjective" one. The one is a protest against the other. And both are a protest against Marx. The first one negates economic theory, i.e. the knowledge in this field, in principle in order to negate Marx, whereas the other one negates the only – objective – research method that first turned political economy into a science.

Certainly the social science book fair every month brings whole mountains of products that result from bourgeois industriousness to the market. And the thickest volumes written by ambitious, modern professors are put out at large-scale capitalist, machine-like speed. But in such diligent monographs either research buries its head like an ostrich into the sand of small, fragmented phenomena so that it does not have to see broader connections and only works for daily needs. Or research only simulates thoughts and "social theories" that are in the last instance just reflexes of Marx's thoughts that are hidden under overloaded tinsel ornaments that appeal to the taste associated with commodities of the "modern" bazaar. Autonomous flights of thought, a daring glance into the distance or an invigorating deduction are nowhere to be found.

And if social progress has again created a new series of scientific problems, then again only the *Marxian* method offers ways for solving them.

So it is everywhere just theorylessness, epistemological scepticism, that bourgeois social science is able to oppose to Marxian knowledge. Marxian theory is a child of bourgeois science, but the birth of this child has cost the mother her life.

Therefore, the upturn of the working class has knocked the weapons out of bourgeois society's hands that the latter wanted to use on the battlefield against Marxian socialism. And today, 20 years after Marx's death, bourgeois society is all the more powerless against him, but Marx more alive than ever.

Of course, contemporary society has one comfort left. While society struggles in vain to find a means to overcome Marx's theory, it does not notice that the only real means of doing so are hidden in this theory itself. Because it is through and through historical, Marxian theory only claims temporally limited validity. Because it is through and through dialectical, it carries in itself the definite seeds of its own dissolution.

Karl Marx, by Rosa Luxemburg

If we abstract from its unchanging part, namely from the historical method of research, then Marxian theory in its most general outlines consists of insights into the historical way that leads from the last "antagonistic" form of society, i.e. societies that are based on class conflicts, to the communist society that is built on all members' solidarity of interests.

Marxian theory is especially, just like earlier classical theories of political economy, the mental reflex of a particular period of economic and political development, namely the transition from the capitalist to the socialist phase of history. But it is more than just a reflex. The historical transition that Marx identified can namely not take place without Marxian knowledge having become the knowledge of a particular class in society, the modern proletariat. That Marx's theory becomes the working class' form of consciousness and as such an *element* of history is the *precondition* for the realisation of the historical revolution formulated in Marx's theory.

Marx's theory proves to be true continuously with every new proletarian who supports class struggle. So Marx's theory is at the same time part of the historical process and is also itself a process. Social revolution will be *The Communist Manifesto*'s final chapter.

Consequently, the part of Marxian theory that is most dangerous to the existing order of society will sooner or later be "overcome". But only *together* with the existing order of society.

10.3 Karl Marx & Rosa Luxemburg, by Christian Fuchs

10.3.1 Dead or Alive?

Rosa Luxemburg's reflections on Karl Marx were published in German on 14 March 1903, in *Vorwärts*, the newspaper of the Social Democratic Party of Germany. It is a text about Karl Marx's life and death, the life and death of his ideas and politics, the life and death of socialism, class struggles and alternatives to capitalism. Karl Marx was born on 5 May 1818, and died on 14 May 1883. Just like Marx's critical political economic theory and progressive politics were much needed 20 years after his death, they are also needed and remain alive more than 200 years after his birth and more than 135 years after his death. Marx is alive as the ghost that keeps on haunting capitalism as long as the latter continues to exist.

Luxemburg stresses that bourgeois ideologues try to declare Marx's ideas and politics dead. They did so in 1903. They do so in 2018. Writing in 1903, she says: "In the twenty years since Marx's death, we have seen a constant series of attempts to destroy Marx's spirit in the labour movement's theory and praxis". 115 years later, the situation is not so different. Much attention is given to Marx on the occasion of his bicentenary. One can discern a bourgeois from a socialist engagement with Marx: bourgeois readings of Marx today argue that he was wrong and his ideas died with him or were already dead while he was alive. What they mean is: "TINA – There is no alternative to capitalism". Socialist readings acknowledge two facts: (a) Marx's ideas and politics continue to be of high relevance for understanding and criticising contemporary capitalism. (b) Marx's thought is dialectical and historical, which means that his basic categories have also evolved with the history of capitalism and the development of Marxian theory. They are not static and fixed, but need to be dialectically developed for today. There is a dialectic of continuity and change of capitalism that manifests itself in the way that Marxian theory uses Marx's categories to explain capitalism today.

Many of us are today probably less optimistic than Rosa Luxemburg in 1903 about socialism's subjectivity because far-right ideology has in recent years been much more strengthened than left worldviews and politics. But in objective terms, socialist and Marxian analyses and politics remain absolutely vital: Capitalism has since 2008 been in a deep crisis that has evolved from an economic into a political and ideological crisis. It cannot be ruled out that a new World War will be the result of proliferating new nationalisms. Capitalism's crisis and the high levels of inequality, precarious life and precarious labour in the world do not just show how much we need Marx's ideas today. The political-economic situation evidences the need of socialism as an alternative to capitalism and social struggles for Democratic Socialism and Socialist Humanism.

10.3.2 Bourgeois Readings of Marx

When the socialist movement became larger and larger at the time of Rosa Luxemburg, bourgeois thinkers' criticisms of Marx proliferated. So for example in 1896, Eugen Böhm-Bawerk published *Karl Marx and the Close of His System*. Böhm-Bawerk came from an aristocratic family (his full family name was Böhm *Ritter von* Bawerk) and was Minister of Finance of the Austrian part of the Austro-Hungarian Empire from 1895 until 1904. At the very start of his essay, Böhm-Bawerk (1949/1896, 3) leaves no doubt that he advances a critique of Marx because the latter had become known to "wide circles of readers". Böhm-Bawerk for example argues that the "fundamental proposition that labour is the sole basis of value" is "dialectical hocus-pocus" (Böhm-Bawerk 1949/1896, 77) and that Marx's theory is "a house of cards" (Böhm-Bawerk 1949/1896, 118). Today, also, criticisms of Marx proliferate together with the wider attention that is given to his works. So for example ideological media such as *Frankfurter Allgemeine Zeitung*, one of the ideological mouthpieces of German capital, claim that Marx was a "false prophet" and that "his central predictions were quite wrong" (FAZ 2017).

How right Marx's assumption was that a theory of economic value is a theory of time and labour in capitalism, still becomes evident in at least two respects today: a) Capital regularly reacts negatively to demands for the legal reduction in working hours without wage cuts. b) There is a tremendous mismatch between those working overtime on the one hand and those who are unemployed or precariously employed or conduct unremunerated labour on the other hand. Capital tries to maximise the hours worked per year by a single employee and to maximise the average amount of commodities workers produce per unit of time in order to increase profits. "Economy of time, to this all economy ultimately reduces itself " (Marx 1857/58, 173).

10.3.3 The Working Class

Luxemburg stresses that Marx's most important insight was that production, class relations, the exploitation of the working class and class struggles form the heart of modern, capitalist society. Given Luxemburg's stress on the importance of the working class in Marx's works, politics and thought, reading her text today brings up the questions: Who is part of the working class today? What are the prospects for working class struggles?

The composition and qualities of the working class have changed since the times of Marx and Luxemburg. Class theory today needs to account for phenomena such as precarious freelance labour, knowledge and service labour, the transformation of labour by digital media technologies (digital labour), the vast amount of the unemployed, new forms of unremunerated labour, etc. In addition, working-class consciousness poses a complex problem today whose analysis requires the combination of class analysis and ideology critique. Where is the working class today? Who is part of it? What does its consciousness look like? What are the prospects for the self-emancipation of the working class today? Peter Goodwin (2018) pinpoints these and other important questions that Marxist theory needs to answer today in respect to the transformation of society's class structure.

Luxemburg speaks of the "immensity of the work of Marx's thought", whereby she points to the fact that Marx was an intellectual worker. He partly worked as a journalist to earn a living, but by and large depended on Engels and other sources of funding for financing his and his family's life. He had to lead a life in poverty. Today, as the general intellect has become an immediate productive force, intellectual work has become generalised. Higher education and as a consequence highly skilled labour has become much more prevalent. Knowledge work has become an important form of labour accounting for a significant share of value-added. We have experienced the rise of mass intellectuality. Mass intellectuality has under capitalist conditions been accompanied by new forms of precarity and exploitation and does not imply that knowledge workers are automatically conscious of their class status.

10.3.4 Praxis

Luxemburg's text shows a somewhat exaggerated historical optimism that considers socialist revolution as highly likely. But these passages should not be mistaken for historical determinism and the automatic breakdown of capitalism. In the paragraph where she refers to the passage from Marx's capital that says that capitalism creates its own negation, Luxemburg uses the conditional form "If the contemporary labour movement [...wins]", which indicates that the "final victory" is all but certain and depends on the unpredictable outcomes of class struggles.

In the context of the First World War, she stressed this openness of the historical process in a pointed manner by arguing that in situations of severe crisis we face the choice between "the reversion to barbarism" and socialism (Luxemburg 1915, 388). "*This world war* means a reversion to barbarism. The triumph of imperialism leads to the destruction of culture [...] Thus we stand today, as Friedrich Engels prophesied more than a generation ago, before the awful proposition: either the triumph of imperialism and the destruction of all culture, and, as in ancient Rome, depopulation, desolation, degeneration, a vast cemetery; or, the victory of socialism, that is, the conscious struggle of the international proletariat against imperialism, against its methods, against war" (Luxemburg 1915, 388–389). "Socialism will not fall as manna from heaven. It can only be won by a long chain of powerful struggles" (Luxemburg 1915, 388).

Luxemburg in her essay makes clear that the transition from capitalism to communism can only become a reality if the content of Marx's theory guides political consciousness. The implication is that if ideologies (such as nationalism, racism, xenophobia, anti-socialism, neoliberal entrepreneurship, etc.) and other developments forestall critical consciousness and critical action, then capitalism will continue to exist (unless society as such breaks down because of nuclear war or other disasters).

Norman Geras writes in his book *The Legacy of Rosa Luxemburg* that Luxemburg's Marxism is radically different from "that determinist science of iron economic laws which is the usual foundation of fatalism and spontaneism" (Geras 2015, 19). He argues that passages stressing necessity and chance of social development can be found next to each other in many of Luxemburg's works. Formulations such as the one about "socialism or barbarism" imply that "[t]here is not one direction of development, there are several, and the role of the proletariat under the leadership of its party is not simply to accelerate the historical process but to decide it. Socialism is not the inevitable product of iron economic laws but an 'objective possibility' defined by the socio-economic conditions of capitalism" (Geras 2015, 28). Geras points out that for Luxemburg, barbarism signifies capitalism's collapse. Every economic crisis is a partial collapse of capitalism. But barbarism also entails fascism, warfare, genocide, nuclear devastation, the ecological crisis, etc., which are all immanent potentials and realities of capitalism. So capitalism itself is barbarism. For Luxemburg, the collapse of capitalism and the creation of socialism are not identical (Geras 2015, 35). Luxemburg's interpretation of Marx fuses "objective laws with the revolutionary energy and will, which, on the basis of that theory, attempt actually to change the world" (Geras 2015, 37).

It should be noted that in the passage from *Capital Volume 1* that Luxemburg discusses, Marx (1867, 929) speaks of a "natural process" and not, as incorrectly translated in the version used in the Marx & Engels Collected-Works, of a "law of Nature" (see Fuchs 2016, 69–70, for a discussion of the translation of this passage from German to English). The difference is that in 19th-century science, laws of nature were considered deterministic, whereas processes in nature always have a certain level of unpredictability. The full passage reads:

> But capitalist production begets, with the inexorability of a natural process, its own negation. This is the negation of the negation. It does not re-establish private property, but it does indeed establish individual *property on the* basis of the achievements of the capitalist era: namely co-operation and the

possession in common of the land and the means of production produced by labour itself.

(Marx 1867, 929)

What Marx says here is that communism is the negation of the negation of capitalism and entails co-operative work based on the common ownership of land and the means of production. Capitalism negates itself in its own development through crises. Communism is capitalism's negation of the negation. The preceding paragraph ends with Marx's famous call and demand that the "expropriators are expropriated" (Marx 1867, 929). This formulation implies that the process Marx talks about only takes place if there are active subjects who in the course of a revolution take the means of production into common ownership. The question of the revolutionary negation of the negation is for Marx not one of automatic breakdown, but of class struggle and revolution (see Fuchs 2016, 322–324 for a detailed discussion of this passage).

10.3.5 Materialism

Luxemburg stresses Marx's materialist concept of society. But what does it mean that the production of material life conditions society, including individual and collective consciousness? Matter in society is neither simply the economy nor tangible things we can touch. By matter in society, Marx refers to the process of social production. That consciousness is grounded in material life means that the human individual, its thoughts and language, are not isolated and cannot exist in isolation, but only in and through social relations with other humans that are relations of production, in which they co-produce the economy, political and cultural life: "The ideas which these individuals form are ideas either about their relation to nature or about their mutual relations or about their own nature. It is evident that in all these cases their ideas are the conscious expression – real or illusory – of their real relations and activities, of their production, of their intercourse, of their social and political conduct. [...] Men are the producers of their conceptions, ideas, etc., and precisely men conditioned by the mode of production of their material life, by their material intercourse and its further development in the social and political structure" (Marx and Engels 1845/46, 36). The implication is that ideas, communication, politics, culture, art, science, philosophy, etc. do not form a superstructure detached from an economic base, but are themselves realms of economic production that have at the same time non-economic qualities. Whereas the base/superstructure metaphor is misleading, it is preferable to talk about the material character of society as a dialectic of the economic and the non-economic.

10.3.6 Left Socialism's Revolutionary Realpolitik

Luxemburg interprets the politics that Marx stands for as revolutionary Realpolitik. She opposes revolutionary Realpolitik to "revolutionary-socialist utopianism" and "bourgeois Realpolitik". At the time of Luxemburg, the bourgeois Realpolitik of the Left took on the form of revisionist social democracy that stood under the influence of Eduard Bernstein's doctrine of reformism and society's mechanical evolutionary development into socialism. Left utopianism took on the form of the anarchist propaganda of the deed.

Isn't the situation of the Left today quite similarly facing the two dead ends of utopianism and bourgeois Realpolitik? On the one end, we find bourgeoisified social democrats, who advance a purely reformist parliamentary politics that has succumbed to neoliberal ideology. The meaning of social democracy today is as a result completely opposed to the meaning it had at the time of Luxemburg as well as at the time of Marx. On the other end, we find radical social movements, who believe in the power of horizontalism and prefigurative politics. They limit politics to civil society and in an anarchist manner want to change society without taking power. Such movements overlook that the state is itself an important terrain of struggle, that it is a mistake to leave this battleground to bourgeois parties, and that changing society simply cannot start from the outside of society, but requires power and resources that come from the inside of the system and are in a dialectical process of revolutionary sublation turned from the inside out. So whereas contemporary social movement politics is by and large a version of abstract, idealist anarchist romanticism, social democracy has completely adapted to the system. Rosa Luxemburg reminds us that Marx argued for the politics of revolutionary reformism that is based on a dialectic of reform and revolution. Parliament and governments are terrains of struggles that should be strategically appropriated for improving the conditions of struggles. The Left needs both a civil society wing and a party that interact dialectically.

If the Left does not want to leave politics to the forces that dominate today – nationalists, the far-right and neoliberals – then it needs to reinvent a left socialism that in a similar vein to the political understanding of Marx and Luxemburg is based on dialectics of party/movements, organisation/spontaneity, leadership/masses, reform/revolution. Michael Hardt and Antonio Negri (2017, 278) argue in this context: "The taking of power, by electoral or other means, must serve to open space for autonomous and prefigurative practices on an ever-larger scale and nourish the slow transformation of institutions, which must continue over the long term. Similarly practices of exodus must find ways to complement and further projects of both antagonistic reform and taking power".

10.3.7 Against Positivism

Rosa Luxemburg in her reflections on Karl Marx also advances a critique of positivist science and positivist social theory. Positivist research is eclectic, fragmented, theoryless, and follows trendy fashions: "Autonomous flights of thought, a daring glance into the distance or an invigorating deduction are nowhere to be found". Positivism cannot explain society's big problems and questions, the large connections of moments within society. It lacks a focus on society as dialectical totality. The academic war that neoliberal academia and postmodernism have for decades waged against Marxist theory has in contemporary society resulted in an academic landscape that is quite similar to the one that Luxemburg criticises.

There is much talk about interdisciplinarity, but in reality interdisciplinarity lacks critical theory and philosophy and is little more than a fancy catchword that aims at turning the university into a business school and corporation and research via the focus on STE(A)M into corporations' and capitalism's vassal. In the social sciences and humanities, postmodernism has resulted in a focus on small-scale micro-studies (typically studies of micro-phenomenon A in country or city B), a neglect of understanding society as totality, and a neglect of the development of grand social theories. While academia gets ever more uncritical, society's global problems get worse. The rise of computational social science and big data analytics is a typical example of how the focus on positivism (in this case via large-scale data analysis) and the lack of grand theories threaten and destroy the critical potentials of the social sciences and humanities (Fuchs 2017). Marxian theory poses a counter-model. It is a true form of inter- and transdisciplinarity that allows situating specific phenomena in their broadest academic and societal context and aims at producing knowledge that helps advancing human emancipation.

200 years after Marx's birth, his approach is urgently needed in research, theory, politics and society at large. That "Marx is needed" means nothing more than that the critique of capitalism and class is an urgent theoretical and political task. Only Marxian theory and praxis can advance knowledge and a form of politics that help us to overcome the severe problems posed by nationalism, inequalities, ecological devastation, authoritarianism, wars, genocides, and economic and political crises. We need to repeat Marx today.

Notes

1 Explanatory remark [Christian Fuchs]: Casimir Pierre Périer (1777–1832) was a French banker and politician, who served as France's ninth Prime Minister (1831–1832).

2 Explanatory remark [Christian Fuchs]: It should be noted that in 1903, when Luxemburg published this text, no linguistic distinction was drawn between social democracy and communism. Communist parties had not yet been differentiated from social democratic parties. When Luxemburg therefore speaks of social democracy, she means movements and parties that aim at the fundamental transformation of society that brings about the abolition of capitalism.

3 Explanatory remark [Christian Fuchs]: The Chancellor of the German Empire Otto von Bismarck (1815–1898) introduced the "Law against the public danger of Social Democratic endeavours" (better known as *Sozialistengesetz* – anti-socialist law) in 1878. This law was in effect until 1890 and prohibited meetings, publications, unions, and associations guided by socialist principles.

4 Wilhelm Weitling (1808–1871) was an early communist writer and activist.

5 Explanatory remark [Christian Fuchs]: Luxemburg here alludes to the fact that the socialist Alexandre Millerand participated as Minister of Commerce, Industry, Posts and Telegraphs in the bourgeois French government of Prime Minister Pierre Waldeck-Rousseau from 1899 until 1902.

6 Explanatory remark [Christian Fuchs]: In April 1902, there were wildcat strikes in Belgium that turned into a general strike for the abolishment of the plural voting system that privileged the rich. Under the impression of these working class protests, the leader of the Belgian Labour Party, Emile Vandervelde, introduced a motion for the introduction of universal suffrage to the Belgian Parliament. The motion was defeated. Introducing universal suffrage required another general strike in 1913 and took until 1919. Representatives of the Liberal Party were, just like the Belgian Labour Party, opposed to the absolute majority rule of the Catholic Party under Prime Minister Paul de Smet de Naezer, but repeatedly opposed electoral reforms.

7 Explanatory remark [Christian Fuchs]: Before the end of the German Monarchy in the November Revolution 1918 and the founding of the Weimar Republic, the German Reichstag did not have full political power. Political decisions were often taken by the government independent of the Reichstag.

8 Explanatory remark [Christian Fuchs]: In 1903, Dutch railroad workers organised a general strike in solidarity with other workers for the right to strike and unionise.

9 Explanatory remark [Christian Fuchs]: Rudolf Stammler (1856–1938) was a legal theorist and the main representative of neo-Kantian legal philosophy in Germany.

References

Böhm-Bawerk, Eugen. 1949/1896. *Karl Marx and the Close of His System*. New York: Kelley.

Engels, Friedrich. 1887/88. Anti-Dühring: Herrn Eugen Dührings Revolution in Science. In *Marx & Engels Collected Works (MECW) Volume 25*, 1–309. London: Lawrence & Wishart.

Engels, Friedrich. 1886. Ludwig Feuerbach and the End of Classical German Philosophy. In *Marx & Engels Collected Works (MECW) Volume 26*, 353–398. London: Lawrence & Wishart.

FAZ. 2017. Der falsche Prophet. *FAZ Online*, July 8, 2017.

Fuchs, Christian. 2017. From Digital Positivism and Administrative Big Data Analytics towards Critical Digital and Social Media Research! *European Journal of Communication* 32 (1): 37–49.

Fuchs, Christian. 2016. *Reading Marx in the Information Age. A Media and Communication Studies Perspective on Capital Volume I*. New York: Routledge.

Geras, Norman. 2015. *The Legacy of Rosa Luxemburg*. London: Verso.

Goodwin, Peter. 2018. Where's the Working Class? *tripleC: Communication, Capitalism & Critique* 18 (2): 535–545.

Hardt, Michael and Antonio Negri. 2017. *Assembly*. Oxford: Oxford University Press.

Luxemburg, Rosa. 1915. The Crisis of German Social Democracy (The Junius Pamphlet). In *Rosa Luxemburg Speaks*, ed. Mary-Alice Waters, 371–477. New York: Pathfinder.

Marx, Karl. 1867. *Capital Volume I*. London: Penguin.

Marx, Karl. 1859. Preface to A Contribution to the Critique of Political Economy. In *Marx & Engels Collected Works (MECW) Volume 29*, 261–265. London: Lawrence & Wishart.

Marx, Karl. 1857/58. *Grundrisse*. London: Penguin.

Marx, Karl. 1845. Theses on Feuerbach. In *Marx & Engels Collected Works (MECW) Volume 5*, 3–5. London: Lawrence & Wishart.

Marx, Karl and Friedrich Engels. 1845/46. The German ideology. In *Marx & Engels Collected Works (MECW) Volume 5*, 19–539. London: Lawrence & Wishart.

Chapter Eleven
Conclusion

11.1 Critical Theory

This book asked: What are important elements of a Marxist-Humanist critical theory of society? It engaged with some of the key thinkers, approaches, and elements of a critical theory of society in order to work out elements of the foundations of a critical theory.

All social scientists want to be critical. But often critique and being critical is simply understood as asking questions or trying to falsify dominant approaches and paradigms. This is the positivist understanding of critique. The tradition that goes back to Karl Marx has a different understanding of critique. It is interested in a critical theory of society (sometimes also termed "critical social theory" but "critical theory of society" is a more precise term).

Critical theory is an approach that studies society in a dialectical way by analysing political economy, domination, exploitation and ideologies. It is a normative approach that is based on the judgment that domination is a problem, that society free from domination is needed. It wants to inform political struggles that want to establish such a society.

Dialectical reason is critical theory's epistemology. Critical theory's ontology includes the critique of political economy, the critique of domination and exploitation, and ideology critique. Critical theory is also a praxeological approach, a method that wants to inform and reflects on human praxis, i.e. social struggles.

Karl Marx is the founding figure of the tradition of the critical theory of society. There have been a variety of debates within and about critical theory. In the 20th century,

DOI: 10.4324/9781003199182-11

such debates included, for example, the debate between critical and administrative/ positivist research, debates about the relationship of postmodernist theory to Marxist theory, debates about humanism and structuralism in critical theory, and debates about the relationship of class and identity (politics).

Critical theory debates have and will continue in the 21st century as a means for clarification and moving critical theory forward in the context of changes of society. One such critical theory debate has been the one between Nancy Fraser and Axel Honneth on the relationship of redistribution and recognition in critical theory. Their discussion has reflected on the rise of identity politics since the 1970s. Such politics has often downplayed or denied the importance of class politics that is focused on the critique of the political economy of capitalism. Fraser and Honneth ascertain that both strands of politics are important for the Left and critical theory. Honneth argues for a moral monism that sees recognition as the super-category that unites all forms of and struggles for justice under the rubric of recognition. Fraser advances a dualism where struggles for redistribution and recognition are both equally important, interact, and are different.

The present author has advanced a dialectical approach of how to think about the relationship of recognition and redistribution. This approach is based on a model of society that is grounded in humans' social production. In modern, alienated societies, social production takes on the form of the accumulation of power that alienates humans from the structures and systems they live in. The consequence is the unequal distribution of power, including wealth, decision-power/influence, and reputation/ definition-power. Questions of justice are therefore questions of production, distribution, power, and social struggles. In capitalist society, the logic of accumulation shapes the most important realms of society, namely the economy, politics, and culture. Capitalism, patriarchy, and racism are three modes of power relations that each have an economy, a politics, and a form of ideological culture. Capitalist society is a formation of society that is shaped by the logic of accumulation. In capitalist society, capitalism, patriarchy, and racism interact in a variety of ways that constitute a specific form of an alienated society. Questions of identity are not independent of capitalism and class, but are always related to questions and dimensions of class and capitalism. In capitalist society, class relations, racism and gender relations have their common foundation in the capitalist labour relation, which means that wage labour, racialised labour, reproductive labour, and unpaid labour constitute the common foundation of class, racism, and patriarchy.

In another critical theory debate, Luc Boltanski and Axel Honneth ask the question of what role empirical research and philosophy should play in critical theory. Honneth argues for the importance of moral philosophy as part of what he calls a "critical sociology" that stands in the classical tradition of the Frankfurt School and is theory-oriented. Boltanski calls for a "sociology of critique" that studies empirically how alienation is experienced and resisted. The approach the present author has advanced understands itself as a *critical sociology of critique* that combines social theory, empirical social research, and moral philosophy.

A critical theory of society uses a variety of terms but often is organised around a central category that defines the understanding and critique of society. In a trialogue, the critical sociologists Klaus Dörre, Stephan Lessenich, and Hartmut Rosa have suggested different key categories for critical theory: Landnahme (grabbing/seizure/appropriation/subsumption of territory), activation (Lessenich), acceleration (Rosa). The result of their debate was that Landnahme is the spatial, activation the social and acceleration the temporal dimension of critical theory.

Space, time, and action/practices are certainly important aspects of society and therefore of any social theory. In general sociological terms, social production is the foundational aspect of society that organises humans and human relations in and across space-time (Fuchs 2020). At the level of society in general, the present author sees social production as the key category. Contemporary modern society is a capitalist society, which means it is a society that is based on the logic of accumulation, which implies profit-orientation, the accumulation of money-capital, commodity production and the class relation between capital and labour in the economy; the logic of competing interest groups that struggle for the accumulation of decision-power in the political system; and the production and diffusion of ideologies in the cultural system that create hierarchies of reputation. In the critical theory the present author works on, capitalism is the key category at the level of the analysis of contemporary society. A critical theory of society is also transcendent in that it informs struggles for a better society. In this respect, the present author considers Democratic Socialism as key transcendental category. Social production, capitalism, and Democratic Socialism together form a framework for the analysis of society in general, contemporary society, and the transcendence of alienation. These are key categories for a Marxist-Humanist version of critical theory. These categories form dialectics and each notion is composed of multiple entangled dialectics. Social practices are the production and realisation processes of society's dialectics. In stratified society, class and social struggles are the key social practices that reproduce and transform society.

Critical Theory

The debate between Nancy Fraser and Rahel Jaeggi shows the actuality and importance of the question: What is capitalism? Both theorists hold and advance the argument that we live in a capitalist society. After decades of neoliberal and postmodern denial of the capitalist and class character of society, we have since the 2008 world economic crisis experienced a renewed interest in Marx, socialism, and the analysis of capitalism and class. Fraser and Jaeggi reflect this renewed interest in Marx and the analysis of capitalism.

Fraser and Jaeggi both integrate aspects of postmodern theory that focus too much on plurality into their approaches at the expense of the Marxist-Humanist focus on what it is that humans and societies have in common. To take a Marxist-Humanist approach in social theory, as the present author does, in no way means or wants to suggest that all societies, societal formations, spheres of society, practices, and human beings are the same. To the contrary, the notions of plurality and diversity only are complete if conceived of in a dialectical relation to unity. There is no plurality without unity in plurality. The logic of postmodernism in contrast just sees plurality without unity.

Hegel explains the dialectical logic of unity in plurality as the dialectic of the One and the Many:

> In consequence, the One proves to be what is strictly incompatible with itself, it expels itself out of itself, and what it posits itself as is what is many. We can designate this side of the process of being-for-itself by the figurative expression 'repulsion'. [...] it is the One that is just what excludes itself from itself and posits itself as what is many; each of the many, however, is itself One, and because it behaves as such, this all-round repulsion turns over forthwith into its opposite – *attraction*. [...] But the *many* are each one what the other is, each of them is one or also one of the many; they are therefore one and the same. Or, when the repulsion is considered in itself then, as the negative *behaviour* of the many ones against each other, it is just as essentially their *relation* to each other; and since those to which the One relates itself in its repelling are ones, in relating to them it relates itself to itself. Thus, repulsion is just as essentially *attraction*; and the excluding One or being-for-itself sublates itself.
>
> (Hegel 1991, 154–155 [Addition to §97; §98])

Paraphrasing Hegel, we can say about human beings: the many humans are each one human being just like other humans. Each human being is one of many human beings. Humans are therefore one and the same. There is a relation of humans to each other.

By relating itself to other humans, the human individual relates itself to itself. The human being sublates itself as one human being that relates itself to many other human beings.

We can say something similar about the dialectic of the economy and society: the many spheres of society are each one sphere of social production. Each social sphere is one of the many different spheres of social production. Each social sphere is economic. Society's spheres are therefore one and the same. There is a productive relation of social spheres to other social spheres. By being related to other spheres of social production, each sphere of social production relates itself to itself. Spheres of social production sublate themselves. They are therefore simultaneously economic and non-economic.

Postmodernism's consequence is an understanding of the world that welcomes and politically advances the fragmentation and split-up of social spheres and humans, whereby it supports and legitimates the logic of neoliberalism. The best one can do is that humans not just actively work towards the death of neoliberalism but along with it towards the death of postmodern logic, i.e. the cultural logic of late capitalism (Jameson 1991) and flexible accumulation (Harvey 1989). The postmodern logic is not simply a cultural logic, but an ideology. "The rhetoric of postmodernism is dangerous for it avoids confronting the realities of political economy and the circumstances of global power" (Harvey 1989, 117). Marxist and Socialist Humanism is a viable alternative to both neoliberalism and postmodernism.

11.2 The Dialectic

Thinkers such as C.L.R. James and Theodor W. Adorno stress the importance of mediation in the dialectic. Mediation is the dialectical process of the reflection of contradictory moments that negate each other into each other. Moment A stands in a contradiction to moment B. A reaches into B. B reaches into A. A is reflected into B and B is reflected into A. Mediation means that contradictions create tensions, a negativity that is the source and potential for change. Mediation and media can be found in all dialectical processes.

Dialectical philosophy is an approach that understands the world in its dynamics and as continuous process that develops through contradictions and ruptures. Transformation is for Hegel the process of *Aufhebung* (sublation), the simultaneous elimination, preservation, and uplifting of being to a new level. The end point of a negation of the negation is a specific result of the dialectic that becomes the starting point of a new contradiction and dialectical process. Žižek (2012, 2014) stresses that this is the retroactive character of the dialectic (see also Fuchs 2014 for a discussion of Žižek's interpretation of Hegel and dialectical materialism).

Based on Heraclitus, the dialectic can metaphorically be described as a fire that extinguishes and kindles itself. In nature, this means that matter is organising and producing itself. In society, *crises and antagonisms condition radical changes, but do not call them forth.* The dialectic of society takes place through human practices. In class societies, class struggle is the key mover of society's dialectic. Class society is based on a class antagonism, which constitutes its negativity. The sublation, the negation of the class antagonism, is not an automatic process and therefore not determined. Many factors shape the reality of class struggles and the question whether or not humans organise collectively and struggle against exploitation and alienation or accept and reproduce such power structures. Collective practices in complex causal networks of reality shapes possibilities and adds to or limits the space of possibilities. Praxis and practices can create new possibilities that did not exist before. A specific quality of society is that humans can actively intervene into the objective dialectic by their subjective collective actions. They act based on specific goals and posit the attainment of these goals in and through their practices, which is what Georg Lukács calls teleological positing (see Fuchs 2016, chapter 2; Fuchs 2020, chapter 4; Fuchs 2021, chapter 6).

Teleological positing means that humans through the production process bring about the "intervention into concrete causal relations in order to bring about the realization of the goal" (Lukács 1980, 67) – "the positing of a goal and its means" (Lukács 1980, 22). This involves that the human being is the "conscious creator" (Lukács 1980, 5) of society. Marxist-Humanist approaches stress the importance of asking not just what society and capitalism are, but what the human being is and what its role is in society and in capitalist society. They are based on Marx's insights that humans are both social beings and producing beings. Social production is the materiality of humans and society.

In non-economic spheres, human production results in the creation and sustenance of structures that have their own logics and are dialectically mediated with the economy. Non-economic realms and practices are at the same time economic and non-economic. There is a dialectic of the economic and the non-economic in society.

In Soviet Marxism, the dialectic became a dogma and ideology. Stalin reduced the dialectic to a catechism and assumed that it means that society is driven by natural laws. The true meaning of the dialectic was lost. This does, however, not mean that critical theory should give up the notion of the dialectic. It in contrast needs to work out the democratic-humanist-socialist relevance of the dialectic in society. In society, the dynamic character of production is based on conscious, social actions of human beings who are producing, social, conscious, thinking, creative, moral, anticipatory-imaginative (i.e. capable of imagining the future and acting based on such anticipations) beings. Society is based on a dialectic of human practices and structures, in which human processes of social production play a key role.

Engels's dialectics has often been associated with Soviet Marxism's mechanistic and deterministic worldview. The present author stresses that Engels put an emphasis on the role of praxis and class struggles in history and the development of society and that Engels should therefore be seen as a socialist humanist. Engels stresses that in class society, class and social struggles are the processes, by which humans make their own history. The term scientific socialism that Engels introduced doesn't mean that society is governed by mechanical laws, but that socialist research studies society based on the combination of critical social theory and critical empirical social research.

C.L.R. James and Max Horkheimer/Theodor W. Adorno stress that capitalism's is based on a negative dialectic so that there is the potential and danger that capitalism turns into barbarism and fascism. Democratic, Socialist Humanism is the best antidote and movement against capitalism and therefore also against fascism and barbarism. Capitalism's negative dialectic has taken on a new form in the 21st century. Also today, we are faced with the alternative between socialism and barbarism.

11.3 Alienation

Alienation is a key Marxian category that has played an important role in Marxist-Humanist versions of critical theory. Alienation is on the one hand the process and condition where workers do not control the means of production and goods they produce because these structures are in capitalist society the private property of the capitalist class. In the capitalist economy, alienation constitutes the class relation between the working class and the capitalist class.

On the other hand, alienation is also a more universal process in the economy, politics, and culture where humans do not control the structures, relations, and systems that shape their everyday life. Alienation is the separation of humans from the means and products that organise and shape their lives. Alienation is the universal form of domination, in which humans are not in control of the structures that affect their everyday lives.

In all forms of alienation, humans face asymmetric power relations and conditions that hinder their control over certain objects, structures or products (external nature, the means of production, the means of communication, the political system, the cultural system, etc.) so that aspects of their subjectivity are damaged (concerning human activities, well-being, consciousness, mind/psyche, body, worldviews, social relations). Alienation is neither purely objective nor purely subjective, but a negative relationship between social structures and humans in heteronomous societies.

David Harvey (2018) speaks in this context of the universal character of alienation and coined the notion of universal alienation. alienation is universal in three respects:

1. alienation extends beyond production into the realms of realisation distribution and consumption;
2. alienation extends beyond the economy into politics, culture, social relations, and subjectivity;
3. alienation has in neoliberal capitalism been generalised as the commodification of (almost) everything and accumulation by dispossession.

Sustainability is the basic survival capacity of humans in society. It means an institutional, social, economic, political, environmental, technological, and cultural design of society that allows future generations to survive and to satisfy basic human needs for all. Universal alienation is the cause of the unsustainability of capitalist society. It has produced global crises that hamper the survival capacities of humans, society, and nature.

In class societies, those who are rich in terms of the amounts of the wealth, income and power they control, are likely to be less affected by unsustainability because a) resource inequality is itself a form of unsustainable development and b) those controlling significant amounts of money, influence, reputation and social relations can more easily escape unsustainable living conditions. Class is an important factor in all forms of unsustainable development. Marx was an early theorist of sustainability: he argues that the private ownership of the world hinders that the world is handed down to "succeeding generations in an improved condition" (Marx 1894, 784).

In capitalist society, powerful actors control natural resources, economic property, political decision-making, and cultural meaning-making, which has resulted in the accumulation of power, inequalities, and global problems, including environmental pollution as well as the degradation and depletion of natural resources in the nature–society relation, socio-economic inequality in the economic system, dictatorships and war in the political system, ideology, and malrecognition in the cultural system.

Cornel West stresses that alienation means dehumanisation. Alienation robs humans of possibilities to lead a fully developed and good life. It makes society and exploited and oppressed individuals and groups fall behind their possibilities so that a gap is created between society as it is – as class society – and society as it could be. "Alienation is an impediment for this true common life of people" (West 1991, 47–48)

Alienation also plays a role in the realm of consciousness: ideology tries to create alienated consciousness, the belief in the truth of distorted images and views of reality that do not correspond to the world as it really is, the world's essence. Ideology tries to distract attention from class structures and domination in order to legitimate, justify, and defend class society, capitalism, and domination. In the 21st century, ideology has played an important role in the form of new forms of racism, nationalism, authoritarianism, and fascism that try to distract attention of social inequalities' grounding in capitalism and the class structure of contemporary society.

Racism is an ideology that propagates and practices the inferiority of certain groups that are identified as "races" or cultures or nations or ethnicities. It is also a mode of governance, a politics that discriminates against racialised groups. And it is a mode of production in which racialised groups face high levels of exploitation. Racism is a system of power that brings together specific forms of economic, political, and cultural alienation.

Capitalism, racism, and patriarchy are three major systems of alienation that each combined economic, political and ideological alienation in particular manners. Socialist thinkers such as Cornel West, Adolph L. Reed Jr., and C.L.R James stress that alienation does not simply mean a diversity of various forms of oppression without unity. In capitalist society, class relations, racism and gender relations have their common foundation in the capitalist labor relation, which means that wage labour, racialised labour, reproductive labour, and unpaid labour constitute the common foundation of class, racism, and patriarchy.

Alienation

Alienation means that class structures and capitalism in contemporary society create the unity of the diversity of oppression. All forms of alienation are related to the exploitation of labour and have to be. West, Reed, and James stress that in order to attain a just, fair and humane society, black and white workers, male and female workers, workers from different countries and backgrounds, blue- and white-collar workers, etc. have to unite beyond their differences in a universal socialist movement that struggles for socialism. Another implication is that postmodern thought advances an approach that sees a plurality without unity of alienation that ends up in identity politics operating at micro-levels and in micro public sphere and thereby fails to challenge the totality of alienated society. Identity politics without class politics drifts off too easily into liberal equal opportunity politics. Equal opportunity politics is a reductionist politics. It is satisfied when in a crisis such as the COVID-19 pandemic, the share of different social groups among the dead corresponds to their overall share in society. But the suffering and death caused by the COVID-19 pandemic as such is the scandal. Inequalities cause an overrepresentation of certain groups, but reducing their share of the dead is not enough. Progressive politics must aim at avoiding deaths in crises by strengthening the welfare state and health care system so that it can properly respond to such crises so that all groups in society are protected. Equal opportunity politics is satisfied with lay-offs and low-wages as long as the composition of the managerial and capitalist class taking these decisions reflects the general representation of identities in the population. But unemployment and low wages are inhumane and a catastrophe for those affected independent of who takes these decisions. Every layoff and every low wage employment is an act of inhumanity.

Nancy Fraser comments on Facebook COO Sheryl Sanderg's remark that the world would be better off if half all "countries and companies were run by women", "This is a remarkable vision of equal opportunity domination: one that asks ordinary people [...] to be grateful that it is a woman, not a man, who busts their union, orders a drone to kill their parent, or locks their child in a cage at the border. [...] Will we continue to pursue 'equal opportunity domination' while the planet burns?" (Arruzza, Bhattacharya, and Fraser 2019, 2 & 4).

Equal opportunity politics legitimates and helps reproducing the inhumanity of capitalism, class society, and alienated society. The alternative is a universalist socialist movement that brings together different groups in their common role as workers and humans in the struggle for a socialist society that abolishes exploitation and domination.

The present author has argued that the logic of accumulation unites the spheres of capitalist society (Fuchs 2020). It originates in the capitalist economy and shapes the spheres of capitalist society where accumulation takes on relatively autonomous logics that are based on and mediated with the logic of capital accumulation. The non-economic spheres of capitalist society are at the same time economic and non-economic, realms of production and accumulation and realms that have emergent qualities that go beyond capital accumulation and are dialectically mediated with capital accumulation.

Capitalist society is a society that is shaped by the logic of accumulation and in-strumental reason. In the economy, accumulation means the accumulation of capital. In the political system, accumulation means the accumulation of decision-power. In the cultural system, accumulation means the accumulation of reputation and attention. Accumulation results in alienation that creates structures that cause injustices. Injustice means that humans are denied a good life, the realisation of their potentials, and control of the conditions that shape their lives. Accumulation and alienation are forms of inhumanity.

Accumulation results in alienation that creates structures that cause injustices. Injustice means that humans are denied a good life, the realisation of their potentials, and control of the conditions that shape their lives. Accumulation and alienation are forms of in-humanity. Table 11.1 provides an overview of the three forms of injustice as alienation.

TABLE 11.1   Alienation as injustice

Sphere	General features	Structure	Process	Antagonism	Injustice
Economy	Production of use-values	Class relation between capital and labour	Capital accumulation	Capital vs. labour	Capitalist exploitation: capital's private ownership of the means of production, capital, and created products implies the working class' non-ownership and exploitation
Politics	Production of collective decisions	Nation-state	Accumulation of decision-power and influence	Bureaucracy vs. citizens	Domination: citizens' lack of influence on political decisions as consequence of the asymmetric distribution of decision-power and influence
Culture	Production of meanings	Ideologies	Accumulation of reputation, attention and respect	Ideologues and celebrities vs. everyday people	Invisibility, disrespect: lack of recognition as consequence of an asymmetric attention economy and ideological scapegoating

11.4 Socialism

Socialism is a classless society that is based on wealth for all, collective ownership of the means of production, participatory democracy, cultural unity in diversity. It realises an inclusive and democratic welfare state and an economy that operates not for profit but rather for the benefit of all humans. Socialism is the sublation of class society, capitalism, and domination.

Today, we are in a situation of deep crisis that means a crossroads where the future is open and undetermined. The future of society will be decided by the outcome of class struggles. We are at a crossroads where humanity faces the choice between barbarism and the struggle for socialism.

Critical theory that is inspired by Marxist Humanism analyses society as realms of production that today constitutes a capitalist society that is full of relations of alienation, i.e. full of exploitation and domination. Marxist Humanism is praxis-oriented: it tries to inform class struggles for a society that corresponds to human capacities and potentials, i.e. class struggles for Democratic Socialism.

Another society is possible. Democratic Socialism is possible. Democratic Socialism is needed.

References

Arruzza, Cinzia, Tithi Bhattacharya and Nancy Fraser. 2019. *Feminism for the 99%. A Manifesto.* London: Verso.

Fuchs, Christian. 2021. *Marxist Humanism and Communication Theory. Communication and Society Volume One.* New York: Routledge

Fuchs, Christian. 2020. *Communication and Capitalism. A Critical Theory.* London: University of Westminster Press. https://doi.org/10.16997/book45

Fuchs, Christian. 2016. *Critical Theory of Communication: New Readings of Lukács, Adorno, Marcuse, Honneth and Habermas in the Age of the Internet.* London: University of Westminster Press. https://doi.org/10.16997/book1

Fuchs, Christian. 2014. The Dialectic: Not Just the Absolute Recoil, but the World's Living Fire that Extinguishes and Kindles Itself. *Reflections on Slavoj Žižek's Version of Dialectical Philosophy in "Absolute Recoil. Towards a New Foundation of Dialectical Materialism".* *tripleC: Communication, Capitalism & Critique* 12 (2): 848–875. https://doi.org/10.31269/triplec.v12i2.640

Harvey, David. 2018. Universal Alienation. *tripleC: Communication, Capitalism & Critique* 18 (2): 424–439. https://doi.org/10.31269/triplec.v16i2.1026

Harvey, David. 1989. *The Condition of Postmodernity. An Enquiry into the Origins of Cultural Change.* Cambridge, MA: Blackwell.

Hegel, Georg Wilhelm Friedrich. 1991. *The Encyclopaedia Logic (with the Zusätze). Part I of the Encyclopaedia of Philosophical Sciences with the Zusätze.* Indianapolis, IN: Hackett.

Jameson, Frederic. 1991. *Postmodernism, or, The Cultural Logic of Late Capitalism.* Durham, NC: Duke University Press.

Lukács, Georg. 1980. *The Ontology of Social Being. 3: Labour.* London: Merlin

Marx, Karl. 1894. *Capital. Volume 3.* London: Penguin.

West, Cornel. 1991. *The Ethical Dimensions of Marxist Thought.* New York: Monthly Review Press.

Žižek 2014 Žižek, Slavoj. 2014. *Absolute Recoil. Towards a New Foundation of Dialectical Materialism.* London: Verso.

Žižek 2012 Žižek, Slavoj. 2012. *Less than Nothing. Hegel and the Shadow of Dialectical Materialism.* London: Verso.

References

Index

Note: Page number in **bold** and *italics* indicates table and figure respectively. Page number followed by n indicates notes.

Taylor & Francis Group
an **informa** business

Taylor & Francis eBooks

www.taylorfrancis.com

A single destination for eBooks from Taylor & Francis
with increased functionality and an improved user
experience to meet the needs of our customers.

90,000+ eBooks of award-winning academic content in
Humanities, Social Science, Science, Technology, Engineering,
and Medical written by a global network of editors and authors.

TAYLOR & FRANCIS EBOOKS OFFERS:

A streamlined
experience for
our library
customers

A single point
of discovery
for all of our
eBook content

Improved
search and
discovery of
content at both
book and
chapter level

REQUEST A FREE TRIAL
support@taylorfrancis.com

Routledge
Taylor & Francis Group

CRC Press
Taylor & Francis Group

For Product Safety Concerns and Information please contact our EU
representative GPSR@taylorandfrancis.com
Taylor & Francis Verlag GmbH, Kaufingerstraße 24, 80331 München, Germany

www.ingramcontent.com/pod-product-compliance
Lightning Source LLC
Chambersburg PA
CBHW050341270326
41926CB00016B/3557